The
MYSTERY
of
ISRAEL
and the
MIDDLE EAST

Other Books by James W. Goll

Deliverance from Darkness
The Discerner
Exploring Your Dreams and Visions
The Feeler
Finding Hope
Hearing God's Voice Today
The Lifestyle of a Prophet
The Lifestyle of a Watchman
The Lost Art of Intercession
The Lost Art of Practicing His Presence
Living a Supernatural Life
Passionate Pursuit
Prayer Storm
Praying with God's Heart
The Prophet
The Prophetic Intercessor
A Radical Faith
Releasing Spiritual Gifts Today
The Scribe
The Seer
Strike the Mark
Tell Your Heart to Sing Again

With Michal Ann Goll:
Angelic Encounters
Dream Language
God Encounters Today
Heroines of the Faith

The
MYSTERY
of
ISRAEL
and the
MIDDLE EAST

A PROPHETIC GAZE INTO THE FUTURE

JAMES W. GOLL

Chosen

a division of Baker Publishing Group

Minneapolis, Minnesota

© 2021 by James W. Goll

Published by Chosen Books
11400 Hampshire Avenue South
Bloomington, Minnesota 55438
www.chosenbooks.com

Chosen Books is a division of
Baker Publishing Group, Grand Rapids, Michigan

Library of Congress Cataloging-in-Publication Data
Names: Goll, Jim W., author.
Title: The mystery of Israel and the Middle East : a prophetic gaze into the future / James W. Goll.
Description: Minneapolis, Minnesota : Chosen Books, [2021] | Includes bibliographical references and index.
Identifiers: LCCN 2021015688 | ISBN 9780800762520 (casebound) | ISBN 9780800799816 (paperback) | ISBN 9781493433643 (ebook)
Subjects: LCSH: Bible—Prophecies—Jews. | Jews—Restoration. | Israel (Christian theology) | Christianity and other religions—Judaism. | Judaism—Relations—Christianity.
Classification: LCC BS649.J5 G65 2021 | DDC 231.7/6—dc23
LC record available at https://lccn.loc.gov/2021015688

Portions of this book were previously published in *The Coming Israel Awakening: Gazing into the Future of the Jewish People and the Church* and *Praying for Israel's Destiny: Effective Intercession for God's Purposes in the Middle East* by James W. Goll

Cover design by Bill Johnson

21 22 23 24 25 26 27   7 6 5 4 3 2 1

Contents

Foreword by Don Finto   9

Acknowledgments   11

Section 1   Prophetic Beginnings

1. The Birth of a Nation   15
2. When the Walls Came Tumbling Down   37
3. The Winds of Awakening   55

Section 2   The Prophetic and Prayer

4. Appointed a Watchman   73
5. Praying for the Fulfillment of Aliyah   91
6. The Mordecai Calling   107

Section 3   The Prophetic Promise

7. The Descendants of Hagar   131
8. The Descendants of Sarah   149
9. The Descendants of Keturah   165

Section 4   Prophetic Gaze into the Future

10. Jerusalem: A City of Destiny   181
11. God's Road Map   199
12. The Great Hope   217

    Appendix A: Overview of Israel's History   241
    Appendix B: Come Humbly to Israel! by Don
       Finto   267
    Appendix C: Praying for Israel and the Middle
       East   279
    Notes   287
    Glossary   295
    Index   303

Foreword

I am smiling as I consider James Goll and his newest book, *The Mystery of Israel and the Middle East*. I have walked this path with Israel and the Jewish people for years, and have traveled to Israel and the Middle East every year—often two and three times a year for more than two decades—yet still I am intrigued and blessed with James's insights.

If you have been wondering why so many believers take such a keen interest in the Jewish people, the nation of Israel and their surrounding neighbors, this book is for you. Yet for those of us who for years have loved and prayed for this chosen host people, this book is for us. You will love the way James weaves together Scripture with history, and biblical prophecy with the present-day prophetic movement that is such a part of James's life.

In chapter 5, you will begin to see the parallels between the prophetic fulfillment that happens with the Jewish people and the corresponding prophetic work among the Church. When Israel gains land, the Church gains land—the side-by-side birth of Zionism (the Jewish return to the land) and the Pentecostal outpouring of the early twentieth century; the birth of the nation of Israel in 1948 and the birth of the healing revival; Israel's restoration to Jerusalem in the Six-Day War of 1967 and the beginning of the Jesus Movement and the charismatic renewal.

As you read this book, I guarantee that you will gain insights that are fresh or even new to you. Never have I heard anyone explore more beautifully the inheritance given to all of Abraham's sons—not only to Isaac, the son of destiny through whom the Messiah was to come, but the blessings to Ishmael and, yes, even to the six sons of Abraham's wife Keturah, the wife Abraham chose after Sarah's death.

James understands that this is not all about Israel, but Israel's God. Listen to his words:

> Please understand that this is not an ethnic issue. This is a God issue. The primary issue is not about a race of people. This is about a promise-keeping God who is faithful to fulfill His plan for a people, a city and a nation through which He has chosen to display His splendor.

James himself is a remarkable man of God, a living example of the truth expressed in Paul's letter to the Romans that "suffering produces perseverance; perseverance, character" (5:3–4 NIV), and the insight from the writer of Hebrews that God's discipline, which often includes suffering, can produce "a harvest of righteousness and peace for those who have been trained by it" (12:11 NIV). James has chosen to walk tightly with God through the death of his wife, Michal Ann, and the intense physical pain that has so often been part of his life.

I recommend to you both James and his book.

Don Finto, founder, Caleb Global; pastor emeritus, Belmont Church; author, *Your People Shall Be My People*

Acknowledgments

This book has deep roots and has been in the making for approximately 25 years. This is a new book filled with historical perspectives. It has its origins in three former books of mine, all related to the subject of the rebirth of the nation of Israel as a fulfillment of prophetic Scripture.

Exodus Cry! with Regal Books was my first attempt at penning on this subject, with Larry Walker as my primary assistant, along with a tremendous research team. Then came *Praying for Israel's Destiny* with Chosen Books, with David Sluka as my right-hand man. Next came *The Coming Israel Awakening*, also with Chosen Books, with the skillful writing assistance of Kathryn Deering.

Finally, we have the consolidation of much material, new and old, to bring us the tapestry of *The Mystery of Israel and the Middle East*, once again with Chosen Books. Angela Rickabaugh Shears was my writing assistant, under the watchful eye of Jane Campbell, Chosen's editorial director. Along the way there were those who acted as advisers, assistants and helpers. Some of these are Avner Boskey, Sandra Teplinsky, Don Finto,

Derek Prince Ministries, Michal Ann Goll, my ministry staff and prayer shield, and many others.

I want to push pause for a moment before we go into the meat of this complex and delightful subject of the mystery of Israel and the Middle East. I have had three people who were the primary influences on what became my writing career. Jane Campbell became, by far, the primary shaper who spoke into this lump of clay and called forth the potential of a prophetic treasure. Thank you, Jane, for seeing what I did not see, giving me skills I did not possess and inching me forward when I did not know where you were steering me. Thousands of people are grateful today because you took time to invest in a man who was hungry to learn. I am most grateful!

Thank you to the great company of people who have served the Lord and His purposes by helping give birth to a teaching guide to help us gaze into the future and into a mystery unfolding progressively in Christ Jesus.

Prophetic Beginnings

1

The Birth of a Nation

Who has heard such a thing? Who has seen such things? Can a land be born in one day? Can a nation be given birth all at once? As soon as Zion was in labor, she also delivered her sons.

Isaiah 66:8

I was born in 1952, only four years after the rebirth of the "land," the nation of Israel, which occurred in 1948, so I can almost say this happened in my lifetime. People worldwide have asked me, "In the past fifty years or so, what is God's greatest prophetic event?" I always give the same answer: The greatest prophetic occurrence in the past hundred years is the restoration of the Jewish people to their Land of Promise, which today is the country of Israel.

Over the years, the word *aliyah* ("ascent") has become very dear to Jewish people and believing Gentiles alike, as prophetic

Scriptures about the regathering of the Jewish people from the ends of the earth are fulfilled right before our eyes. *Aliyah*, simply put, means to go from a lower place to a higher place—the process of returning to the homeland.

I believe that, throughout this book, the Holy Spirit is going to open your eyes so you realize that the God of the Bible is at work even in the crucible times for the Jewish people, ordaining that they would come from the ends of the earth to be restored, returned to their homeland.

Isaiah 11:11–12 says,

> Then it will happen on that day that the Lord will again recover with His hand the second time the remnant of His people. . . . And He will lift up a flag for the nations and assemble the banished ones of Israel, and will gather the dispersed of Judah from the four corners of the earth.

This prophecy is extremely important. Let me add that for every verse I give throughout this book, I can give many more that complement it. The Word of God confirms itself again and again, especially concerning His children.

The well-being of the Jewish people has always hinged on the balance of the level of their obedience to God, His faithful promises to their ancestors and His eternal purpose and love for them. In general terms, when God's people obey Him, they prosper. When they do not, they are judged. This principle comes from Deuteronomy 28, and we see it repeatedly in action in the history of Israel (for example, in Judges 2:6–23). This biblical law of sowing and reaping still applies, even under the grace of God received through the finished work of Jesus Christ.

Over the millennia, Jacob's descendants have suffered greatly and have been greatly blessed as well. British Bible teacher Lance Lambert says of them:

> No other nation in the history of mankind has twice been uprooted from its land, scattered to the ends of the earth and then brought back again to that same territory. If the first exile and restoration was remarkable, then the second is miraculous. Israel has twice lost its statehood and its national sovereignty, twice had its capital and hub of religious life destroyed, its towns and cities razed to the ground, its people deported and dispersed, and then twice had it all restored again. Furthermore, no other nation or ethnic group has been scattered to the four corners of the earth, and yet survived as an easily identifiable and recognizable group.[1]

The first exile took place under Babylonian rule. As for the second great exile, Roman forces serving under the Roman commander Titus destroyed and dismantled Jerusalem in August AD 70, exactly as Jesus prophesied 37 years earlier. The Romans killed 600,000 Jewish residents and deported 300,000 more to locations scattered around the Empire.[2]

Sixty-five years later, the forces of Roman Emperor Hadrian crushed the last Jewish uprising, led by Bar Kokhba. Those Roman forces hated and persecuted Jewish and Gentile followers of Christ. Some observers believe this might have helped plant early seeds of anti-Semitism in the fledgling Church.

Hadrian's hatred for the Jews burned so brightly that he changed Jerusalem's name to "Aelia Capitolina" (his given name was Aelius) and declared it "a Roman city forever which no Jew could enter under pain of death." He built a temple to Jupiter on the site of the former Temple, where sacrifices had been made to Jehovah.[3] Then he renamed the land "Syria Palaestina" (Latin for *Philistia*).

Caesar overlooked an important detail: Unlike the power-less gods of Rome, the God of Israel was and is alive and well.

The Jewish people in Jerusalem and Judea were recaptured, died violent deaths or were scattered to distant lands. This second dispersion following the death and resurrection of Jesus the Messiah lasted far longer than the first. It would not end after five hundred—or even a thousand—years.

The devastated city of Jerusalem became the most contested urban real estate on earth, as for two thousand years various nations, empires and religious factions battled for its possession. All the while, its builders and original residents—the Jewish people—were forced to seek refuge in Gentile cities and nations around the world, which none could call home. That all changed in one day, as you will learn toward the end of this chapter. Eighteen hundred and thirteen years after the destruction of Jerusalem under Hadrian, a new nation emerged from the birth pangs of World War II and the horrible Holocaust, just as Isaiah prophesied (see Isaiah 66:8).

Before every birth must come birth pangs. The Scriptures clearly predicted the two great dispersions and the persecutions they represented. They also describe the regathering of the Jewish people and the rebirth of Israel.

The Rebirth Begins

In 1855 Hudson Taylor, a Christian physician and missionary to China, saw in the Spirit that a great end-time revival would occur in the land of the north. Taylor was full of the Holy Spirit and entirely surrendered to God. Known as a man of great self-denial, heartfelt compassion and powerful prayer, he interceded for the salvation of the Chinese every morning for forty years.

While on a ministry furlough in England, Taylor suddenly stopped in the middle of a sermon and for a few moments stood speechless with his eyes closed. Finally, he explained to his audience:

> I have seen a vision. I saw in this vision a great war that will encompass the whole world. I saw this war recess and then start again, actually being two wars. After this, I saw much unrest and revolts that will affect many nations. I saw in some places spiritual awakenings. In Russia I saw there will come a general, all-encompassing, national, spiritual awakening, so great that there could never be another like it. From Russia I saw the awakening spread to many European countries, and then I saw an all-out awakening followed by the coming of Christ.[4]

Twenty-six years later, in 1881, Russia's tsar, Alexander II, was murdered, and his son, Alexander III, succeeded him. Alexander III hated the Jewish people, and that year a "pogrom"—an organized massacre or persecution of Jewish people—swept through Kishinev, the capital of Moldova, adjacent to Romania and Ukraine.

As life for the persecuted Jews became more difficult under the tsar, Zionist ideas about a Jewish homeland gained strength and followers. Some Jewish leaders began to search for a place of refuge, a homeland for the world's displaced Jewish population. The term *anti-Semitism* entered the English language around 1870, referring to hostility toward Jews as a religious,

19

ethnic or racial group. The first aliyah, or immigration, to Israel took place in 1882. Jewish immigrants established a Jewish colony called Rishon LeZion.

The First of the Fishermen

During this time of rebirth, God sent prophetic voices of Christian and Jewish "fishermen" and "hunters" to His chosen people:

> "However, the days are coming," declares the LORD, "when it will no longer be said, 'As surely as the LORD lives, who brought the Israelites up out of Egypt,' but it will be said, 'As surely as the LORD lives, who brought the Israelites up out of the land of the north and out of all the countries where he had banished them.' For I will restore them to the land I gave their ancestors. But now I will send for many *fishermen*," declares the LORD, "and they will catch them. After that I will send for many *hunters*, and they will hunt them down on every mountain and hill and from the crevices of the rocks."
>
> Jeremiah 16:14–16 NIV, emphasis added

These divine messengers, "fishermen," used neither nets nor force; gently and persistently they warned the Jewish people and wooed them toward God's plan to deliver those who took heed, before the "hunters" appeared. In virtually every case, which we will see in the next pages, His goal was to preserve a remnant and return them to their ancient Land of Promise.

In the same year that the first aliyah to Israel took place, a prominent Jewish leader named Joseph Rabinowitz (1837–1899) journeyed from Kishinev to Palestine, as Israel was called at that time. He was an unofficial delegate representing some like-minded Jews who wanted to see if Palestine was the right place to establish a Jewish homeland.

Rabinowitz was a Haskala ("Enlightenment") Jew who first searched for truth while studying the Talmud with a Chassidic rabbi, and later sought understanding through extensive reading of more liberal writings by so-called enlightened Jewish teachers. He loved his people deeply; the disappointments he experienced and witnessed finally convinced him they would find safety among Gentile nations only as long as it was convenient for their unwilling hosts.

During a brief stay in Palestine, Rabinowitz went to the Western Wall in Jerusalem—the Wailing Wall, part of the expansion of the Second Jewish Temple—at the beginning of a Sabbath day. Palestine was controlled at that time by the sultan of Turkey from his capital in Constantinople. Rabinowitz watched in dismay as Jews who had gathered there for prayer struggled to worship and weep at the wall amid "the jibes and harassments of the Muslims."[5] The level of desolation Rabinowitz witnessed in the Promised Land, coupled with the plight of the Jewish people in Europe and around the world, shocked him.

Just before sunset one evening, Rabinowitz visited the Mount of Olives. He sat down on a slope near Gethsemane. As he pondered the troubling scene of jeering and mocking at the Western Wall, a passage from the Hebrew New Testament he had read fifteen years earlier flashed in his mind: "If the Son therefore shall make you free, ye shall be free indeed" (John 8:36 KJV). In that moment he began to realize that Jesus was the King and Messiah, the only One who could save Israel. Rabinowitz returned to his temporary residence, where he read John's gospel. He was struck by John 15:5: "Without me ye can do nothing" (KJV).[6]

When Rabinowitz returned home to Kishinev, Moldova, he studied the Hebrew New Testament. Later he played a key role in distributing Bibles to other Jewish people. He told his Jewish friends about his Mount of Olives experience. He did not claim to know if the land of Palestine was the hope of the Jewish people, but, touching his chest, he would say, "This is the land, the land of the heart. It is what God wants us to obtain." He would sometimes add, "The key to the Holy Land lies in the hands of our brother, Jesus."[7]

In Kishinev, Rabinowitz and forty families established the world's first modern-day Messianic (or Hebrew-Christian) congregation, called Israelites of the New Covenant.[8] Rabinowitz's ministry and writings had great impact in Russia and Europe and were known worldwide.

In 1888 Rabinowitz said, "I have two subjects with which I am absorbed: the one, the Lord Jesus Christ, and the other, Israel."[9] A year later, while visiting London, he said, "Russia is like the ocean; the Jews there are like shipwrecked people; and since by God's mercy my feet are on the Rock [which is Jesus], . . . I am shouting and signaling to my shipwrecked people to flee to the Rock."[10]

The establishment of Rabinowitz's Messianic congregation in Kishinev marks the beginning of the time of fishermen were sent to the Jewish people in Europe, and specifically in the land of the north. It was the start of a paradigm shift!

Some fourteen years after Rabinowitz viewed the sunset on Jerusalem's Mount of Olives, Theodor Herzl, a Jewish attorney and writer, penned an essay titled *Der Judenstaat*, "The Jewish State." That essay, published in 1896 and subtitled *An Attempt at a Modern Solution to the Jewish Question*, changed the course of Jewish history. Herzl dreamed of reestablishing a sovereign Jewish state on Jewish soil. Under the prophetic anointing of a true fisherman from God—God can speak prophetically through anyone He chooses—Herzl wrote:

> In the world as it is now, and for an indefinite period will probably remain, might precedes right. It is useless, therefore, for us to be loyal patriots, as were the Huguenots, who were forced to migrate. If we could only be left in peace . . . but I think we shall not be left in peace.[11]

Herzl also wrote:

> The idea [of a Jewish state] must radiate out until it reaches the last wretched nests of our people. They will awaken out of their dull brooding. Then a new meaning will come into the lives of all of us. . . .
> Therefore, I believe that a wondrous generation of Jews will spring into existence; the Maccabees will rise again . . . and we shall at last live as free men on our own soil, and die peacefully in our own homes.[12]

In 1897 Herzl orchestrated the first worldwide gathering of Jews since AD 70. The delegates to the First Zionist Congress, held in Basel, Switzerland, established the World Zionist Organization. Herzl became its first president.

Amazingly, I was in Basel in the fall of 1997, one hundred years to the day after the First Zionist Congress met. I was to speak at one of the first prophetic conferences that had been held there in many years. The conference was actually located within blocks of the site where Herzl and his Jewish friends had gathered.

In his inaugural address Herzl prophesied, "We are here to lay the foundation stone of the house which is to shelter the Jewish Nation."[13] In his diary entry for September 3, 1897, shortly after he returned from the Zionist Congress, Herzl went one step further and wrote:

> Were I to sum up the Basel Congress in a few words—which I shall guard against pronouncing publicly—it would be this: "At Basel I founded the Jewish State." If I said this out loud today I would be answered by universal laughter. Perhaps in five years, and certainly in fifty, everyone will know it.[14]

In November 1947, fifty years later, the General Assembly of the United Nations (U.N.) recognized the right of the Jewish people to have their own state.

God raised up and released fishermen to pursue and save the Jewish people in both the religious and secular realms. Both Rabinowitz and Herzl brought hope and direction to their people, but the work of Rabinowitz revealed the greater plan of the God of Abraham, Isaac and Israel.

Birth Pangs

The shadows of World War I settled on the nations of the world even as God's fishermen began to draw His people back to their biblical homeland. Yet the borders and gates of Israel remained in the antagonistic grip of the Turks until God intervened supernaturally.

Here is what happened. During the war, Britain ran out of acetone, the solvent used in making cordite, the essential naval explosive at that time.[15] Until war broke out, Britain had purchased all of its acetone from Germany, now its principal enemy. The acetone shortage put the entire nation at risk. In desperation Winston Churchill, then first lord of the admiralty, summoned the brilliant Jewish chemist Chaim Weizmann to the British War Office. He asked him to develop a synthetic version of cordite that did not require acetone, and he placed every available government facility at his disposal.

While British forces under General Edmund Allenby battled Turkish troops for control of Palestine, Dr. Weizmann developed and produced 30,000 tons of an acetone-free synthetic cordite that was even more explosive than the original version. When Weizmann was asked what he wanted in return for his vital service to Great Britain, he said, "If Britain wins the battle for Palestine, I ask for a national home for my people in their ancient land."[16] Chaim Weizmann would later become the first president of the reborn nation of Israel.[17]

Weizmann received his answer on November 2, 1917, when British foreign minister Arthur James Balfour issued a statement on behalf of the British government, with the approval of the cabinet:

> His Majesty's Government views with favour the establishment in Palestine of a national home for the Jewish people, and will use their best endeavors to facilitate the achievement of this object, it being clearly understood that nothing shall be done which may prejudice the civil and religious rights of existing non-Jewish communities in Palestine, or the rights and political status enjoyed by Jews in any other country.[18]

Through a miracle on December 11, 1917, General Edmund Allenby took possession of Jerusalem without firing a single shot. Before entering what is called the Old City, the general sent planes over Jerusalem during daylight hours to learn the size and deployment of the Turkish troops within its walls. He also had the planes drop leaflets calling for the Turks to surrender—and for some reason the Turkish forces fled the city during the night.

Author Ramon Bennett reported:

> The dropped leaflets, signed with the name of "Allenby," were taken by the Turkish Muslims to be a directive from "Allah" for them to leave the city. No shots were fired in the capture of the Old City of Jerusalem. General Allenby, a devout Christian, would not ride his horse into the city. He dismounted, and cap in hand, led his horse and his troops into the City of the Great King.[19]

Britain finally forced Turkey to sign an armistice in October 1918. The area the world called Palestine was in British hands.

At the end of the war, Britain was given a mandate, or official authority, to administer most of the Middle East. After years of political maneuvering and high-level betrayals, however, more than *seventy percent* of the land promised to the Jewish people was placed in Arab hands in 1921 and named "Transjordan." Yet there was One who remembered His promises to the Jewish people. He was unmoved by riches, politics or the schemes of people and nations; and His promises would come to pass.

The British government imposed severe immigration quotas on Jewish immigrants who wanted to go to the Promised Land. Yet despite seemingly impossible obstacles, determined Zionist groups defied the quotas and established colonies in Eretz Israel, "the land of Israel."

The labor pangs of the nation of Israel grew stronger and more violent with each decade, signaling that birth was imminent, echoing Isaiah 66:8. When would Zion come forth? As soon as Zion travailed. As always, the dragon of old waited and schemed to destroy the divine seed of God's will before its birth or immediately after delivery. Satan is always positioned to try to prevent anything given birth to by God—particularly if of great prophetic and strategic importance. The dragon is waiting there to devour the offspring.

While the voices of many fishermen such as Herzl raised the alarm of danger to the Jewish people in Germany, Russia and the Balkans, only a fraction of those people heeded the warning. Meanwhile the world was experiencing violent labor pangs of its own.

In Russia the doctrines of Marx, Lenin and Trotsky ignited fires of violent change. In 1917 those fires plunged Russia into the darkness of atheistic Communism, producing an ungodly broth bitter to both Christians and Jews.

Meanwhile Germany struggled with economic and social woes after her humiliating loss in World War I. A little-known man from Austria—born seven years after Rabinowitz had pondered the truth of the Messiah on the Mount of Olives—penned a journal of hate called *Mein Kampf*. Adolf Hitler rose rapidly in Germany's political ranks on a wicked wave of anti-Semitism and his extremist nationalistic doctrine of Aryan supremacy.

Adolf Hitler is one more in a long line of historical examples of a hunter who has been released, per the Jeremiah passage we looked at earlier:

"I will send for many fishermen," declares the LORD, "and they will catch them. After that I will send for many hunters, and

27

they will hunt them down on every mountain and hill and from
the crevices of the rocks."

Jeremiah 16:16 NIV

As Hitler's grip tightened on the reins of the German government, nation after nation ignored him and the Nazi phenomenon. Global leaders overlooked the growing army of Brown
Shirts that surrounded the Nazi kingpin. But the One who never
sleeps knew what was afoot. Once again God sent fishermen to
warn His people before the coming trauma was fully released.

Ze'ev Jabotinsky (Jeb Zabotinsky) was one such fisherman.
An early Jewish pioneer in Israel, he traveled in 1933 throughout
Europe—and Germany in particular—warning Jews, "There
is no future for you here. Come back to your land while the
doors are still open."[20] Thousands heeded the admonitions of
Zabotinsky and others to flee the north, but millions of Jewish
people in Germany, Austria and the Balkan countries did not.

Nuremburg and the Camps

Hitler came into power as chancellor that same year and began
depriving Germany's Jews of rights, segregating them from the
rest of German society. Discrimination intensified as he con-
solidated power as the *Führer* (literally, "the leader") in 1934.
The next year the Nuremburg Laws were enacted, denying Jews
any legal or citizenship rights.

While the world observed, Hitler established camps for Jewish people within Germany's borders, starting with Dachau—
not only concentration camps, but forced labor camps, killing
centers and others.[21] Hitler's actions, he claimed, were legal
under international law, since the camps dealt with an internal

"Jewish problem" that had nothing to do with the citizens of other nations. Most world leaders accepted this argument, reasoning that the Jewish people had no country or government, per se.

By 1938 Hitler felt that his power was strong enough to defy world opinion on a larger scale, so he suddenly "annexed" neighboring Austria into the Third Reich in what was called the *Anschluss*. Steve Lightle in his book *Operation Exodus II* aptly depicts the scene: "Overnight Hitler did in Austria what took him five years to do in Germany. He took away all the rights of the Jewish people, confiscating their businesses and instituting his atrocities immediately."[22]

The League of Nations, the toothless precursor to the U.N., had neither the power nor the will to stand up to the bully ruling Germany. When the League of Nations failed to act, American President Franklin D. Roosevelt called a meeting of national leaders. He wanted them to discuss ways to rescue the Jewish people from Germany and Austria.

Fifteen weeks after Germany took Austria, representatives of 32 nations met in Évian-les-Bains, France. On July 6, 1938, the conferees argued for hours over which delegate would chair the meeting. After two days of halfhearted wrangling, no nation, not even Great Britain or the United States, was willing to take in more than a token number of Jewish immigrants.

Hitler sent spies to monitor the opinions and determinations of the nations represented in Évian. According to *Operation Exodus II*, these spies reported to the Führer, "You can do anything you want to the Jews; the whole world does not want them." According to Lightle, one German newspaper, referring to a Nazi plan to sell Jewish lives to the nations, declared in a headline, "Jews For Sale, Who Wants Them? No One."[23]

Once Hitler's spies confirmed that none of the nations whose representatives met at Évian was prepared to protect or offer sanctuary to more than a few Jewish people from Germany, Austria or Eastern Europe, Hitler knew that nothing stood in the way of his "final solution." Evidently the report also convinced Hitler that he was dealing with sheep, because less than two months later, Germany's armies engulfed Poland in a *blitzkrieg*, or "lightning war," and catapulted the world into World War II. Barely one month later, in November 1938, the Germans went on a rampage called *Kristallnacht*, "The Night of Broken Glass," during which they smashed the windows of synagogues, Jewish businesses and homes, marking the full-scale beginning of the Holocaust.

By 1942 Hitler was ready to expand his extermination of Jewish people beyond the borders of Germany and Austria to include all of Europe. At the Wannsee Conference in Berlin, he essentially authorized the annihilation of the Jewish population in Europe, exactly as he had envisioned in his demonically inspired book, *Mein Kampf*. The Nazi war machine brutally murdered six million defenseless European Jews, around two-thirds of Europe's Jewish population, before it was finally stopped in 1945.

Pastor Ulf Ekman of Sweden wrote in his book *The Jews: People of the Future*:

> There are no words to describe the suffering it inflicted. It is impossible to depict the wretchedness and misery in its wake. That it was perpetrated at all is heinous. That it was committed by a nation that was considered the cultural elite of Europe is incomprehensible; and that it was done by Christians is a shame beyond words.[24]

First God sent Jewish and Gentile fishermen to warn the Jewish people of their danger, but only an estimated 600,000 heeded the warning in time to flee. Once the hunters gained momentum, they exterminated two-thirds of the nine million remaining Jews. Not one nation represented at the Évian meetings had clean hands. Nor, as we shall see in the next chapter, was the Church guiltless in this unspeakable tragedy.

In spite of the hatred that led to the massacre of six million Jewish victims, God still had a plan to restore His ancient covenant people to their land. The world would learn firsthand that nothing and no one can stand in God's way.

The nations of the world were shocked to see images of the atrocities carried out by Hitler's henchmen at 27 main Nazi concentration camps, including Auschwitz, Treblinka, Dachau and Bergen-Belsen. For a brief window of time after the end of World War II, people in most of the Allied countries softened their attitudes toward the Jewish people who survived the Holocaust.

Israel Becomes a Nation

Throughout World War II the British fought another war of sorts—a war to end Arab-Jewish conflict in the Holy Land. Still administering official authority in the Middle East, the British were caught in an age-old struggle. The Arabs rejected Jewish immigration by conducting a nonstop campaign of vandalism and terrorism against the settlers. To defend themselves against the Arabs, the settlers organized underground vigilante and defense groups such as the Irgun, the Stern Gang and the Haganah.

At first most of these groups limited their activities to defense; but as Arab atrocities increased, the Jewish groups kept pace, especially the violent Stern Gang. In an effort to appease the Arabs, the British limited Jewish immigration to the Promised Land. Despite Britain's best efforts to stop it by imposing severe quotas on Jewish immigrants, the Haganah worked tirelessly to help rescue desperate refugees from the Holocaust in Europe.

By 1947 the British occupation forces and the British people were so exhausted with the struggle that the Empire returned the "Palestine problem" to the U.N. A committee was formed to investigate, and eventually recommended to the General Assembly that the Promised Land be divided, or "partitioned," equally between Jews and Arabs.

What happened next could be attributed only to the intervention of God.

Russia, hungry for the petroleum reserves in the Middle East, wanted desperately to see Great Britain remove her military forces from the region. The best way to make that happen was to back Israel's desire for independence. In his book *The Miracle of Israel*, the late Gordon Lindsay, founder of Christ For The Nations, described what happened next:

> The Russians, witnessing Britain's dilemma, had secretly facilitated the migration of 100,000 refugees through Central Europe. Soviet officials helped them get on ships at Black Sea ports. Andrei Gromyko, Soviet foreign deputy of the U.S.S.R., pled their case before the U.N. saying:
>
>> It would be unjust if we deny the Jews the right to realize these aspirations to a state of their own. During the last war the Jewish people underwent indescribable suffering. Thousands are still behind barbed wire. The time has come to help these people not by words but deeds.

Because the Russian bloc voted in favor of the Jews (vote 21–20), the Jews gained the right to plead their case before the U.N.[25]

That day in the subcommittee marked the first time in U.N. history that the U.S.S.R. (the Union of Soviet Socialist Republics, or the Soviet Union) and the United States jointly supported a major decision. Finally, the Partition Plan came to a vote in the General Assembly, where a two-thirds majority was needed for passage. Jewish people in Israel and around the world kept their ears glued to their radios. The U.N. resolution to partition the land and allow the Jewish people to reestablish the nation of Israel passed on November 29, 1947. Jewish people around the world danced for joy.

Within three days more than 40 million Arabs pitted themselves against the 600,000 Jews already living in Israel. Declaring *jihad*, holy war, Arab leaders vowed publicly, "We are going to kill all Jews or drive them into the sea."[26] They were so confident that they warned all the Arabs living peacefully within the borders of the Jewish partition to move out of their homes for a few days until the Jewish people were wiped out. This, ironically, is the origin of the Palestinian refugees.

The battle for survival went on for months during the time between the U.N. vote authorizing the partition of the Promised Land and the final withdrawal of Britain from the region. As it prepared to end its administration, the British government did little to stop the violence, but was careful to continue deporting every Jewish immigrant without a visa. Only the determination and organization of the Haganah defenders saved the Jewish people from annihilation in their own land.

In the U.N., opponents to the formation of a Jewish state worked feverishly to stop Israel from declaring independence, but they became entangled in red tape. At midnight on May 14, 1948, the British mandate for Palestine ended. Earlier that day David Ben-Gurion, head of the Jewish Agency, proclaimed the establishment of the State of Israel. U.S. President Harry S. Truman officially recognized the new State of Israel that very day, May 14, and extended full diplomatic privileges. The U.S.S.R., eager to make sure the British never returned to the Middle East, shocked the world by quickly recognizing the nation of Israel as well.[27]

The next day, May 15, her Arab neighbors attacked. Tiny Israel faced the armies of four Arab nations—Egypt, Syria, Transjordan (present-day Jordan) and Iraq—in what became the 1948 Arab–Israeli War. She survived her war for independence but did not gain full control of her capital city. The city of Jerusalem was subsequently divided in two—with Israel controlling half and the Arabs controlling the other half—until the Six-Day War in 1967. (For a more detailed explanation of this period in Israel's history, see Appendix A, "Overview of Israel's History.")

Gordon Lindsay wrote:

On December 4, 1948, thousands gathered around the tomb of Herzl, raised their right hand and took the oath, "If I forget thee, O Jerusalem, let my right hand forget her cunning." Mr. David Ben-Gurion summed up the feelings of the people of Jerusalem and all Israel when he declared, "Israel's position on the question of Jerusalem found a clear and final expression in statements by the government and all parties of the Knesset [the Israeli equivalent of Congress or Parliament] on December 5. Jerusalem is an inseparable part of Israel, and her eternal capital."[28]

Yes, Jerusalem is in the center of God's heart and attention. It is the only city mentioned in the entire Bible for which all peoples in all generations are to pray by name. The existence of Jerusalem under Jewish rule is a modern-day miracle—an authentic fulfillment of the prophetic Word of God. Indeed, God's jealousy rests over the destiny of this great city. Prophecy is written about this ancient, walled dwelling place. Our posture toward the reunification of the city of Jerusalem under Jewish rule is important to God. And what is important to God must become important to His people.

Friend, this is our story. This is God's story. I want you to see the fingerprints of God throughout world history as well as throughout His Word. God is faithful who promises and keeps His promises.

Israel is the only nation on earth that was born in a day. The supernatural intervention of God prepared the ancient homeland for His displaced covenant people, and now He is once again sending out fishermen to forewarn the Jewish people dwelling in "the land of the north" (Jeremiah 16:15) of the growing danger lurking in the land. More on that as you read further.

◇ **A Personal Prayer** ◇

Holy and mighty God, I marvel at the details of Your ways. I declare that Your Word has not returned empty and void, but You have watched over Your Word to fulfill it. The fishers and the hunters came, but through it all, You brought forth a homeland for Your covenant people. I declare, therefore, that the prophecies of Isaiah and Jeremiah are true, and I rejoice in their fulfillment. Amen and amen.

2

When the Walls Came
Tumbling Down

"How great are His signs and how mighty are His miracles!"

Daniel 4:3

I will never forget watching television reports of East German youth tearing down the Berlin Wall. Nearly delirious with joy, they swung sledgehammers, iron bars, chisels and anything else they could find. Emotions flowed freely in a frenzied attempt to topple the twelve-foot walls that had separated Germany and imprisoned East Berlin for 28 years. It was a historic spectacle!

The dramatic scene unfolded on Thursday, November 9, 1989, barely a month after East Germany had celebrated its fortieth and final anniversary as a country. Major news organizations from around the world showed up after jubilant Germans began to disassemble sections of the 87-mile-long Berlin Wall. The border guards merely watched without interfering.

Before the "wall came a-tumbling down," I participated in a prophetic gathering in Kansas City, Missouri, in which Paul

Cain announced prophetically, "Communism is going to be commun-wasm." A few years before that I had ministered with seer prophet Bob Jones and heard him share that the Russian Jews would come forth from the land of the north, after which would come the need for "cities of refuge." Sure enough, Cain's prophetic word was fulfilled, and the Wall was removed. I have a piece of the Berlin Wall that I brought back from one of my intercessory visits to Berlin. I keep it as a reminder that, in God, all things are subject to change.

The fall of the Berlin Wall signaled the inevitable collapse of the Communist regime that overshadowed Russia and her satellite states. Day by day people around the world watched as the Soviet machine disintegrated until, about two years later, in 1991, we learned that Soviet leader Mikhail Gorbachev would step aside and the Soviet Union as we knew it was no more. Newly chosen president Boris Yeltsin and the Commonwealth of Independent States (CIS) took the lead, 74 years after the Communists seized power under the atheistic direction of Vladimir Lenin.[1]

The Berlin Wall was not the first fortress around a city to tumble. Millennia ago another bulwark fell, sending shock waves throughout the surrounding nations. That event, too, signaled catastrophic and convulsive change in the affairs of humankind and in the balance of power over the world's most contested real estate:

> Now Jericho was tightly shut because of the sons of Israel [who surrounded it]; no one went out and no one came in. But the LORD said to Joshua, "See, I have handed Jericho over to you, with its king and the valiant warriors. And you shall march around the city, all the men of war circling the city once. You shall do so for

six days. Also seven priests shall carry seven trumpets of rams' horns in front of the ark; then on the seventh day you shall march around the city seven times, and the priests shall blow the trumpets. It shall be that when they make a long blast with the ram's horn, and when you hear the sound of the trumpet, all the people shall shout with a great shout; and the wall of the city will fall down flat, and the people shall go up, everyone straight ahead."

Joshua 6:1–5

In a sense, the walls of Jericho were more formidable than the Berlin Wall. The Jericho rampart was wide enough for six chariots to run abreast. The walls were not designed to keep unarmed people in; they were designed to keep the strongest armies out. Yet they fell. Why? Was it the force of arms or the fierce attacks of skilled soldiers that brought them down? No, they collapsed upon themselves under the power of what I call prophetic acts of prayer. In other words, they disintegrated in obedience to God's direct command.

For seven days the people did not shout or utter a word in their time of battle. Just imagine, not even a word of criticism could be heard! They walked around the city in silence because God had told their leaders to do so. But then came a sound at the end of the seventh march on the seventh day, a shout of prophetic declaration from the people, and down tumbled the walls! Believers of the one true God obeyed His command in faith, and the impossible was made possible.

The East German army erected the mighty Berlin Wall in 1961. At the end of World War II Berlin was divided, with West Germany controlling a portion. But the city lay completely within the borders of East Germany. The Wall went up because over a twelve-year period, 2.7 million people had fled the nation into West Berlin.[2] The Wall was built to keep the East Germans inside, not to protect them against dangers from the outside. It was fortified by armed soldiers, tanks, tank pits, machine guns, concertina wire and a whole slew of other devices. Yet not one bullet or tank shell was involved in its demise. What happened to bring it down? How could such a thing come to pass?

In actuality, the fall of the Wall was merely the final fruit of events that occurred beyond the realm of the once-feared Iron Curtain, a political boundary isolating the nations controlled by the Soviet Union, of which East Germany was part. The Berlin Wall collapsed on itself because the demonic principalities and powers upholding the Iron Curtain were dislodged. Like the walls of Jericho, the Berlin Wall fell because God's power prevailed. Just as shouts of praise preceded the fall of the walls of Jericho, a mighty movement of prayer preceded the collapse of the Berlin Wall in our day. This resulted in a dramatic shift of power that triggered an unprecedented movement of people across national borders.

The Events Behind the Fall

"God events" played a part in the fall of a modern superpower. Let's look at a few of them.

The Christian Embassy

In a strategic public move, godly believers established the International Christian Embassy Jerusalem with the goal of comforting God's people and summoning the Church to pray for Israel. On Passover 1980, the Embassy held its first of many Mordecai Outcry events to publicly expose the mistreatment and imprisonment of Russian Jews.

Simultaneously God launched an invasion in the spirit realm. Amid His love for the Russian people groups within the U.S.S.R., He had no love for the antichrist spirit motivating and sustaining the Communist regime. That government's dismal track record of persecuting Christians and Jews within its borders finally reached the point of no return in the heavens.

Prayer Commandos

God began to lead small groups of "prayer commandos" to strike from strategic places in the U.S.S.R. at the root of key historical events that had launched evil into the world. God also sent prayer teams into East and West Germany to battle in the spirit realm.

The prayer commandos entered these nations armed only with the name of Jesus Christ, the Word of God, the power of the Holy Spirit and a divine commission to release prophetic prayers in strategic places. It was a replay of the battle between little David and the monolithic Goliath, whose people ruled the north.

International intercessory prayer movement leaders Kjell Sjöberg, Johannes Facius, Steve Lightle and Gustav Scheller, who carried a forerunner anointing on their lives, assembled a prayer conference in Jerusalem. Participants prayed for Israel and the release of Soviet Jewry. During the gathering the Holy Spirit set apart Lightle, Facius and two other intercessors for a prayer mission to the U.S.S.R.

One month after Soviet leader Mikhail Gorbachev took power in 1985, the four-person team arrived, commissioned with a mandate from Isaiah 62:10 to "go through the gates" of the U.S.S.R. and prepare the way for Jewish Russians to return to their biblical homeland.

Strategic Prayer

Team members felt led to follow a strategy found in Zechariah 1:18–21. Dubbing themselves "the Four Smithskis" after the blacksmiths, or craftsmen, described in this passage, they set out in Jesus' name to "terrify . . . and throw down these horns of the nations who lifted up their horns against the land of Judah to scatter its people" (verse 21 NIV). In both Old and New Testaments, the term *horn* is often used to refer to the leaders or the power of nations or empires.

In many of the U.S.S.R.'s Jewish centers, the team circled giant statues of Lenin, then proclaimed the idols would fall. The intercessors sought key transportation locations along the "exodus route" to Israel and asked God to open up a highway of departure for the Jewish people who would leave the land of the north.

The team went to the Potemkin Stairs, the formal entrance into Odessa, a port city in Ukraine, which at the time was part of the Soviet empire. This famous staircase features a broad series of massive steps leading from the waters of the Black Sea to the city's opera house in the city square.

Obeying the leading of the Lord, the four intercessors prayed in the Spirit as they walked up and down the staircase. The ever-present Communist secret police (KGB) followed them closely down the stairs, apparently trying to decipher their words. When the prayer team members reached the bottom of the staircase, they quickly turned around to retrace their steps. The red-faced secret agents were so close and surprised, according to the intercessors, that they ran back up the massive staircase as fast as they could![3]

The Lord uses different people at different seasons. He always has His forerunners who go before and pave the way for others so that they, too, can take their turn carrying His baton in this prophetic relay race. I, along with others, have stood on those same stairs in Odessa, at the edge of the Black Sea. As intercessory watchmen, we spoke forth that this port would remain open, and we lifted up a cry from Exodus: "Let My people go!" Years later Scheller and others watched the first shipload of Russians leave for Israel from that very port.

Invasion Mission

From late December 1985 to early January 1986, Facius and Lightle returned to the Soviet Union along with twelve other intercessors from a number of nations. This would be their most important and historic prayer assignment behind the Iron Curtain. It could be called an invasion mission. Their first assignment was to launch a "spiritual missile" at the office—specifically, the spiritual principality behind the office—of Soviet President Mikhail Gorbachev in the Kremlin.

On New Year's Eve 1985, during a bitterly cold afternoon, the fourteen praying men marched double file "just like a commando unit carrying a spiritual missile."[4] One of the intercessors had previously been to Gorbachev's office and was able to guide the others right to the target. Lightle later wrote about what happened:

> The sign to launch our missile was for me to take off my hat, although the wind was blowing and it was snowing. . . . I'll never forget what happened. It was wild, because we had to march like a commando unit, but God gave us tremendous joy. . . . As we were marching, we had big smiles on our faces. We turned the corner. . . .
>
> I had not seen so many police, KGB and army people before. No Russian person walks down that sidewalk, but there

we were. The KGB came running across the street, about forty or forty-five of them. They were stunned as they walked along with us. They didn't know what we were planning to do, but it didn't affect us a bit. When we got right in front [of the door leading to Mr. Gorbachev's office] to where I could reach out and touch the door, I took off my hat.[5]

While the men smiled at their anxious and confused KGB escort squad, they also spoke into the spirit realm and released a deadly missile from God's Word. It was the same word that brought down another king who had dared to reject God's commands. Thousands of years earlier, Samuel the prophet had delivered that fatal missile from heaven, dislodging King Saul, a Jewish ruler who had misused his authority:

> "Because you have rejected the word of the LORD, he has rejected you as king. . . . The LORD has torn the kingdom of Israel from you today and has given it to one of your neighbors—to one better than you."
>
> 1 Samuel 15:23, 28 NIV

With the divine payload delivered to its target, the fourteen men turned around abruptly and walked away from Gorbachev's office. Going back the way they had come, they left their bewildered and unsuspecting KGB escorts scratching their heads.

Six years later to the week, on Christmas Day 1991, as Scheller and his wife were watching television in Odessa, Ukraine, Gorbachev came on the air and announced, "I hereby discontinue my activities at the post of president of the Union of Soviet Socialist Republics." Scheller summed it up: "With him disappeared the Soviet Union."[6]

Breaking the Spirit of Death

During the same trip in late 1985 and early 1986, the prayer team invaded Lenin's tomb on Red Square in Moscow. It is reported that many Russians had called the tomb "holy," even though they did not believe in God. For decades line after line of schoolchildren had been brought to the tomb to honor the spirit of death hovering over the remains of the father of the Communist revolution.

But now, through divine intervention, the intercessors found themselves alone at what amounted to one of the Soviet Union's most "holy" shrines to the spirit of death. The Lord had arranged miraculously for the guards in the tomb to be distracted. Responding to a problem outside the mausoleum, they rushed away, leaving the team alone to drop their "bomb" in the Spirit. God had dispatched a commando team of prophetic intercessors to destroy the demonic power behind this idol.

As team members, miraculously alone in the mausoleum, encircled the decaying body of Lenin encased in glass, they broke the power of the spirit of death in that place in the name of Jesus Christ.[7]

First Prayer Mission

In the 1980s Tom Hess led a 24-hour prayer watch in Washington, D.C. In 1985, he led a team to Egypt and Israel. While praying on Mount Sinai for the Jewish people, the Holy Spirit told Hess he was to go to America and Russia to help prepare for the future exodus. And in the fall of 1986, Hess felt he was to take a team of 38 Jewish and Gentile believers on a prayer journey to Russia and Israel.

They were greeted at the airport in Leningrad by the KGB, but later they managed to meet with and encourage Russian Jewish dissidents called *refuseniks*, so named because they were refused permission to emigrate. The team traveled to Moscow and completed a prophetic Jericho march around the Kremlin. At Red Square they prayed for the release of the Jewish people living within the borders of the Soviet Union. On Yom Kippur the team visited a Jewish synagogue in Moscow, where they provided clothing and Bibles to many Russians. Members also serenaded their KGB escorts with "O Come, Let Us Adore Him," something neither group will ever forget.

This strategic visit took place simultaneously with the summit meeting in Iceland between U.S. President Ronald Reagan and Soviet Union President Gorbachev. When Hess's group finally reached Jerusalem, they stood on the Mount of Olives and issued a prophetic command to the land of the north to release the Jewish people in the name of the Lord. Within a few days, the Soviet Union unexpectedly agreed to release within one year twelve thousand Jewish people who wanted to emigrate to Israel.[8]

Second Prayer Mission

Hess led a second prayer mission to the U.S.S.R. in the spring of 1987, with a specific assignment to strike at the root of the Communist ideology that, at the time, was enslaving virtually seventy percent of the human race. In Moscow God ministered to the group from Daniel 12:1, revealing that the archangel Michael was arising to deliver the Jewish people out of the Soviet Union. It was no coincidence that they visited a sixteenth-century church in the Kremlin called Cathedral of the Archangel (which now also served as a museum) and prayed for their release.[9]

46

The team marched Jericho-style around the Kremlin. Then they moved on to Leningrad to visit an atheistic museum, housed in an old church building that had been converted into an anti-God memorial. On the lower floor of the church stood a statue of a large, nude male figure surrounded by little cherubs or demons and an eerie portrait of Vladimir Lenin. These items aptly portrayed the god of Communism. Hess described the twisted scene in detail and explained what God sent the prayer team to accomplish:

> The central focus is a picture of Lenin with all the religions and cultures of the world being subjugated by communism. The cross is broken in two. The American, British, Swiss and other flags are torn in two, and the hammer and sickle [is triumphing] over the world. We did another Jericho march around the atheistic museum and with the Sword of the Spirit laid the axe to the spiritual root of communism in the very city where Lenin instituted this demonic ideology in 1917.[10]

By the turn of the century Hess had led ten teams of Jericho-type prayer marches in Russia. Today he is setting his sights toward organizing similar on-site prayer ventures in the United States and other lands.

What Brought the Walls Down?

Lightle also took a twelve-member prayer team to Moscow in 1987, on the seventieth anniversary of the October Revolution of 1917. The prayer team's heavenly mission was clear and seemingly impossible: They were sent to cancel the Soviet Constitution signed by Lenin and rewrite a new one based upon God's Word.

Canceling the Soviet Constitution

After a series of adventures, the twelve prayer commandos gathered in a circle in front of the building where Lenin signed the constitution into law. (The building now houses the Bolshoi Theatre.) The four KGB agents tailing them were so desperate to learn their plans that one of them accidentally poked Lightle in the back with his elbow as he strained to understand their words, and another was literally cupping his hands to his ears to hear. Lightle wrote, "I don't know why he was doing that. I was praying in the Holy Spirit, and I know he couldn't understand that."[11]

God had one more assignment for the commando prayer team. Because Gorbachev, "the pharaoh of the north," refused to give up God's people, God had revealed to the intercessors that He was going to shake up the world economy, especially the economy of the Soviet Union and the Communist bloc nations.

Armed with a prophetic word and a key Scripture passage from Ezekiel, the team visited the Soviet financial district. On the night of October 17, 1987, the intercessors "prayed judgment concerning the finances of the world, especially in the Communist bloc countries." Lightle wrote, "When we left the Soviet Union and found out about the stock market crash just two days later, on Monday, October 19, we understood our prayer."[12] In a global economy, what happens on Wall Street reverberates around the world.

During that same season I was participating with an intercessory team in New York City. The Lord had given me a vivid dream of a crash on Wall Street with the words, *When Wall Street hits 2600, this is a demarcation. Count forty days after.*

By divine direction we were interceding in New York City exactly forty days prior to the financial collapse. We had spent hours in prayer that day and then felt released to go on site at the New York Stock Exchange. As we stood in the encased glass balcony overlooking the trading floor, we began to intercede. Then, like an arrow shot from its bow, a prayer was released that hit the target, and we all knew it.

At that moment the time clock changed to 1:26:00 P.M., while at the same time the trading hit 2600. Isn't it amazing to see how God can orchestrate these things? Then, just as the dream had stated, we began to "count forty days after." Sure enough, forty days later the U.S. stock market suffered a devastating but temporary crash.

Interesting, isn't it? The Lord had people who did not know one another and who were in two different parts of the world engaged in the same prophetic intercessory activity!

Repenting for Évian

July 6, 1988, marked the fiftieth anniversary of the international travesty that took place in Évian, the conference we talked about in chapter 1. In that small French town, situated on the shores of beautiful Lake Geneva, the leaders from 32 nations failed to properly answer the question "How do we rescue the Jewish people from Germany and Austria?" No nation, as we saw, was willing to take in more than a token number of Jewish immigrants. As a result six million Jews perished at the hands of the mad Austrian dictator, Adolf Hitler.

Fifty years later, in what may be seen as a prophetic year of jubilee for the beleaguered Jewish people, intercessory and prophetic leaders representing each of the 32 nations that had sent delegates to Évian in 1938 assembled for a prayer conference in Berlin. A small group of them also went to Évian.

These prophetic delegates met together under a mandate from God to conduct solemn acts of "identificational repentance"— a form of intercession in which one confesses the generational sins of the family, ethnic group, city and/or nation of one's background—for the sins committed fifty years earlier against the Jewish people. They were to restore the breach created when their fathers, mothers, ancestors, nations and even the Church herself forsook the Jewish citizens of Germany and Austria in their hour of greatest need.

I wanted ardently to participate in those gatherings because the Lord had placed those issues on my heart years before. Moreover, He had given me a personal mandate to teach and impart to others many of the truths concerning identificational intercession and repentance. The problem was that my wife, Michal Ann, was nine and a half months pregnant with our third child. With his birth two weeks past due, I opted instead to intercede from home at the same hour the delegates began to gather and pray in Berlin.

At 1:17 A.M. I was praying in my living room in Kansas City, Missouri, confessing the sin American Christians committed when they failed to raise their voices on behalf of the Jewish people in 1939. The intercessors in Berlin were dealing with the same subject at about the same hour. While I was in prayer, an angel appeared and stood in the doorway of my living room. The angel, dressed in a military uniform, looked right at me.

Many things were revealed in that supernatural encounter that I will not go into, but finally the angel said, "It is time for you to go and lay your hands upon your wife and call forth your son, Tyler Hamilton."

My conviction was that the angelic message referred to something greater than the birth of my son, as important and wonderful as that was. The angel arrayed in military attire was sent to tell me that it was a time of birthing and a time of war.

Sure enough, when I laid hands on Michal Ann, she started to have contractions, and our child was born hours later—on 7-7-88. Seven is the number of completion and eight is the number of new beginnings. On this day we had doubles! In both the natural and the spiritual realms, it was a pivotal day of completion followed by new beginnings, new openings and birthing.

Just as birth happens once the birth canal is opened, so the solemn acts of identification, intercession and repentance of the Church trigger a completion on the one hand and a birthing on the other. Our prayers of repentance for our historical sins against the Jewish people closed the circle of pain, and in a moment released new freedom and life.

The natural and the spiritual often mirror one another. In 1988 believers around the world entered into identificational repentance, triggering a simultaneous new spiritual birth. In the same way, prayer preceded a new era in history. Just before the Berlin Wall fell, Soviet President Gorbachev visited East Germany and told German Chancellor Helmut Kohl that the Soviet Union had abandoned the Brezhnev Doctrine. Moscow would no longer use force to keep its satellite states from adopting democratic forms of government or free market economies. This was an unprecedented miracle.

Prayers Overflow

By September 11, 1989, neighboring Hungary had pulled down the Iron Curtain around her borders, and within six months 220,000 East Germans fled to the West through Austria or sought political asylum in West German embassies in Hungary. To put this into perspective, before the miracle of 1989, only a few East Germans managed to escape to West Berlin, and at least 327 people died trying to flee.[13]

The fall of the Iron Curtain had an even greater effect on the emigration of Russian Jews to Israel and Western nations. Russia had a long history of anti-Semitism, but it crossed an invisible line when Soviet leaders chose to persecute the Jewish people living under their control and to deny emigration to Israel.

The *refuseniks*—persecuted Soviet Jews—received worldwide coverage when they opted to risk life and limb to protest the bureaucratic denial of their applications for immigration. Jewish people in Russia knew that simply by applying to leave the U.S.S.R. for Israel, they would probably lose their jobs, be denied basic privileges and endure harassment from the KGB and local Communist officials. They also realized that they could possibly face prison time. Nevertheless, thousands of *refuseniks* applied. They had Eretz Israel on their minds and in their hearts.

As I taught in my book *The Lost Art of Intercession*, "What goes up must come down!" The prayers ascending from a radical remnant of the Body of Christ must have filled to the brim a golden bowl in heaven—one of the "golden bowls full of incense, which are the prayers of the saints" (Revelation 5:8)—and started to overflow back down to earth. Many believe the answers to these prayers started to appear in 1988 when Gorbachev changed part of the Soviet Constitution and initiated a total rewrite one year later. By 1990 Jewish people were already emigrating from Russia in unprecedented numbers, and the best was yet to come.

Partnering with God

On November 9, 1989, sixteen months after the acts of iden-tificational repentance made before God in Berlin and Évian, the Berlin Wall came down. The Iron Curtain of the Soviet Union followed. The Soviet Union ceased to exist on December 31, 1991. It marked the beginning of a remarkable decade in which Jewish people could leave Russia and return freely to Israel. Since then an estimated 1.2 million Russian-speaking Jews have moved from the former Soviet Union to the Promised Land,[14] where Russian is now the most popular language in Israel.

Just as they did in Jericho of old, amazing things happen when God partners with people and when people partner with God. Even walls called immovable start tumbling down. It has happened before and it will happen again!

◇ **A Personal Prayer** ◇

Father, in Jesus' great name, I am grateful that, in the days of Joshua, the walls of Jericho came tumbling down through the power of warfare praise. And I am grateful that, in more recent history, the Berlin Wall of division, once thought impenetrable, also came down. I take these biblical and historical examples of intervention through Christ's intercessions, and declare that the walls are still coming down today. So I thank You, Lord, and I praise You. God almighty, I arise to be a watchman on Your walls to give thanks for all You have done and the extra-ordinary things You are about to do. For the glory of God. Amen and amen.

3

The Winds of Awakening

Regarding the angels He says, "He makes His angels winds, and His ministers a flame of fire." . . . Are they not all ministering spirits, sent out to provide service for the sake of those who will inherit salvation?

Hebrews 1:7, 14

In early December 2006, I was supposed to fly to Long Island, New York, to be the first speaker at the Open Heavens Conference with revivalist Matt Sorger. But God had other plans. Prior to my flight, I came down suddenly with a flu-type sickness. The conference planners quickly reshuffled the order of the invited speakers, while I took the day to rest and recover at my home in Franklin, Tennessee.

As I lay in bed that day, the Holy Spirit kept telling me, *The winds are coming! The winds are coming!* I did not understand what He meant and could not get any more information than that. All day long as I rested, I heard the same declaration: *The winds are coming!*

The next day I felt well enough to fly. As the first leg of my flight headed from Nashville to Baltimore, we encountered unusually strong winds. The plane was bouncing around like crazy. The pilot came on the intercom to say that we were hitting fierce winds of 160 knots. When we finally landed safely in Baltimore—in winds that were still blowing forty to sixty knots on the ground—the plane was shuddering and shaking. Believe me, I was praying in tongues for angels on each wing to help steady the plane.

I wondered how I would make my connecting flight, but I soon discovered that it did not matter. Nobody was going anywhere. As it turned out, the entire East Coast was affected by this weather pattern, and all the airports in New England were closed down. That meant I would have to lay over in Baltimore for a day. I began to wonder if I would make it to this conference at all.

That night, lying awake in my hotel bed, I heard the same words once again: *The winds are coming.* What? More winds?

By morning the winds had died down enough to fly, and I made it to Long Island in time to address the closing session of the conference. As I sought the Lord beforehand, I felt that He wanted to give me words of knowledge for people at the beginning of the service—which is not my typical modus operandi— and again I heard, *The winds are coming.*

The winds are still coming? I thought they had come and gone.

During the worship portion of the service, I was worshiping our awesome God, enjoying His presence and minding His business with my eyes closed. Suddenly I felt a wind blow across my face. I opened my eyes to see if I could find the air vents. I could not see any vents, so I went back to worshiping.

Again I felt a wind blow. In an instant the atmosphere shifted, and I began to scribble down words of knowledge as fast as the Holy Spirit gave them to me—people's names, cities and diseases. The air was permeated with the spirit of revelation.

Then a third time I felt the wind. This time when I opened my eyes—*whoosh!*—an angel suddenly appeared in front of me, hovering and looking right at me. The angel was carrying a shofar and wearing a glowing white robe with a gold sash that went from the left shoulder to the waist. On the sash I could read the words *Israel Awakening*. The angel blew the shofar right in my face and then vanished.

I had experienced angelic encounters before, but had never been given the name of the angel. Was "Israel Awakening" the name of this angel? Though I did not ask, I believe it was. But whether that was the angel's name or not, I do know that the angel had come from the throne of the Ancient of Days to convey a message to His people.

I am captivated by the revelation that God is releasing angels of awakening specifically for the Middle East and especially for an Israel awakening. The angel "Israel Awakening" had come like a wind in our day to blow a trumpet and to awaken the Body of Christ in a new way. This particular messenger from heaven had been released to this generation to blow the shofar and to keep blowing it. The winds had come. The winds would continue to come. The atmosphere had shifted. The time had come for Israel to be awakened, for the Jewish people worldwide to wake up to the fullness of their identity in the Lord their Maker.

A new spirit of adoption seemed to have become available from the Lord Jesus Himself to help prepare the Body of the Messiah to fulfill her call in these last days. Simultaneously the time had come for the Gentile Church to awaken to her intercessory mission of compassion, to say yes to her calling to stand in the gap for God's purposes in Israel and wherever the Jewish people reside on the globe.

Israel Awakening

I believe the angel named "Israel Awakening" was the head of a legion of angels released to bring spiritual awakening to both the Jewish people (regarding God's purposes within Israel) and to the Body of the Messiah, the Church of Jesus Christ (concerning her role of supporting Israel in the end times, when the dispersed of Israel shall be gathered into the Kingdom of God). Centuries ago the prophet Isaiah said, "The Lord GOD, who gathers the dispersed of Israel, declares, 'I will yet gather others to them, to those already gathered'" (Isaiah 56:8).

First God had sent winds in the natural realm, and then He sent them in the spiritual. Why had the Spirit made such a point of telling me, *The winds are coming*? Because the angels are winds: "He makes His angels winds, and His ministers a flame of fire" (Hebrews 1:7). Why had they come? Because they are "ministering spirits, sent out to provide service for the sake of those who will inherit salvation" (verse 14). The Word of God will interpret the revelation sent from God.

After writing down the revelations God had given me, and my encounter with the angel, I pulled out my sheet of paper with the various names and words written on it and began to minister to the people at the conference. Sure enough, present in the meeting were a man named Daniel and twelve women named Elizabeth, just as the Holy Spirit had indicated to me. I prayed for these people, and then I started to recount the angelic encounter. My host, revivalist Matt Sorger, was ecstatic because he, too, had written on a piece of paper that an angel had entered the meeting with me that night and that the angel's name was "Israel Awakening." The Lord had confirmed His word!

But the word God gave me that night was not only for the people at the conference. Neither was it a word meant only for people who already have a heart for Israel. It is a word for you, whether you identify yourself as a Gentile or as a Jewish person, whether you believe that Yeshua (the Jewish name for Jesus) is the Messiah or not. Every one of us is going to be awakened to a new degree.

To be awakened implies that we are currently asleep, and to some degree all of us are indeed slumbering. Individually and corporately, our eyes are shut and we are sleeping. But God is giving us a heads-up. The alarm clock is going off even as dawn is breaking on a new day. It is time to wake up to God's prophetic purposes in our generation.

Romans 11 gives the New Testament apostolic view of what authentic awakening in Israel will look like. The blinders will come off Israel's eyes (as a nation and individual Jewish people in diaspora around the world) so she can behold the goodness of the Lord even in the midst of a time of great trouble. Israel will rise to her prophetic destiny and role in the Middle East as descendants of Abraham. God will apprehend the Jewish people, and they will know their one true Messiah.

The Priority of Israel

The Church will be awakened. The Gentile (non-Jewish) Church, part of the Body of Christ, will be awakened by the supernatural activity of God. She will be awakened to her strategic and sovereign role in the last days. The sleeping Bride of Christ needs to wake up and assume her rightful place of intercession and cooperation with the Son of God.

This Israel awakening also includes a fresh revelation to the Body of Messiah concerning the priority of Israel in God's heart in the last days, and the Gospel of the Kingdom being preached and demonstrated to the ends of the earth, preparing the way for the Messiah's return. The Body of Christ will awaken to the place of the Jewish people in the Word of God, in the heart of God and in the move of God; and to her responsibility to watch on the walls for Jerusalem's sake:

On your walls, Jerusalem, I have appointed watchmen; all day and all night they will never keep silent. You who profess the LORD, take no rest for yourselves; and give Him no rest until He establishes and makes Jerusalem an object of praise on the earth.

Isaiah 62:6–7

The Church, the Body of Messiah, will be awakened out of a place called "replacement theology," which neuters us, the Church. Simply defined, replacement theology teaches that the Christian Church is the replacement for Israel and that many of the biblical promises made to Israel have been fulfilled in the Church, not in Israel. I do not subscribe to such a theology.

The Gospel of the Kingdom will be praised and demonstrated—not only preached but also revealed in action with power.

This gospel of the kingdom shall be preached in the whole world
as a testimony to all the nations, and then the end will come.

Matthew 24:14

The phrase *the Gospel of the Kingdom* is also cited in Mark
and Luke. They mention not *the Gospel of the Church* but
the Gospel of the Kingdom. Jesus never told anyone to invite
people to church. I am not saying that is wrong—but why invite
them to church? We *are* the Church. We are the *ekklesia*—
which referred originally to "a ruling assembly of citizens in
the Grecian democracy to govern its city-states." That noun
translated *assembly* is translated *church* elsewhere in the New
Testament.[1]

The word God speaks to His Church today is "Pray, be in
unity, and go." The Gospel of the Kingdom will be preached
in the marketplace and demonstrated to the ends of the earth,
preparing the way for the Second Coming of the Messiah and
the coming Church awakening.

Parallelism

Parallelism between the natural and the spiritual occurs during awakening. When natural Israel is restored, the Church is
restored. When Israel gains more land, the Church gains more
land. A parallel awakening has occurred, is occurring and will
occur in the Church of the Lord Jesus Christ and in Israel taking her proper role in God's destiny.

When Israel was formed in 1948, there was a major move
of the Holy Spirit.

In 1967, during the Six-Day War, the Holy Spirit opened the
spiritual floodgates, and from that flow emerged three important movements that continue to immerse the Body of Christ

and draw people worldwide: the charismatic renewal; the Jesus People movement;[2] and the Messianic movement. (I am a product of the first two movements.) Jewish Voice Ministries International estimates that "there may be as many as 250,000 Messianic Jews in the United States and Canada at the present time" and as many as 15,000 Jewish believers in Israel."[3] Those numbers are surely growing.

In 1973, during the Yom Kippur assault, the move of the Holy Spirit brought hundreds of thousands of people to faith in the Lord Jesus.

There will be a parallel restoration, a parallel awakening, that will occur in the Church when Israel takes her proper place and role in God's destiny. I firmly believe that restoration in the Body of Christ happens according to the Jewish calendar—prophetic foreshadows. Restoration is the heart of God. As the Jewish people return to their land, God restores the Church to her land of promise as well.

Three Awakenings

Several years ago the voice of the Holy Spirit came to me and said, *There will be a gentle awakening, followed by a rude awakening, which will all work together toward the Great Awakening.* When I receive a word like that, I know it is not my natural thinking. In fact, a rude awakening sounds rather offensive! But that is what I heard. There will be a gentle awakening, followed by a rude awakening, that will work together for good unto the Great Awakening.

We can see these three awakenings in world events and Church history, as well as in the Bible. Let's dig deeper into these concepts.

The Gentle Awakening

Three primary aspects have characterized outpourings of the Holy Spirit's presence.

First, an intercessory prayer movement of unprecedented proportion—one that today shows no signs of waning. In the gentle awakening, there is an invitation from God for a more intimate relationship with Him through prayer. This is followed by the personal place of intimacy, the gifts of the Spirit and a prophetic movement in which the voice of God is heard. So the first characteristic of an outpouring of the Holy Spirit is prayer, followed by a release of giftings, particularly in hearing God's voice.

Second, we have seen an amazing upsurge of interest today in prophetic words from God, and a corresponding increase in the technological means of transmitting what He says. No longer does the word *prophetic* bring to mind odd predictions of distant future events uttered by strange wilderness prophets. As God speaks through a variety of people, His word is welcomed by those with open hearts.

Third, prophetic restoration has come on the heels of the restoration of evangelism: "Go, therefore" (Matthew 28:19). This is an important task of the Church.

Each of these—prayer, prophecy and evangelism—is an aspect of God's gentle, invitational awakening.

Throughout the Word of God, invitations were sent to people. Today is no different. Let's consider an upcoming wedding.

These days, even before an invitation is sent, hosts send a "Save the Date" notice so busy people can schedule the event, even a year in advance. Later an official invitation is sent. Most invitees are excited about the event and anticipate a nice time with friends and family. But not everybody who receives an invitation accepts it. When people refuse to wake up to the Lord's gentler awakenings—His invitation—they set themselves up to be shaken rudely awake. God wants to wake up as many people as possible in time for the Great Awakening that lies in the near future.

When people refuse the gentle invitational awakening, forerunners help prepare the way. And when people refuse, the alarm goes off and they are shaken out of their slumber—yet it all works together for good. Remember why? Because God wants as many as possible to be alert, vigilant and cooperative. He wants people to line up their lives and lifestyles with the plumbline of His own righteousness.

Since my father was a carpenter, I practically grew up in a lumberyard. I have fond memories of being in a massive truck sitting next to my daddy's large, Popeye-muscle arms. I would ride along with him to Kansas City to pick up an entire load of lumber at a wholesale place and bring it to his lumberyard in Braymer, Missouri, where he worked as a manager. When that lumber was used to build a home, school, church, whatever, the walls had to be "true to plumb" or they would not stand.

As my father invited me to journey with him, our heavenly Father invites us to sit beside Him and journey through life leaning on Him and becoming Kingdom builders.

The book of Amos mentions that when the plumbline is dropped, it determines whether what is being built is perpendicular: "So He showed me, and behold, the Lord was standing by a vertical wall with a plumb line in His hand" (Amos 7:7).

These developments are part of what I call the "gentle awakening" in which God woos His people. In His kindness and mercy, God wants to restore people to righteousness and true life. When they do not respond to His repeated gentle overtures, because of His kindness and mercy, He resorts to what the Holy Spirit, speaking to me, called a "rude awakening."

The Rude Awakening

Rude awakenings are not pleasant and often drive people to their knees in surrender to the sovereign Lord. Central to the Lord's awakenings is holiness. In the passage we looked at in the previous section, Amos describes how God drops His plumbline to see how the obedience of His people measures up. When God's plumbline—His perfect standard of righteousness—reveals how sinful people are, He brings a rude awakening, shaking everything that can be shaken.

So if you are going through a shaking, do not be discouraged. I have good news for you: You are exactly where God wants you. He wants you to wake up more than you want to be awakened. It is the kindness of God that ruthlessly awakens us and the Church, and it awakens Israel to her greater place of sovereign destiny. The plumbline of God's character and Word is dropped to see if the house we are building will withstand the turmoil surrounding us.

The whole world is gripped in war. This global war touches every continent. It features human rights abuses, genocide, corruption and overt hatred—which are, more often than not, clothed in religious terminology. It is a spiritual war with physical manifestations. And it is going to get worse.

The right response is not fatalism or denial; it is prayer—and lots of it. It is time for a prayer storm to strike the nations! Pray for protection and relief, and do not forget to focus sharply on the real goal: awakening.

Nobody should sleep through such a rude awakening. It is time to wake up. Why? Because God also declares it is going to get better! The dark will get darker, and then light will shine forth and penetrate this temporary present darkness. Amen!

> [Know] the time, that it is already the hour for you to awaken from sleep; for now salvation is nearer to us than when we first believed. The night is almost gone, and the day is near. Therefore let's rid ourselves of the deeds of darkness and put on the armor of light.
>
> Romans 13:11–12

Yes, God will have His way—the coming global Great Awakening.

The Great Awakening

On the other side of the gentle and the rude is the promise of a great global awakening, a time when Joel 2:28 is fulfilled:

> "It will come about after this that *I will pour out My Spirit on all mankind*; and your sons and your daughters will prophesy, your old men will have dreams, your young men will see visions."
>
> emphasis added

I have said many times, "It takes a young man's vision to fulfill an old man's dreams."

There are multiple waves or movements, I believe, even in the Great Awakening. There are the "suddenlies" of God, as in the book of Malachi: "The Lord, whom you are seeking, will suddenly come to His temple" (3:1). And there is the "always-been-there," as in "Jesus Christ is the same yesterday and today, and forever" (Hebrews 13:8) and "Behold, I am with you always, to the end of the age" (Matthew 28:20).

We have experienced the First Great Awakening (1730s–1740) and the Second Great Awakening (early nineteenth century), and I believe we are crossing over into the beginning of the Third Great Awakening. In the last days, the Body of Christ will be awakened to her strategic role by the supernatural activity of the Holy Spirit. The once-sleeping Bride of Christ will be awakened by the kisses of intimacy by her Master, her Lord, the Lover of her soul, to assume her rightful place of intercession and destiny in the purposes of God—the gentle awakening.

Awakening to Love

A great awakening is centered on two major commandments: "You shall love the Lord your God with all your heart, and with all your soul, and with all your mind" (Matthew 22:37) and "You shall love your neighbor as yourself" (verse 39). If you are to love someone else as you love yourself, you have to learn to receive the Father's love. Our good Father releases security and identity, and you learn to rest in His love.

So it is actually a three-pronged issue of love. First, "We love him, because he first loved us" (1 John 4:19 KJV). Then that love sinks into our souls and heals us as we worship Him. We learn not just to accept ourselves, but that we are uniquely and fearfully and wonderfully made. Second, we stop negative self-talk and accept the fact that Jesus came to heal the brokenhearted and free those who are bruised. And finally, we are commissioned to love one another.

Years ago the voice of the Holy Spirit came to me. One morning my left ear popped, and it was as if the dove of God was perched right beside my ear and whispered to me, *I will have a revival of kindness. I will have a revival of kindness.*

How noble for the Body of Christ to be awakened in love and kindness, walking in the fruit of the Spirit and in the gifts of the Spirit and with the wisdom ways of God. We will be awakened as an international family of affection, overflowing with the love of God. I see Israel as the eldest son in God's family. The firstborn inherits substantially, which means that the Jewish people will have the extra measure, a double portion, of blessing—and the added responsibilities.

The Israelites have been called to do something with what they have been given. They are called to serve. They are called to speak out, like the nation of prophets that they are, proclaiming God's coming to the world and telling what He is like. So I believe the winds are coming, and a gentle awakening followed by a rude shaking will work together for the Great Awakening comprising Scripture-based prophetic prayers and awakening by the winds of God.

Just as I experienced the winds of God to deliver a strategic message, as I described in the beginning of this chapter, so will it be in this global Great Awakening, with an unprecedented move of the Holy Spirit—a wonderful closing to the narrative of the earth. The last days are upon us. Whether you are a Gentile or a Jew, wake up! Do not miss the day of His manifest presence, His soon coming.

By the way, consider this thought. He is coming *to* us before He is coming *for* us—because it is all about preparing Christ's Bride.

Gentiles have taken off their blinders, in part, over the past two thousand years, embracing Jesus as Savior and thereby becoming God's primary instrument for establishing His Kingdom on earth, while Israel has remained blind to her Messiah. This situation, however, is not meant to be permanent (see Romans 11). Israel is not out of the picture. She has not disqualified herself from God's redemptive plan. God has not given up on using His chosen ones to establish His Kingdom on earth.

Remember, God remains faithful when we are unfaithful. Great is His faithfulness! In fact, He plans to raise up and fully restore His original covenant people:

> Then He said to me, "Son of man, these bones are the entire house of Israel; behold, they say, 'Our bones are dried up and our hope has perished. We are completely cut off.' Therefore prophesy and say to them, 'This is what the Lord GOD says: "Behold, I am going to open your graves and cause you to come up out of your graves, My people; and I will bring you into the land of Israel. Then you will know that I am the LORD, when I have opened your graves and caused you to come up out of your graves, My people. *I will put My Spirit within you and you will come to life, and I will place you on your own land.* Then you will know that I, the LORD, have spoken and done it," declares the LORD.'"
>
> Ezekiel 37:11–14, emphasis added

An awakening of unprecedented proportions will occur, hand in hand with unprecedented troubles that will make God-fearing Jewish people in the land of Israel cry out to the one true God. Their prayers will rise alongside those of compassionate Gentile believers around the world.

Yes, the sleeping Bride of Christ will be awakened so that she assumes her rightful role. And yes, the land of Israel will experience a corresponding awakening. But in addition to all this, a fresh move of God will blow across the nations of the earth, wherever Jewish people reside, and Jewish people worldwide will be awakened.

During the Jesus People movement, which began in 1967, hundreds of Jewish people came to faith in Jesus as their Messiah. Signs and wonders accompanied this new outpouring of grace. More than a generation has gone by since then. Far from having dwindled into a historical anomaly, this move of God has become a steadily growing tide.

And something new is still happening. As angels such as "Israel Awakening" are released worldwide, fresh oil is still being poured out. The scope of what God is doing takes my breath away. The more I find out about it, the more meaning I find in the daily news and the more specific prayers I pray.

In the chapters that follow in section 2, I will take a closer look at the well-orchestrated details of the past, present and future for God's people.

An awakening is coming. Indeed, it has already begun. Yes, Israel will be awakened for such a time as this.

◇ **A Personal Prayer** ◇

Father God, in Jesus' mighty name, I welcome the winds of God into my life, my family and my sphere of responsibility and authority. And I call forth an invasion of heaven's angelic army into the earth realm. I declare that a supernatural movement of signs and wonders is already here. Father, use the gentle and even the rude awakening to create the climate and culture of the greatest global awakening, for Your holy name's sake. Amen and amen.

The Prophetic and Prayer

4

Appointed a Watchman

"For the earth will be filled with the knowledge of the glory of
the LORD, as the waters cover the sea."

Habakkuk 2:14

Some years ago I was teaching from the Scriptures that the glory
of the Lord will cover the earth as the waters cover the seas. The
topic, to a certain degree, was theoretical. Then the Holy Spirit
asked me, *How will that happen?* Not knowing the answer, I
said back to Him, *Oh, how will that happen?*

Always remember, the best way to answer a question from
God is to ask Him what the answer is. He does not ask a question because He does not know the answer. Every question He
asks is an invitation into greater partnership with Him.

So while I was teaching the class and declaring God's Word, I
was actually having a personal exchange with the Holy Spirit, although the students did not know about this behind-the-scenes
discussion.

When I returned the question to God, He answered, *One*

clay pot at a time. I will fill the earth with My glory one clay pot at a time.

We are those clay pots. We are the clay pot watchmen who are to be ready and prepared to cover the earth with the glory of the Lord.

Did you know that God has a calendar with appointments waiting to be fulfilled? Watchmen remind God of the appointments on His calendar that have not been fully met and fulfilled. The task of a watchman is by appointment. It means being chosen for the divine privilege of composing history before the throne of the Almighty.

I want to be a history-maker. That is the goal of my life. Are you ready to make a difference? The recipe for enduring change is that simple. Yes, prayer provokes change!

Are you taking your biblical place on the wall for Israel's sake? Just as the call for watchmen went out in Isaiah's time, the Holy Spirit is releasing this strategic call again in the 21st century.

It seems as if God has been conducting a monumental chess game throughout the ages, waiting for the strategic moment in history to make His move. Yes, the playing board has been set and the pieces have been chosen. The call for watchmen is the strategic positioning of His intercessory knights and prophetic bishops being brought together for a sweeping move— one that all the world will observe closely. No eye will miss this mysterious and fascinating time. We must pray, therefore, for our eyes to be opened with spiritual understanding.

Seeing through God's Eyes

After our move from Kansas City to "Music City," the first conference that my wife, Michal Ann, and I hosted in Nashville was on "The Mystery of the Church and Israel." Our friends Avner and Rachel Boskey of Final Frontier Ministries in the Beersheva region of Israel led the worship. During one of the worship times, I saw an open vision of an eye staring right at me. In the middle of this eye, I saw the Star of David. As I gazed more intently upon the vision, I saw a Scripture reference written in the middle of the Star of David. The Scripture I saw was Zechariah 2:8.

I did not have the foggiest idea what Zechariah 2:8 was, so I found it in my Bible: "The one who touches you [Israel], touches the apple of His eye."

Some other translations render the phrase *apple of God's eye* as *the pupil of God's eye*. The pupil is the opening that allows light into the eye, beginning the process of sight. So he who touches Israel touches the center of God's eye—the center of God's sight.

If you want an accurate prophetic perception of life, Scripture and God's purposes on earth, especially in the days before Christ returns, you must have God's vision, seeing through God's eyes and then holding dear to your heart the things that are closest to His heart. Since Israel is at the center of God's vision, we need to see through the lens of Israel's destiny if we are to see correctly and clearly.

Moses tells us in Deuteronomy 32:9–11,

> For *the LORD's portion is His people*; Jacob is the allotment of His inheritance. He found him in a desert land, and in the howling wasteland of a wilderness; He encircled him, He cared for him, *He guarded him as the apple of His eye*. As an eagle that stirs up its nest, and hovers over its young, He spread His wings, He caught them, He carried them on His pinions.
>
> emphasis added

Please understand that this is not an ethnic issue. It is about a promise-keeping God who is faithful to fulfill His plan for a people, a city and a nation through whom He has chosen to display His splendor. We cannot afford to poke at God's eye with prejudice and wrong concepts such as replacement theology, sensationalism and other false teachings. This is about God's faithful character being on lavish display for all to observe and know.

A phrase in a famous hymn says, "His eye is on the sparrow, and I know He watches me." Well, because God's eye is on the sparrow, we know His gaze has never lifted from the center of His attention. That center is Israel, and His eye is ever gazing on them.

Seven Reasons to Pray for Israel

I have been interceding as a watchman for Israel for well over 25 years. From this vantage point, I would like to share with you seven reasons I pray and take a stand for Israel. I believe that you, too, should be a watchman on the wall who cries out to God on Israel's behalf. Ready for your assignment?

1. The Apple of God's Eye

Pray and take a stand for Israel because Israel is very close to God's heart. I have already shared Zechariah 2:8: "The one who touches you [Israel], touches the apple of His eye." And Psalm 148:14 declares, "He has lifted up a horn for His people, praise for all His godly ones, for the sons of Israel, *a people near to Him. . .*" (emphasis added). I love that!

The first reason I pray for Israel, then, is not profound. I pray for Israel because I want to be close to God's heart and in alignment with His sight. If God says that Israel is the apple (or pupil) of His eye, then I want to pray with insight—with His sight.

Do you want to be close to the heart of God? Then be close to the things, people and purposes that are close to His heart.

2. *Time for Compassion*

Pray for Israel's destiny to be fulfilled in the Middle East in order to be in union with God's heart of compassion. For me this is not just a biblical accuracy issue; it is a heart issue. Our prayers must go beyond mere words; we need to pray for Israel by being filled with compassion for Israel's condition. Psalm 102:13–14 says:

> You will arise and have compassion on Zion; for it is time to be gracious to her, for the appointed time has come. Surely Your servants take pleasure in her stones, and feel pity for her dust.

The time has come!

When I recorded the vocal prayer tracks for *Prayers for Israel*, I was in a small, out-of-the-way studio in Kelowna, British Columbia, Canada. It was chilly in that little building! But while I was praying through Psalm 102 for the cut "It's Time to Have Compassion," the Holy Spirit came upon me and my heart burned with the fire of God. I started to weep. Perhaps I was releasing a measure of God's heart at that moment.

You see, God wants us to pray, not with a clenched fist of self-righteous anger, but with a compassionate heart. I have cried out to the Lord to tenderize my heart. You, too, can ask the Holy Spirit to give you His heart of compassion for Israel.

I was asked in an interview what my prayer times are like. I thought, *How can I answer that? Prayer has taken many different forms over the years.* I responded something like this:

> Well, I started out by praying the Word, and engrafted the Word into my life. I prayed the Scriptures for hours. Then I came to a time when I learned to worship and sing and pray in the Spirit. I was taught by my tutor, the Holy Spirit, to pick up the warrior's mantle of prophetic intercession and exercise the authority of a believer in Christ. This led to another turn in the journey of prayer—prayer of the heart that does not even have language. It is simply being there with Him. But the primary way that I pray today is with tears. Something happens inside and I just begin to weep. God puts into me His contrite heart, and I begin to feel what God feels over a situation, a place, an individual or a group of people.

God wants to give His heart to us so we can pray over Israel with compassion—even to the prayer of tears. It is time to have compassion on Zion. Will you join me?

3. Establishing Jerusalem

Pray and take a stand for Israel because God wants to establish Jerusalem and make her a praise in the earth. Listen again to the Scripture at the beginning of this chapter:

> On your walls, Jerusalem, I have appointed watchmen; all day and all night they will never keep silent. You who profess the LORD, take no rest for yourselves; and give Him no rest *until He establishes and makes Jerusalem an object of praise on the earth.*
>
> Isaiah 62:6–7 (emphasis added)

We are to give Him no rest until *what* is established? Jerusalem! He did not say Washington, D.C., or Paris or London. He did not say Constantinople, Athens, Damascus, Moscow or Cairo. He said until *Jerusalem* is made a praise. A *praise*!

News reports state that Jerusalem is far from being a praise. In fact, many people curse Jerusalem and call the Jewish people names I will not even dare repeat. So we must lift our voices in prayer until she becomes a praise—a glorious praise—in all the earth.

Let's understand something very clearly: This is not for the sake of the Church. It is for the sake of Zion!

Our ministry hosts weekly prayer watches for Israel. It is not always easy, but it is a delight. No form of prayer is convenient. But as you put your hand to this plow, you will find that even more distractions come your way. Reasons not to pray, reasons to slack, distractions, interruptions in your schedule. Just set your heart to be resolute. Pray until!

4. Israel's Salvation

Pray for Israel so that Israel will be saved.

I have shared that God wants to give us His heart of compassion—His tears—for Israel. But tears and compassion are not God's end objective. He wants us to receive His heart so that we can pray with accuracy and discernment for the salvation of Israel. The apostle Paul wrote, "I have great sorrow and unceasing grief in my heart. . . . My heart's desire and my prayer to God for them is for their salvation" (Romans 9:2; 10:1). Paul also declared, "I could wish that I myself were accursed . . . for the sake of my countrymen . . . who are Israelites" (Romans 9:3–4). Paul was willing to be separated from Christ so that his brethren might know their

Messiah. What a sacrifice he was willing to make for the sake of Israel!

At the conferences that our ministry hosts, we normally include a special Israel Prayer Watch so that believers can listen, agree, receive, learn and participate. At one of these Israel Prayer Watches, I was given a wonderful, interactive visionary encounter. I entered into rays of God's brilliant white light. As I stepped into this light, I saw a man standing at the end of a tunnel of God's vast love. Suddenly it was as though my being soared in the air and leaped into the heart of the man standing in the light of God's love. An apostolic heart of God was pounding loudly within him. Words in rhythm with the heartbeat of God were echoing in the heart of this man, who appeared to be a representation of Paul the apostle. Then I heard, "My heart's desire is that all Israel be saved." My own heart was pierced once again. I wept and wept for Israel's salvation.

We must pray for Israel's salvation to go forth like a burning torch. Boldly I say that there is only one way to our Father—through His one and only Son, the Lord Jesus Christ (see John 14:6). One of the greatest gifts the Jewish people have given the world is the Bible. All 66 books (with the possible exception of Luke) were penned by Jewish people. God's Son has a Jewish bloodline inheritance. Jesus is the way. Do you pray with a burning heart of desire for Israel's salvation?

5. The Peace of Jerusalem

Pray and take a stand for Israel because God wants to bless Jerusalem and her inhabitants with His peace and goodness. David, the warrior psalmist, loved Jerusalem and fought many battles for her. Wars and heated conflicts continue to rage today over this small piece of land in the Middle East.

We must continue to pray and sing David's exhortation in Psalm 122:6–7 today: "Pray for the peace of Jerusalem: 'May they prosper who love you. May peace be within your walls, and prosperity within your palaces.'" The heart of God is revealed in many other psalms, too. He hears "the desire of the afflicted" (Psalm 10:17 NIV); He "will save [the helpless] on a day of trouble" (Psalm 41:1); and He "secures justice for the poor and upholds the cause of the needy" (Psalm 140:12 NIV).

The apostle Paul loved not only Israel but Jerusalem and was concerned for the city and the welfare of her inhabitants. He wrote to the Romans that he was "going to Jerusalem, serving the saints" (15:25).

Today, despite hundreds of thousands of new immigrants, the downturn of tourism during the global pandemic, the "Boycott, Divestment and Sanctions" (BDS) movement, terrorism, wars and rumors of wars, Israel's economy has seen continued growth.

We must pray for the shalom of God—*shalom* is the Hebrew word for peace—for the city of peace. But we must do more. I have often quoted intercessor S. D. Gordon: "You can do more than pray after you've prayed. But you cannot do more than pray until you have prayed."

The Lord said to Abram:

"I will make you into a great nation, and I will bless you, and make your name great; and you shall be a blessing; and I will bless those who bless you, and the one who curses you I will curse. And in you all the families of the earth will be blessed."

Genesis 12:2–3

6. Life to the World

Pray and act for Israel because the Jewish people's acceptance of the Messiah, Jesus, will lead to worldwide revival of unprecedented magnitude. Romans 11:15 says that if Israel's rejection of Christ "proves to be the reconciliation of the world, what will their acceptance be but life from the dead?" Wow!

I was once interviewed for a documentary focused on the literal raising of the dead. I was asked, "What would be the greatest resurrection you would like to see?" My response? "One of the greatest resurrections would be that the Body of Christ is raised from the dead, and that we would take our place on the walls for Israel's sake." I firmly believe that we are that important for Israel's salvation—and because her salvation is a key to worldwide revival. If Israel's rejection of Christ meant that the Gentile world was given the Gospel of the Kingdom, resulting in reconciliation with God, what will be Israel's reward be for their acceptance of Christ as the Messiah? God's Word says, "Life from the dead."

This prophecy of Isaiah—"In the days to come Jacob will take root, Israel will blossom and sprout, and they will fill the whole earth with fruit" (27:6)—refers to more than just natural fruit. Praying for Israel, as we have just seen, is one of the major keys to world revival. The Jewish people being awakened out of their sleep and beholding their Messiah will create a divine acceleration into a time when hundreds of thousands, if not literally millions, turn to Jesus as their Messiah. There is nothing more potent than a Jewish believer telling others about the God of Abraham, Isaac and Jacob.

Israel's acceptance of her glorious Messiah will be used to create the greatest spiritual awakening this planet has ever seen.

The whole earth will be filled with the fruit of revival. I pray toward this end! Will you join me?

7. Jesus' Second Coming

Pray and take a stand for Israel because the Second Coming of Christ is linked to Israel's response to Him. Jesus prophesied before His death, "I say to you, from now on you will not see Me until you say, 'Blessed is the One who comes in the name of the LORD!'" (Matthew 23:39). Jesus thus linked His Second Coming to Israel's national returning, or turning, to Him.

Johannes Facius, founder of Intercessors for Denmark, helped launch prayer initiatives in at least 45 nations. He writes:

> Now get the picture here! The Lord is not saying to the Jewish inhabitants of the city of Jerusalem that they shall never see Him again. He is saying that they shall not see Him until they are ready to welcome Him. When He came the first time He was not welcomed. The Messiah has no intention of repeating this situation. Jesus is saying that His Second Coming will not take place until there is a Jewish population in Jerusalem who will welcome Him with all of their hearts. Before that can happen, the descendants of the Jews who were exiled nearly two-thousand years ago will have to return to Jerusalem.[1]

Do you want to see Jesus come back in your lifetime? Is it possible to hasten the day of His appearing (see 2 Peter 3:12)? Do you want to see Jesus come again? Then pray that the blinders on the Jewish people's eyes will fall off (see Romans 11:25) and that they will welcome their Messiah with open hearts.

Anna and Simeon spent their time in the Temple preparing the way for the first coming of our glorious Savior and Lord (see Luke 2:25–38). So will it be before the Second Coming of our glorious Messiah. Hundreds and thousands of Annas and Simeons will arise across the nations, taking their place in worship and intercession, with watching and fasting, preparing the way for the Second Advent of our Jewish Messiah, Yeshua.

Why pray and take a stand of action for Israel? Because Jesus said to, because Isaiah said to, because David the psalmist said to and because today the Holy Spirit is saying to—to pray and take a stand of action. Let's take our place on the wall and pray for Israel to be awakened, because as we do, we are praying not just for one race of people, but for a move of Holy Spirit in the Middle East and the entire globe.

Let the Cry Arise!

The Lord answers when we cry out to Him. And Israel's history shows a clear pattern of people who, time and again, found themselves in trouble, cried out to the Lord and saw Him deliver them out of their adversity.

It is my conviction, and that of many other leaders in the Body of the Messiah, that the Holy Spirit is opening a strategic window of opportunity for the Gentile Church to arise "for such a time as this" (Esther 4:14). We must pray and take a stand as never before in all of Church history for God's purposes to be fulfilled in Israel, in the Jewish people and in all the descendants of Abraham. We will talk more about them in section 3.

The Church in this pivotal hour is recovering the lost weapon of fasting. Spiritual crisis intervention is launched from the biblical foundation of prayer with fasting. God's Word provides many examples; perhaps the greatest is that of Queen Esther and her cousin, Mordecai, who in a time of life-and-death crisis called a solemn three-day fast from all food and drink. God provided them with a way of escape that ultimately saved the Jewish race from annihilation; and He will provide one for Israel today if we respond as they did.

Like Queen Esther, we must consider our role in saving God's chosen people from demise. The Holy Spirit is issuing a prophetic invitation to history-making intercession with fasting. When we seek God's heart earnestly concerning the Jewish people and their destiny, we unlock historic action. We are called to be modern-day Esthers and Mordecais on behalf of God's ancient covenant people. Therefore, with faith, humility and a sense of destiny and urgency, I have established "The Cry"—three days of prayer with fasting, every year during the time of Purim (the holiday commemorating the saving of the Jewish people in the time of Esther) until God's purpose is fulfilled among His people, Israel. It is time to take a stand.

According to the Jewish calendar, Purim is held in the month of Adar, which usually falls in February or March. Moses was born in Adar. It is also the month when the Maccabees, the Jewish rebel warriors, defeated the Seleucid Dynasty; and the month when the orders were given to rebuild the walls of Jerusalem preceding the reconstruction of the Temple and the first return of the Jewish people to Israel.

Will you join me? Not everyone can participate in an Esther fast because of health reasons, but some can. Sacrifice releases power, and we can each take our place on the walls and see the eyes of Israel open in a move of the Holy Spirit in unprecedented proportions across the entire face of the earth. Let's pray until Israel's destiny is met and fulfilled.

The night before I was to minister at a conference in Germany, I dreamed that I was going to be asked to speak, and that the Holy Spirit's presence would come into the auditorium so powerfully on the first night that no one would speak. I did not mention the dream to anyone.

The next night, the first night of the conference, while we were worshiping, God's presence rolled into the room to such a degree that about half the attendees lay prostrate on the floor, seeking God. The Holy Spirit instructed me to read the book of Esther as we were all in the presence of God, all in the glory. As I sat in the front row, I read the book of Esther under the manifest presence of God. I have never read a book of the Bible before or since under such an overwhelming dimension of destiny and presence. Under His anointing, I read the book Esther from beginning to end. He gave me a different lens to read it through—the "I" narrative of Mordecai. What was being highlighted to me was not so much about Esther as about Mordecai.

One of my callings in this life, I believe, is to be a modern-day Mordecai, who has a spirit of adoption to help nurture the Bride for her appointment. I am to stand in the gap—the cry in the time of Purim. I am sure many others have this same calling, and I pray we all take this role seriously.

I do not believe there is only one call, training or commissioning for followers of Christ. I actually believe we can have multiple callings throughout our lifetime. We have a calling, a training, a commissioning and a fulfilling—and then we can have another one. These are often progressive in nature.

Over the years, after each of a few close-to-death moments, I asked God, "Why am I still here?" One of the reasons is to teach what I am teaching right now. Another reason is to challenge the Church. Yet one more reason is to wake myself up and wake you up, that we will be part of the gentle, the rude and the Great Awakening—that we will have God's heart and carry the

Jewish people on our shoulders to God with Scripture-based prayers for divine appointment and fulfillment.

Now I have a few questions for you. Will you lift up your voice to fill up every clay pot with His glory? Will you join me? Let the cry arise. Receive your appointment as a vessel of history-making intercession for such a time as this. Allow the Holy Spirit to give you guidance and instruction. He wants to release this spirit of adoption—the calling to be a Mordecai for such a time as this. Accept God's heart to help prepare the Bride for her divine appointment.

Praying the Scriptures

I encourage you to read through the following two Scriptures and pray through each passage using the sample prayer that follows.

> In You our fathers trusted; they trusted and You rescued them. To You they cried out and they fled to safety; in You they trusted and were not disappointed.
>
> Psalm 22:4–5

God, I read in the Bible of Your great faithfulness. When those who trusted in You cried out to You, You delivered each one. I ask, therefore, that the people of Israel would once again put their trust in You, the God of their fathers, Abraham, Isaac and Jacob. In the midst of great difficulty, I ask that they would cry out to You and that You would deliver them from all their troubles. Reveal Yourself to them. Show them again Your great faithfulness and that You are the God who does not disappoint. Amen.

In the days to come Jacob will take root, Israel will blossom and sprout, and they will fill the whole world with fruit.

Isaiah 27:6

Thank You, Lord, for Your eternal Word and Your promises to Jacob. Prosper Israel. Let her take root, blossom and sprout. Jesus said that only those who abide in Him will bear much fruit. We ask that Israel will abide in their Messiah so they can bear much, much fruit and that their fruit will fill the whole world. Let the fruit of revival come to Israel, and from Israel to the ends of the earth. Amen.

Let's seize the moment and arise to our destiny to be watchmen on the walls for Israel's destiny to be fulfilled. Desperate times take desperate measures. Let's not miss the divine opportunity and appointment set before us. Let the prayer army increase in size, purity and effectiveness. This is the time. This is the generation. May a new breed of servant-believers emerge who demonstrate the identity of the Jewish Messiah we serve.

◇ **A Personal Prayer** ◇

Lord God, I ask that a loud cry would arise within me. When I call out to You in times of distress, I know with confidence that You hear and will answer quickly. Hear my prayer, O Lord. Thank You for listening to my cry for help. Listen to the cries of Your people, Israel, and give me Your heart of compassion for them. Arise and have compassion on Your people.

I pray that Your servants would take great pleasure in Israel and have Your heart of compassion for her condition. Give me Your heart, O Lord, and let the apple of Your eye become the center of my vision. Hear Your people's collective prayers. Be gracious to Israel and all people of the Middle East. In Jesus' name. Amen.

5

Praying for the Fulfillment of Aliyah

"Do not fear, for I am with you; I will bring your offspring from the east, and gather you from the west. I will say to the north, 'Give them up!' and to the south, 'Do not hold them back.' Bring My sons from afar and My daughters from the ends of the earth."

Isaiah 43:5–6

When I was about twenty and living in Kansas City, during the Jesus People Movement in the 1960s, I heard international Bible teacher Derek Prince speak about how modern-day Israel and the return of the Jewish people to the land was a fulfillment of prophetic Scripture. This scholarly man, educated at Cambridge, had studied Hebrew and Aramaic at the Hebrew University in Jerusalem, and spoke worldwide about his life-changing experience with Jesus Christ. He had a way of communicating that made me sit quietly and absorb what he was saying. It was the combination of both Word and Spirit that apprehended me. Ever since then, the fulfillment of aliyah—the Jewish people returning to the homeland—has been a favorite subject of mine.

You may remember the word *aliyah* from chapter 1. This term is used commonly in the Semitic languages, especially Hebrew. It has become associated with the journey of Hebrew families in Bible times going up to Jerusalem and the Temple Mount, there to celebrate the three great annual festivals that the Lord ordained. Psalms were written to accompany these joyous occasions. Fathers led their families up the highway to Jerusalem singing the psalms of aliyah.[1]

Over the years, the word *aliyah* has become very dear to Jewish people and believing Gentiles alike. As prophetic Scriptures are fulfilled right before our eyes about the regathering of the Jewish people from the ends of the earth, the term has become a way of describing all that is involved in the process of returning to the homeland.

How could a remnant of scattered and persecuted Jewish people, who went through their darkest hour in Hitler's Holocaust, come forth all at once as a sovereign nation within their age-old boundaries? Surely it was with divine intervention, although many secular Israelis today believe they did it all on their own.

Prophetic Foreshadows

This history of God's providential protection of Israel since her rebirth as a nation in 1948 is a brilliant study in its own right. (Be sure to take a look at Appendix A, "Overview of Israel's History.") The amazing promise of God's restoration and protection of Israel is not based on anything good she has accomplished as a nation. It is, rather, a declaration of God's own nature—His greatness, sovereignty and faithfulness. God and God alone will be glorified as this act of redemption unfolds.

This is what mercy is all about. If Israel deserved pardon, she would not need God's grace. Only through receiving His grace can she restore to Him the glory that her sins robbed from Him. Paul, the Jewish apostle to the Gentiles, paints this picture for us perfectly in Romans 11:6: "If it is by grace, it is no longer on the basis of works, since otherwise grace is no longer grace."

Let's review two remarkable Old Testament prophecies regarding God's grace in Israel's dispersion and regathering.

Jeremiah's Detailed Declaration

Jeremiah, the weeping prophet, gazed through the lens of time to reveal that Israel's covenant-keeping God would graciously offer His stretched-out wings as a place of divine protection, specifically during the time of her gathering to the Promised Land:

> Hear the word of the LORD, you nations, and declare it in the coastlands far away, and say, "He who scattered Israel will gather him and He will keep him as a shepherd keeps his flock."
>
> Jeremiah 31:10

Jeremiah declared God's precise will to the Gentile nations. This was a prophetic declaration that God would perform a sovereign extraction of the Jewish peoples and that aliyah would be fulfilled. Amazing!

In this one short verse we find three great truths. First, it was God Himself who scattered Israel from her homeland. Second, the same God who scattered Israel will gather her back to her own land. Third, God will not merely gather Israel, but will keep her and put a divine hedge of protection around her as she is being gathered. We will look again at this verse, with the verses that lead up to it, later in this chapter.

What a promise! What a God!

Hosea's Piercing Pronouncement

The parabolic prophet Hosea adds another layer of truth. Listen to his penetrating words: "In the place where it is said to them, 'You are not My people,' it will be said to them, 'You are the sons of the living God'" (Hosea 1:10).

This piercing prophetic statement, "You are not My people," was pronounced at a time when Israel languished in a state of rebellion and sin (see Hosea 1:9). But thank the Lord, God's word of judgment included a ray of hope. Isn't it amazing? With every word of judgment comes a silver lining, a promise waiting to be found. God's true word cuts deeply at times, but those cuts are for the purpose of bringing healing and restoration.

On the heels of His judgment, God offered the Hebrew children a phenomenal promise. He promised that "in the place"—in the land of Israel—where they were told they were not His people, they will be told, "You are the sons of the living God."

Contemplate the meaning of this verse with me. Hosea 1:10 speaks not only of a physical relocation and restoration, but also of a spiritual rebirth or revival that will take place among God's covenant people when they have returned to their covenant-given land. God is declaring a miracle of major proportions. This is one of the major reasons aliyah is so important. No wonder the return of the Jewish people is contested so hotly in the spirit world! I agree with Malcolm Hedding, former chaplain of the International Christian Embassy Jerusalem:

Israel's restoration is truly an eschatological event. That is, an event that has to do with the end of one age and with the beginning of another. The world is now in the *terminal season*.[2]

Whether or not you fully accept that premise, you must agree with me that the fulfillment of aliyah is a reflection of the awesome faithfulness of our Father! I once heard Derek Prince declare, "To pass off the restoration of Israel as a political accident is like believing the world is flat." Even after hundreds of years, God is faithful and true to His Word.

Two Regatherings

With the foundation of God's grace and faithfulness in place, let's add a few more building blocks to our understanding. With this next layer I want to expand our appreciation of the Diaspora (the dispersion) of the Jewish people throughout history. William W. Orr stated in 1948:

> There isn't the slightest doubt that the emergence of the nation Israel among the family of nations is the greatest piece of prophetic news that we have had in the twentieth century. Such a significant event requires closer investigation if we are to truly grasp its significance, especially in view of the fact that a nation twice exiled has returned to the very land of its fathers. Such a thing is without precedent in world history.[3]

The First Regathering

Scripture foretold plainly that the Jewish people would suffer two major dispersions, or scatterings, from their own land, followed by two miraculous regatherings.

The first scattering was in the years when the prophets Daniel and Ezekiel were exiled in the land of Babylon, when the Jews of Judea were displaced from their country after the destruction of the Temple and Jerusalem by Nebuchadnezzar (see Daniel 1:1–6). It was around 605 BC when Daniel and his associates were carried away. Their restoration to the land began in 538 BC (see 2 Chronicles 36:22–23; Ezra 1:1–4), and the Temple remained in ruins until 515 BC (see Ezra 6:15), about seventy years after its destruction in 586 BC.

Let's take a moment now to consider the prophetic understanding of Daniel. A prophet of the one true God and a man of excellent character, he was in captivity with the children of Israel in Babylon. It was perhaps their 63rd year of captivity in a foreign land with a foreign culture, foreign gods and foreign ways. Daniel was meditating on the Word of God—"the word of the LORD to Jeremiah the prophet" (Daniel 9:2)—when a revelation based on the promises of Jeremiah came to him:

> "This entire land will be a place of ruins and an object of horror, and these nations will serve the king of Babylon for seventy years. Then it will be when seventy years are completed I will punish the king of Babylon and that nation," declares the LORD.
>
> Jeremiah 25:11–12

> This is what the LORD says: "When seventy years have been completed for Babylon, I will visit you and fulfill My good word to you, to bring you back to this place."
>
> Jeremiah 29:10

Daniel believed the Word and declared it as true for his time and people—that at the end of seventy years of Babylonian captivity, the children of Israel would be released from their enslavement and return to their own land. Daniel sought the Lord for any reasons or blockades that might yet stand in the way of the promise of the Lord being fulfilled (see Daniel 9:3–19). Then, as described in my book on prophetic intercession, *Kneeling on the Promises*, Daniel responded to the word of revelation by humbly and persistently "kneeling on it."[4] He entered with resolution into identificational repentance and confessed the sins of his people as his own.

The following verse summarizes his confession:

"Lord, hear! Lord, forgive! Lord, listen and take action! For Your own sake, my God, do not delay, because Your city and Your people are called by Your name."

Daniel 9:19

This is prophetic intercession at its best. For sure, at the end of seventy years, the Israelites were released from Babylon in fulfillment of prophecy—their first return to their covenant land. The walls of Jerusalem began to be rebuilt. The people returned. Restoration occurred.

Many more cycles of faith, sin, repentance, revival and restoration followed, but the word given to Jeremiah had been fulfilled and God had shown Himself true to His promise. The cycles have continued as the years come and go, but God's faithfulness to His Word remains.

The Second Regathering

Isaiah, one of God's appointed watchmen, not only saw the first dispersion and regathering but also prophesied the second one:

It will happen on that day that the Lord will again recover with His hand the second time the remnant of His people who will remain, from Assyria, Egypt, Pathros, Cush, Elam, Shinar, Hamath, and from the islands of the sea. And He will lift up a flag for the nations and assemble the banished ones of Israel, and will gather the dispersed of Judah from the four corners of the earth.

Isaiah 11:11–12

This Scripture describes clearly a second dispersion and, at some point later, a second regathering. The first dispersion did not send these wandering Hebrews in various directions at once. They remained together as a collective entity in Babylon—a very persecuted yet identifiable people in a foreign land. But the second scattering would send them to regions way beyond the known existence of Isaiah's day—out as far as "the four corners of the earth."

When did the second dispersion occur? It began around AD 70 under the Roman ruler Titus, as we discussed in chapter 1, when the Jewish people ran for their lives and fled their homeland once again. This time the Jewish people were scattered not for seventy years, not for five hundred years, not even for a thousand years, but for approximately 1,900 years they were banished to "the four corners of the earth."

Regarding the regathering from this second dispersion, Ramon Bennett, in his excellent book *When Day and Night Cease*, writes:

The second gathering began with the trickle of Jews into Palestine after the turn of the last century. The trickle became a stream after 1948 and then a river during the 1950s and 1960s.

The river is now in flood stage and in danger of bursting its banks with the masses arriving from the last vestiges of the [former] Soviet Union.[5]

Derek Prince proclaims in his book *Promised Land:*

When I consider all the different intertwining circumstances that make this second deliverance possible, and when I take into account the diverse and numerous crises in the past century in which God sovereignly intervened to bring His prophetic Word to fulfillment, I conclude that this second deliverance is already greater than the first.[6]

What a statement, and what a fact of history!

I love it when the purposes of God unfold right in front of our eyes. From my vantage point, that is exactly what is occurring in the Middle East today. We are continuing to see with our very own eyes the second great regathering. The Holy Spirit is at work today breathing on God's Word, and the children of Israel are being called from the four corners of the earth. Can you pierce through the clouds of confusion and see through God's prophetic lens?

Fulfillment of the Prophetic Promise

When people ask me what the Lord is doing prophetically in the earth today, I tell them about the outpouring of the Holy Spirit in South America, Africa, China and other lands. I mention the river of God's presence in various congregations, cities and nations. But eventually I tell them about what the Lord is doing among the Jewish people worldwide.

Do you hear a trumpet blast? A clarion call of the purposes of God can be heard ringing clearly from Jeremiah's trumpet. Listen to the clear sound of the second great regathering:

"Behold, I am bringing them from the north country, and I will gather them from the remote parts of the earth, among them those who are blind and those who limp, the pregnant woman and she who is in labor, together; they will return here as a great assembly. They will come with weeping, and by pleading I will bring them; I will lead them by streams of waters, on a straight path on which they will not stumble; for I am a father to Israel, and Ephraim is My firstborn."

Hear the word of the LORD, you nations, and declare it in the coastlands far away, and say, "He who scattered Israel will gather him, and He will keep him as a shepherd keeps his flock."

Jeremiah 31:8–10

These verses paint for us a graphic picture of the painful but providential regathering process. We are even told that "the north country" will be one of the primary places of this exodus and returning.

The Lord holds the compass that points to the proper interpretation of His Word. To get the correct reading, however, we must stand in the right place. To understand the regions prophesied, we must take the read from the proper geographical context. As we have seen, Israel is the pupil, the focal point, of God's eye, and we must read the compass of the prophetic Scriptures from this perspective. Yes, the bustling city of Moscow is located directly north of the little piece of land in the Middle East that today we call Israel.

Like many others, I have ministered in "the north country," in Russia. I have been graced to participate in the outreach ministries of the Festivals of Jewish Music and Dance under the direction of Rabbi Jonathan Bernis, to help lead intercessory teams for the opening of the 40/70 prayer window and to minister at other strategic events.

After the Soviet Union fell, millions of Jews left Russia and the former Soviet states for both Israel and the United States.[7] They fled for freedom from the land of the north in cars, airplanes, trains, buses and ships. Most were assisted by Jewish or Christian agencies, individuals and groups. It amounted to the emancipation and transportation of an entire people group from one part of the world to another. Nothing like it has ever happened on such a massive scale. But there are still far more we must reach and rescue.

In the trumpet call from Jeremiah that we read on the previous page, he predicted *how* God's chosen people would be led out: "They will come with weeping, and by pleading I will bring them" (verse 31:9). *Strong's Concordance* renders the meaning of the word *pleading* as "strong prayer." Jeremiah thus gives us the secret to the fulfillment of the prophetic promise. It is preceded by the desperate prayer of the heart (weeping) and by praying the promise back to God (pleading).

For all who read this book, I have a challenge: Will you join me and lift your voice to help fill up the "golden bowls full of incense, which are the prayers of the saints" (Revelation 5:8)?

Praying the Scriptures

I offer the following three prophetic Scriptures with corresponding prayers for the fullness of aliyah to be made complete. May the spirit of prayer and supplication come upon you, and may you lift up desperate prayers from the heart to the One who hears.

> When the LORD brought back the captives of Zion, we were like those who dream. Then our mouth was filled with laughter, and our tongue with joyful shouting; then they said among the nations, "The LORD has done great things for them."
>
> Psalm 126:1–2

Gracious God and King, I rejoice for the day I live in. The dream of Your people returning to their own land is being fulfilled right before my eyes. Indeed, I rejoice in the Lord and my heart is filled with gladness. Thank You for awakening me to the prophetic reality of this time. But Lord of Hosts, I lift a cry to You that the nations will look upon this historic event and know that You are the only God in heaven. As You bring back the Jewish people from the four corners of the earth, let the nations know that the God of the Bible is alive, and give glory to You. Indeed, the Lord has done great things—and the best is yet to come. Hallelujah! Praise the Lord! Let it be!

"However, the days are coming," declares the LORD, "when it will no longer be said, 'As surely as the LORD lives, who brought the Israelites up out of Egypt,' but it will be said, 'As surely as the LORD lives, who brought the Israelites up out of the land of the north and out of all the countries where he had banished them.' For I will restore them to the land I gave their ancestors. But now I will send for many fishermen," declares the LORD, "and they will catch them. After that I will send for many hunt-

ers, and they will hunt them down on every mountain and hill
and from the crevices of the rocks."

Jeremiah 16:14–16 NIV

Dear Lord, as I ponder these days, I stand in awe of Your
redemptive work throughout the pages of history. Demonstrate the power of Your strong arm once again and
bring forth the remaining Jewish people from the land of
the north into their Promised Land of Israel. Send forth
many fishermen, laborers and intercessors to call them
forth from all the countries where they have been scattered. Restore them to the land of their fathers, as You
promise in Your Word. Release a movement of signs and
wonders unprecedented in all of history. Eclipse what You
have done in the past and move by Your great power, for
Your holy name's sake. Amen.

"I will signal for them and gather them in. Surely I will redeem
them; they will be as numerous as before. Though I scatter them
among the peoples, yet in distant lands they will remember
me. They and their children will survive, and they will return."

Zechariah 10:8–9 NIV

Dear Lord, I agree with Your Word and ask that the Holy
Spirit would release a sound, an inner witness and a signal that will be recognized and acted upon by the Jewish
people. Redeem Israel! Though they have been scattered,
regather them from all the distant lands. Cause them to
remember the one true God and to call on His name—
Your name. Release divine protection to them and cause

the fulfillment of aliyah to come to pass in the Messiah's mighty name. Amen and amen.

God's Last Days Mission

Our picture is nearly complete. Aliyah, the regathering of God's chosen people from the farthest corners of the earth, is the great fulcrum around which He is orchestrating these final moments of history. As Israel streams back to the land, God has used aliyah to provoke the nations into confrontation over the increasing number of settlements in disputed territory. Eventually the land will be reclaimed, and Israel will blossom as prophesied.

For the fullness of aliyah to come to pass, demonstrations of God's redemptive work must be completed in the land of the north; among the Sephardic Jews yet living in exile in much of Latin America; among the Jewish people of North America; and among those of Europe. All eyes will end up on the Middle East, searching for answers, as perplexing times and days of pressure mount. Leaders will be groping for answers. But God has "the last word on the Middle East" (the title of a 1982 book by Derek Prince), because God's road map leads to Israel's future.

◇ **A Personal Prayer** ◇

Gracious heavenly Father, I agree with Your Word and ask the Holy Spirit to release a sound, an inner witness and a signal that will be recognized and acted upon by the Jewish people. Redeem Israel, though they have been scattered. Regather them from the distant lands. Cause them to remember the one true God and call on His name. Release divine protection to them and cause the total fulfillment of aliyah—the return to the land and to the God of the land. In the Messiah's mighty name. Amen and amen.

6

The Mordecai Calling

> "If you remain silent at this time, relief and deliverance for the Jews will arise from another place, but you and your father's family will perish. And who knows but that you have come to your royal position for such a time as this?"
>
> Esther 4:14 NIV

The dark spirit of anti-Semitism—or what may be called "the spirit of Haman," named after the man in the book of Esther who plotted to exterminate the Jewish people in the days of King Artaxerxes—is on the move across the world today.

We Christians have a dangerous tendency to consider biblical narratives such as the story of Esther, Mordecai and Haman as myths or children's stories. On the contrary, these stories are real and instructive to us today. The Bible declares, "All Scripture is inspired by God and beneficial for teaching, for rebuke, for correction, for training in righteousness" (2 Timothy 3:16). The fact is, the ancient spirit of genocide yields only to the power of God, which can be released only by a people who, like Esther's cousin Mordecai, pray and fast and even put themselves at personal risk, as Esther did.

A Divine Appointment in Berlin

The reality of this age-old nemesis of the Jews was driven home to me even further in 1992, during one of my first trips to the central European nations right after the fall of Communism. After ministering in the nations formerly known as Yugoslavia and Czechoslovakia, I rode a train from Prague in the Czech Republic to Berlin, Germany. I traveled alone because I needed some special time to seek the Lord. Being a "Goll" of German descent, I have for years carried a heart for the German-speaking world, praying that the wrongs of the past be righted.

I took advantage of the free time on the train to read the book *Daniel: Insight on the Life and Dreams of the Prophet from Babylon* by Paul Yonggi Cho (Creation House, 1990). The book cover featured a striking image of a beastlike character. I was intrigued by this depiction from the ancient Ishtar Gate of Babylon—constructed of glazed bricks by King Nebuchadnezzar in 575 BC—and pondered what it meant. I even wondered if there was a purpose in my reading the book at that time.

Cho writes a remarkable statement in the text:

In order to make a nation stand upright, the evil prince which is behind the nation must be driven away through prayer. The demon which seeks to steal and kill an individual or a family must also be bound in prayer.[1]

The principles revealed in this book flowed right into the revelations presented in a second book I read on that long train trip: *Engaging the Enemy: How to Fight and Defeat Territorial Spirits* by Dr. C. Peter Wagner (Regal, 1995).

Although I had visited Germany previously, I knew only a few phrases in German. I had never been to Berlin. I did not even know where to get off the train or how to find lodging. But my Guide, the Holy Spirit, knew the layout of the land quite well.

The Seat of Satan

My train trip ended at the Berlin Wall. I checked into a hotel, and then did not leave my room for nearly three days. After being holed up in prayer, I sensed God releasing me to walk through the city to pray. That was when I stumbled across a building called the Pergamon Museum on "Museum Island" in the heart of Berlin, a museum I did not know existed. (Pergamon is another name for Pergamum.)

In the book of Revelation, the Spirit said to the angel of the church of Pergamum,

> "I know where you dwell, where Satan's throne is; and you hold firmly to My name, and did not deny My faith even in the days of Antipas, My witness, My faithful one, who was killed among you, *where Satan dwells.*"
>
> Revelation 2:13 (emphasis added)

As far as I know, this is the only mention in the Scriptures of a physical site where Satan's throne could be found. Pergamum was also called the place where the adversary lived. It did not surprise me to learn that in the Greek, *Pergamus* is from *pergos,* "fortified."[2] But I was shocked, when I went into the Pergamon

Museum, to find myself staring at the exact beastlike idol pictured on the front of Cho's book! This was the original—the real thing. How could it be?

I soon learned that sometime between 1878 and 1886 (close to the time Joseph Rabinowitz met the Messiah and took the Good News from the Middle East back to his home in Eastern Europe), German engineer and archaeologist Karl Humann excavated the ruins of the ancient city of Pergamum in what is now Turkey. Thousands of fragments from the friezes of the great altar were removed from Pergamum and shipped to Berlin.[3] They remained in storage until they were reconstructed stone by stone as the Pergamon Altar.

The Pergamon Museum also contains part of a grand walled "processional way" leading into ancient Babylon—a reconstructed section of the Ishtar Gate. I had just read about Daniel, the prophet to Babylon, in Cho's book, only to be confronted by the very pagan deity, the genuine original image, that I had seen pictured on the front of Cho's book. I was viewing remnants from the pagan shrine in the ancient city that the Bible describes as "the seat of Satan." This was the actual graven idol whom men worshiped in Pergamum when John received the warning in the book of Revelation.

To put this in context: On that day in 1992 when I stood before the Pergamon Altar in Berlin, the children of Israel were again in captivity—this time in the land of the north. They had reached the end of another seventy-year period (compare Daniel 9:1–19 with Jeremiah 25:11 and 29:10); and another conquering nation was in turmoil after touching "the apple of God's eye." Not only did the Jewish people begin their journey homeward in Daniel's day at the end of seventy years, but the walls of Soviet Communism also came tumbling down at the seventy-year mark of their origins.

And here I was, staring at the restored ruins of the time about which Daniel spoke.

Spiritual Roots of Anti-Semitism

I wanted to maximize this once-in-a-lifetime divine appointment. I felt it was time to intercede quietly in the Spirit. So I prayed softly that the same God who had enlightened Daniel would now enlighten me.

As I waited on God, the light began to shine. Massive pieces of a jigsaw puzzle started to fall into place. I was beginning to understand what God had orchestrated.

Could the spirit of anti-Semitism with a base of operation here in Germany have some connection with this occultic high place, this altar from Pergamum, being reestablished? Could this be one of the spiritual strongholds that had empowered Hitler's reign of terror? I mused. I listened. I learned.

My dear friend Don Finto, founder of Caleb Global ("to ignite revival in Israel, the Middle East and the nations"), told me that he was in Nuremberg for a conference with some of his Messianic brothers. They went out onto the parade ground where Hitler had held many party rallies. Don writes:

> I was in Nuremberg several years ago with some of my Messianic brothers, including Asher Intrater. We had a conference there and I was one of the speakers. We went out to the parade ground where Hitler had held so many of his rallies. The "stage" from which Hitler spoke was an enlarged replica of the Pergamum throne.
>
> Albert Speer, Hitler's architect, was the fellow who constructed that enlarged Pergamum throne. And he did know, and I believe Hitler knew, and called on demonic powers.

111

I wouldn't step up to the place where Hitler would stand, but Asher did, and declared, "I want all the demons in hell to know that I am a Jew, and we're still here, and Hitler is gone."[4]

Rising Anti-Semitism

From that initial revelation in Berlin, God has continued to reveal to me the spiritual pulse of His heart for His chosen people today. In order to view the future accurately, we must have a proper reading of yesterday's headlines and an accurate pulse on today. What do we see when we gaze into the future? Where are we at this point? What are the current conditions in the nations of the world? Is the spirit of anti-Semitism at work again? What signs might give us some clues?

God has revealed to me that this brooding, antichrist, anti-Semitic spirit is raising its ugly head all around the world, just as it has in the past. And whenever there is a major threat to God's Kingdom, God counters it. Conflict is turned to great purpose. God always has a plan, and "reveals His secret plan to His servants the prophets" (Amos 3:7). The more I pray and seek God's face, the more I sense a prophetic word rising in my heart for the nations concerning the need for a Mordecai calling and an Esther anointing in the Church.

In Russia

In the years that followed my visit to the Pergamon Museum in 1992, pressures began to mount in Russia. Anti-Semitism arose once again with a vengeance. Fire bombings, persecution and violence began to occur on a regular basis. Terrorists vandalized Jewish synagogues and cultural centers and attempted to assassinate leading Jewish figures. Russian Jewish leaders

112

claimed that an "increasing number of [Russian] political figures . . . have with impunity issued anti-Semitic statements as
part of their effort to win popular support."[5] Even the number
of Jewish people granted visas to emigrate to Israel was legally
reduced.

My friend Richard Glickstein, a Jewish-American, had been
working with Messianic congregations in Moscow. As Russians
began to show greater animosity toward Westerners and blame
the United States for their economic woes, Glickstein could have
become a target of harassment. So he moved his family from
Moscow to Germany, where he worked with a pocket of Russian Jews. Then he relocated to Finland so he could be postured
to help the growing number of Russian-speaking Jewish people
wanting to leave the former Soviet states. Today my friend has
relocated to New York to reach out to American Jewry. He is
one of many modern-day Mordecais being positioned for what
is about to come—the second great exodus!

In Europe and the U.S.

Austria, the nation that gave us great composers, philoso-
phers and artists, also produced Adolf Hitler, leader of the Nazi
movement. In the year 2000, a far-right political party headed
by alleged Nazi-sympathizer Jörg Haider placed second in the
parliamentary election to join the ruling coalition of the Austrian government. Although he soon stepped aside, the move
sent shock waves throughout Europe.

Jewish people in Austria and neighboring Hungary have since
felt the growing threat of anti-Semitism once again breathing
down their necks. A poll of fourteen European countries, con-
ducted for the Anti-Defamation League in November 2019,
found that about one in four Europeans hold anti-Semitic beliefs.[6]

The United States, too, has felt the pangs of growing anti-Semitic violence. A report released by AJC (Global Jewish Advocacy) titled "The State of Antisemitism in America 2020" reported "deep anxiety among American Jews and a disturbing lack of awareness among the general public about the severity of antisemitism in the United States."[7]

And just as heart-wrenching:

> Antisemitic incidents in the United States reached the highest on record in 2019, according to a press release from the Anti-Defamation League. More than 2,100 acts of assault, vandalism and harassment were reported last year, according to the ADL, which has been tracking these incidents since 1979.
>
> "This was a year of unprecedented antisemitic activity, a time when many Jewish communities across the country had direct encounters with hate," said ADL CEO Jonathan A. Greenblatt. "We are committed to fighting back against this rising tide of hate and will double down on our work with elected leaders, schools, and communities to end the cycle of hatred."[8]

A Growing Concern

The Lord often spoke to my wife, Michal Ann, through prophetic dreams, and many of her dreams have come to pass. My concern for the Jewish people in the land of the north grew even greater when Michal Ann began to have consistent, vivid dreams about a new European holocaust.

The following is what Michal Ann saw in one of her dramatic dreams in the summer of 2000:

> I saw thousands of Jews trying to escape from within European countries. In this dream they were not only trying to escape

through Finland and across the North Sea to England, but they also were trying to head south through Italy to the Mediterranean Sea. [Their route] included Russia, Germany, France, Austria and the whole European scene.

These countries were providing transportation so the Jews could escape, but their policy toward anyone who wanted to pursue the Jews was: "Whoever wants to go after them may do so. However many you kill is fine. Our official statement is that we are allowing them to leave, and we are providing transportation. Whatever happens to them in transit is not our responsibility."

There were many different modes of escape, but in every case I saw tremendous numbers of people being killed. It was horrible.

I saw railway boxcars filled with Jewish people—just like the images of Jews herded into Nazi boxcars during the Holocaust of World War II. They were packed like sardines. In some cases it seemed like someone had purposely pulled out old train cars from World War II and made these Jews get into the same boxcars. They had also rigged the sliding doors to these boxcars so they would stay open. Then I saw automobiles filled with modern neo-Nazis in uniforms driving alongside these train cars and shooting as many people as they could.

At a later point I saw that only a handful of Jews had survived the train trip. I also noticed that in some of the boxcars, hangman's nooses had been tied to supporting beams. As many as fifty nooses were in a car, and some of them had been used to hang Jewish victims. Their bodies were cut down, but the Nazis left the ends of the nooses hanging in the boxcars to terrorize all the people who might try to escape in the future.

They also used a taxidermy procedure on three Jewish bodies, and their stuffed skins hung in the nooses. Anyone riding in the boxcars was jostled by the carcasses throughout the train ride. I remember riding in one of the cars and bumping up against one of those bodies while looking into its face. It was just horrible.

Then the scene changed, and I saw Jewish people trying to escape in automobiles. Once again I saw carloads of uniformed neo-Nazis pulling alongside them. The Jews were fleeing for their lives, and they had little with which to defend themselves.

I remember one carload of Jewish people in particular because they actually fought back with some boat oars they had found. The only thing they could think to do was to wait until these neo-Nazi soldiers had pulled up alongside. When they did, they rolled down the window to point their guns. The Jews stuck their boat oars through the window and jabbed them into the chests of the soldiers, crushing their sternums. In their desperation, they had no choice but to brutally defend themselves.

Every time the Jews tried to defend themselves, it was with hand tools and in hand-to-hand combat. The enemy always had cars and guns.

It seemed that Italy had decided to open up a portion of its border to the Jews. Many, however, were still being killed—thousands upon thousands. I found myself praying in the dream, "Open the door! Open the door and let them go!"

Finally the few straggling refugees who made it through the gauntlet seemed to arrive at their destination—a large, green pasture surrounded by a dense planting of scrubby oak trees. In one way it seemed like it could be a good defensive place, but to me what seemed to be the issue was that those trees constricted a possible path of escape should one become necessary. And I had a sense of foreboding that the neo-Nazis were still following and that the Jews had no real security at all.

I was one of these refugees, along with two of my children, because in the dream I was Jewish. We experienced these things alongside the Jewish people.

The Jews were provided with some empty, rough cabins, but I don't know if they had any small cots or blankets. It just seemed that all the Jews had were the things they had brought with them.

This was definitely a dream about the Jews being hunted, but it had a twisted, "sporting edge" to it. The Nazis let them think they were escaping, but they were really just playing a mental game with them. The enemy let them run while driving them with fear. They wanted to see how many they could track down and kill, and they wanted to see how they would react.[9]

God sometimes gives us glimpses of unpleasant things not to paralyze us with fear but to energize us to pray in faith. After Michal Ann's dream, I fell to my knees in even greater intercession for my Jewish kindred in the land of the north and other nations.

A Fresh Perspective

I mentioned in chapter 4 that, at a conference in Germany, I read the book of Esther from start to finish, under the anointing of the Holy Spirit.

Today I am convinced that we are destined to relive the book of Esther in this generation. Her older cousin, Mordecai, warned her about Haman's plot against the Jewish exiles (see Esther 3–4).

Let's take a deeper look at the call of God on the man Mordecai. What was his God-given task, his divine assignment?

Mordecai's job was to prepare Queen Esther for her hour of influence before the king. He had raised Esther as his own daughter. He did not bow down or pay homage to Haman, a scheming man of influence in the kingdom, but worshiped only the one true God. When he learned of Haman's scheme to annihilate the Jews, he revealed it with wisdom to the queen, whose Jewish identity was known to no one but him. He walked in prophetic counsel and instilled courage in Esther.

Esther, properly tutored and mentored by her cousin's counsel, seized the moment through prayer and fasting. Alongside Mordecai, Esther entered into an urgent act of crisis intervention: a three-day fast from all food and drink of any kind. No one enters casually into this kind of fast. A life-and-death crisis is a good reason. So is a direct command from God.

Then Esther launched an appeal to the king—who could have had her executed, since he had not summoned her—for the deliverance of her fellow Jews from their sworn enemy. Esther was anointed to intervene and stand in the gap, yet she had to walk in cooperation with the preparation of Mordecai, the spiritual authority God had placed in her life. Her intervention would not have succeeded unless she had first cooperated.

If there had been no Mordecai, then there would have been no Esther. If there had been no Esther, then all the Jews in the empire would have been annihilated.

Prayer gave Esther the right approach, privileged access to the supreme earthly authority, the king, and helped create the favor that extended from him the scepter of grace. God was the true authority, but He chose to work through Mordecai to alert Esther to her destiny and the timing of her intercessory acts on behalf of the Jewish people.

In an hour of crisis, intercessors and those in authority, both spiritual and secular, must learn to walk together. Today, as in Esther's day, millions of lives are at stake. And in the same way, just as intercessors cannot afford to walk an independent road, so spiritual leaders must avoid the temptation to walk and lead in exclusivity, reserving their outreach, leadership and spiritual resources solely for their own gatherings. A marriage must occur between the watchmen on the walls and the gate-keepers of every city.

In the Old Testament, the gatekeepers were elders who sat at the gates. Today they are the spiritual and physical governmental authorities who are to act in a spiritual sense as gatekeepers of His presence.

In Bible times watchmen were posted on the walls to watch every route of approach and announce ahead of time the identity and purpose of those who approached the city. Watchmen today are the intercessors who see what the Lord is doing locally and among the nations. Spiritually they are posted in high places to watch and announce ahead of time the identity and purpose of those who approach the community of God—whether the visitors are ambassadors of goodwill or enemies approaching with evil intent.

Watchmen do not always have the authority to apply the revelation or even to issue the warnings; by God's design their revelation and intercession must be submitted to the governmental authorities who sit at the gates. These gatekeepers, both secular and spiritual leaders, must then determine whether to bar the gates or to open them wide. No matter what opinions or experiences we may have, it is clear from God's Word that these two essential ministries must learn to walk together.

To put it more clearly, the evil, anti-Semitic Haman spirit is once again moving eagerly to wipe out the Jewish people. The Church, represented by Esther, may or may not be ready. It is the job of the watchmen, represented by Mordecai, to recognize the dangers approaching and inform the Church before it is too late, so she can fill her God-ordained role of saving His chosen people.

Window of Opportunity

People gifted with prophetic vision and insight have come to understand that Jewish people are approaching another season of crisis. This Mordecai and Esther call is a historic global window of opportunity for the Church to arise and wash the stains and spots out of our bridal garments. It is our chance to right history. Like a nurse with a fully loaded needle, the Holy Spirit wants to inject into the global prayer movement the burden of the Lord for the Jewish people. We need a potent shot of God's heart into our own hearts. This is why God wants to raise up a Mordecai anointing to prepare Esther for a time of intervention.

My mandate and heavenly burden has become clear. It involves releasing a cry and making a loud, divine declaration: Let the Mordecais and Esthers of the Church come forth! Let these men and women take their stand for God and for the Jewish people. There is no better time than now. We were born, anointed and set in place "for such a time as this" (Esther 4:14).

The Church must throw out life preservers of prayer and fasting to save the Jewish people at risk of being overtaken by a rising flood of demonic and unreasoning anti-Semitism. I am not talking about something that is going to come; no, it has already begun. In fact, it is spiraling to new heights in hot spots around the world, especially in the former Soviet bloc.

When we speak comfort to God's covenant people, we honor Him. We long for the Jewish people to discover and receive their Messiah, yes; but one of the first steps is to reach out in prayer, fasting, love, compassion and practical assistance,

120

particularly to help them return safely to their ancient home of Israel.

Serious crises call for serious strategies. Unbridled attacks from the enemy require our most powerful weapons of warfare. We must tap in to deeper veins of prayer, mixed with fasting, in which we truly seek the face of God. Crisis intervention requires a higher level of strategic discernment. The effective power of authoritative prayer comes only through agreement with others, which requires commitment, consecration and sacrifice.

Such a longing has compelled me to look back at historic times of effective crisis intercession. What was it that worked for our spiritual ancestors when they faced their most difficult trials? I found some answers in Wales.

A Visit with Samuel Howells

In his book *Rees Howells: Intercessor* (Christian Literature Crusade, 1952), author Norman Grubb recounts how Howells and students at Swansea Bible College interceded during crucial moments during World War II.

In May 1940, for instance, Allied forces needed to be evacuated immediately from the beaches of Dunkirk, France, across the North Sea, so they would not be annihilated by the approaching Nazi troops. Rees Howells and the Bible College prayed that Hitler's armored columns driving toward the trapped British and French troops at Dunkirk would be stopped. And on May 24, Hitler gave the order to halt the advance of those columns. On May 26 he gave the tanks the go-ahead again, but by that time the Allies had had time to arrange for the evacuation of those troops. On and after May 28, in what some call "the miracle of Dunkirk," about 338,000 British and French soldiers were rescued from the beaches at Dunkirk.

The reason for Hitler's order to stop his Panzer divisions? It remains unexplained to this day. Did God intervene? Rees Howells and the Wales Bible College believed He did.

I was honored and thrilled, then, when my friends Trevor and Sharon Baker, graduates of Swansea Bible College (also known as the Bible College of Wales), arranged for me to meet with Samuel Howells, the only living son and successor of Rees Howells, the great intercessor.

Sue Kellough, a proven prophetess who was serving on the board of directors for our ministry at the time (who has since gone on to be with the Lord), came with me. Howells, who had succeeded his father as president of the Bible college, was 86 years old when we had tea with him on the Swansea campus. He showed us "the blue room," where many historic prayer meetings had taken place during the dark years of World War II. An elderly lady who had participated in those prayer gatherings also attended the tea.

I had visited other places on the historic crisis intercession map. And I had led a group to Herrnhut, Germany, the site of the Moravian community that started an unprecedented round-the-clock prayer watch in 1727 that was unbroken for more than a hundred years and resulted in the sending of hundreds of missionaries. The Holy Spirit had descended upon the Moravians in an unforgettable manifestation of divine impartation.[10]

It became clear that now, in the 21st century, the Lord had another plan. This was to be a quieter, personal impartation. Why He would choose such a strategy soon became apparent.

During our divine appointment in Wales, I asked Howells some vital questions, knowing that his family and the intercessors at the college had a proven anointing to pray for intervention.

The Key to Authority in Prayer

As soon as we settled down to tea, I asked, "Mr. Samuel [the proper way to address Samuel Howells in Wales], how is it that your father got this revelation? How did he and the people know what to pray for? I know it was not by newspaper reports, and I know it was not by radio. How did he know what armies were in what locations? How did he know what battles to pray through and when? Did it come by dreams or visions? How did it come?"

Howells did not immediately answer. The son of the great intercessor turned to me and said simply, "Don't you think it is time for another crumpet?"

He talked freely about other things. He answered questions and carried on a dialogue without hesitation. But his demeanor changed when I turned to him again and asked, "Mr. Samuel, how is it that your father and all the intercessors in that period of time knew what to pray for? What was the key of authority that the Lord gave you for intervention in that period of time?"

Again Howells looked at me. "Don't you think it is time for a little more tea?"

It was as if he did not hear the questions I asked and would not give the answers I yearned to hear.

I grew bolder. A third time I inquired, "Mr. Samuel, I must know! Did an angel come and announce these things? How did they know? Did it happen by spiritual gifts or through illumination of the written Word? How did they know of the battles and when and how to pray?"

"Enough of this," Howells said.

Then Sue Kellough, older and more tenacious than I, dropped to her knees before Howells, peered up at the veteran intercessor and gave it one last try. "Mr. Samuel, our nation is in great need. And with the days that lie in front of us, we are in great need of the kind of prayer that your father and you and these people have known in the past."

A tear trickled down his cheek as he looked into our eyes. "You must understand," he said, "the Lord's servant"—that is how he referred to his father—"was possessed by God."

Sue and I wept. Then we asked Howells to pray for us.

Later we learned that Samuel Howells rarely met with people. And I have been told that he rarely prayed for people when he did meet with them. Nevertheless, he laid his hands on us and asked the Lord to grant to us the authority of "identification" and "intercession." He asked the Lord to give us the place of purity in prayer; that our hearts would become aligned with God's purposes; and that we would pray out of God's heart. He prayed simply, concluding with the prayer that it would all be centered in Jesus.

What a timely, strategic appointment! Mr. Samuel Howells has now moved on to his heavenly reward. But I left Swansea Bible College that day knowing I had taken part in a divine appointment. This was greater than a mere prayer technique. Howells had reluctantly shared with me a truth that few are willing to implement in their lives: The most effectual, fervent prayer comes when the Lord Himself takes possession of His people. We are not our own. We were bought at a price. We are being called to be possessed with and by God.

This revelation answered all my questions about the key to effective crisis intercession.

I later came across the text of a letter from Dr. Kingsley Priddy of Swansea Bible College. It is reproduced in the appendix of Gustav Scheller's book *Operation Exodus*:

You see, intercession is not prayer, nor even very intense prayer. Anyone may pray, and pray earnestly, for something, and yet not be committed to be irrevocably responsible, at any cost, for its fulfillment. The intercessor is.

In intercession there is identification with the matter or persons interceded for. The intercessor is willing to take the place of the one prayed for; to let their need become his need; to let their need be met at his expense and to let their suffering become the travail of his own heart.

That is how the Lord Jesus "made intercession for the transgressors" (Isaiah 53:12). "He was numbered with the transgressors," and "He was wounded for (their) transgressions" (verse 5). He had to be "identified" with sinners; He secured their pardon by vicariously paying the debt that they owed.[11]

The Mordecai Call

The antichrist spirit of Haman has loosed a fresh plot to destroy the Jewish generation of today. The events of recent years bring me back to the same important questions: Have enough intercessors heard the sound of the shofar? Have enough of us not only listened to but also obeyed the summons? Are we stirring ourselves to respond? Are we moving toward the next (and last) Great Awakening? Will enough of us be awakened in time?

The biblical Mordecai and Esther are gone. The season of Joseph Rabinowitz is over. Now it is time for someone in this generation to step forward, shout and signal to His shipwrecked people to flee to the Rock. As each generation passes on, another must carry the baton. The Holy One of Israel is once again looking for a man, for a woman, for a people to stand in the gap on behalf of His ancient covenant people.

God is seeking Mordecais and Esthers to step forward. He is calling people of prayer to stand in the gap in this generation. It is time to cry out to the Church with a solemn call to a yearly fast, an Esther fast, for the salvation and preservation of the Jewish people around the world. In the name of Jesus Christ, I call forth the Mordecais to prepare Esther, the Church, for her greatest hour of selfless intercession for the Jewish people.

True deliverance comes not in the human realm but in the realm of the Spirit. God is offering an opportunity for the Body of Christ to arise. A window of opportunity has opened, enabling the Church to right history before the throne of almighty God.

I was born for such a time as this. So were you!

When God delivered Israel from Egypt in the first great exodus, He did it through sovereign acts of supernatural intervention. The Hebrews were not delivered from Pharaoh's grip by swords, chariots or mighty armies; they were delivered by the hand of God. Supernatural signs and wonders were the tools of their release.

Most of the Jewish people who have made aliyah since World War II did not arrive in Israel through signs and wonders. They have migrated to Israel by plane and ship. They have made their exodus because of the sacrifices of others. A few miracles occurred along the way, but most of the breakthroughs happened as the result of hard work and astute maneuvering through political mazes.

God will continue to use all these means to free His people. There have been and will continue to be multiple phases of His great work. But my strong conviction is that the completion of the second great exodus is destined to eclipse the first, and it will come about again through the supernatural contending of altars.

We see the altar of the occult and the demonic rising around the world. At the same time, an authentic staff of God is being lifted through the prayers and selfless obedience of the Church. By this means, the supernatural authority of God will once again swallow up the counterfeit powers of the enemy.

The present era of the fishermen (which we discussed in chapter 1) is coming to a close. Another era of the hunters is already beginning. The gentle awakening (which we discussed in chapter 3) is giving way to a rude awakening. As it was in Egypt during the first great exodus, the Jewish people will be pushed out by the hands of the hunters and by the prophetic and the apostolic display of great signs and wonders—all for the glory of God.

We have seen miracle after miracle come to pass in recent years on behalf of the Jewish people in Russia. Everything occurred in response to prayer. There is no other explanation for the rapid disintegration of what was the world's second-ranked superpower. There is no other rationale for the fall of the Berlin Wall after decades of unrestrained terror and bondage. The truth is: Prayer changes things.

With great power and authority, God's people are declaring to the land of the north: "Let My people go!" At such a time as this, we must ask: Where are the Corrie ten Booms and Fritz Graebes, the righteous Gentiles of our day who are willing to identify so closely with the plight of the Jewish people that they will put themselves on the line to see them saved and preserved from destruction? Where are the Dietrich Bonhoeffers who will stand up and declare the truth about God's love for their Jewish neighbors, even in the face of public disapproval and personal danger?

Are we willing to stand and make a difference? Then we must become possessed by God. Do we want to be close to the heart of God? Then we must love the things that He loves—and that specifically includes His covenant people.

Now is the time for Mordecai to rise up and for Esther to be prepared. We must catch the Mordecai anointing and be people who prepare the corporate Esther, the Church, for this critical time. We need to call forth the same anointing for crisis intercession that was upon Rees Howells at Swansea Bible College during World War II.

Together we can make history before the throne of God through the power of effective intercession.

◇ A Personal Prayer ◇

Father, in Jesus' matchless name, I choose to volunteer freely in the day of Your power. I want to be close to Your heart and to love the things and the people You love. Release the mantle of Mordecai to prepare the corporate Esther, the Church, for this critical time. I accept the calling to make history before the throne of God through the power of effective intercession. I lift my desperate cry and pray that You take possession of me to help right the wrongs of the past. For the sake of Your holy name. Amen and amen.

The Prophetic Promise

7

The Descendants of Hagar

He took him outside and said, "Now look toward the heavens and count the stars, if you are able to count them." And He said to him, "So shall your descendants be."

Genesis 15:5

Imagine the scene with me: A teenage lad lay in distress, crying desperately. His mother had laid him under a bush to give him a little reprieve from the scorching heat of the desert. They had no more water—for either their mouths or their souls. The boy's natural father had just turned his back on them and cast them out, sending them away suddenly from the comforts of their home. They were now entirely on their own, left to wander in a wilderness.

The mother, not wanting to watch her son wither away and die, sat down a short distance away and began to weep. When everything seemed bleak, then God—yes, God in heaven—heard the lad crying and sent supernatural assistance to the mother and her boy—who would grow up as a strong young man and become the father of a great nation.

The boy was Ishmael. His mother was Hagar. His father was Abraham.

In a book about praying for the destiny of Israel, you might expect me to focus only on the Jewish people—the descendants of Abraham, Isaac and Israel (Jacob). But in one of our weekly Israel Prayer Watches, through a visionary experience, the Holy Spirit spoke to me and said, *I am calling you to raise up prayer for the descendants of Abraham. Remember that Ishmael also came from Abraham's seed. In fact, Abraham's seed went into three different women.*

The Jews are not the only seed that Abraham produced. In fact, there are three different generational lines making up Abraham's descendants. Together all three represent the descendants of Abraham.

We are going to look first at the descendants of Hagar. Why am I starting with Hagar? Because Hagar brought forth Abraham's firstborn son. We will look at Abraham's descendants in order of birth.

Innumerable Descendants

Abram and Sarai, as they were called before God changed their names, had more than most couples could ask for in terms of wealth, prestige, servants and possessions. But when it came to having what they really wanted, they came up short. Abram and Sarai were barren and, to make matters worse, well past normal childbearing age. Michal Ann and I identify with this pain, as we, too, were once barren until the Lord healed us.

It must have been quite a surprise to Abram when God took him outside and said, "Now look toward the heavens and count the stars, if you are able to count them. So shall your descendants be" (Genesis 15:5). Abram believed God against all odds.

But after years of waiting for this promise to be fulfilled, he and Sarai took matters into their own hands. One day Sarai came to Abram, grieved and frustrated, and said, "See now, the LORD has prevented me from bearing children. Please have relations with my slave woman; perhaps I will obtain children through her" (Genesis 16:2). Abram listened to his wife; and Sarai's Egyptian maidservant, Hagar, conceived right on the spot. As you can imagine, Sarai ended up despising Hagar and thus treated her harshly. So Hagar felt like an outcast, even though she was not responsible for the decision that led to her pregnancy.

In despair Hagar fled from Sarai into the wilderness. Genesis 16:7 says, "Now the angel of the LORD found her by a spring of water in the wilderness." What Hagar heard from the angel must have been quite a surprise: "I will greatly multiply your descendants so that they will be too many to count" (verse 10). Hagar obeyed the angel, returned to Sarai, and bore Abram, at age 86, a son, whom Abram called Ishmael.

Thirteen long years passed. Abram now had a teenage son, and Sarai had a maid she despised with a son who resembled her husband. Somehow I do not think those thirteen years were the most pleasant. Abraham was 99 years old when the Lord appeared to him and said:

> "My covenant is with you, and you will be the father of a multitude of nations. No longer shall you be named Abram, but your name shall be Abraham; for I have made you the father of a multitude of nations. I will make you exceedingly fruitful, and

133

I will make nations of you, and kings will come from you. I will establish My covenant between Me and you and your descendants after you throughout their generations as an everlasting covenant, to be God to you and to your descendants after you. And I will give to you and to your descendants after you the land where you live . . . as an everlasting possession; and I will be their God."

Genesis 17:4–8

After this God instituted the covenant of circumcision with Abraham and his descendants. (We will get back to the initiation of this important covenant in just a moment.) What God said next brought Abraham to his knees in laughter.

Then God said to Abraham, "As for your wife Sarai, you shall not call her by the name Sarai, but Sarah shall be her name. I will bless her, and indeed I will give you a son by her. Then I will bless her, and she shall be a mother of nations; kings of peoples will come from her." Then Abraham fell on his face and laughed, and said in his heart, "Will a child be born to a man a hundred years old? And will Sarah, who is ninety years old, give birth to a child?"

verses 15–17

After enduring decades of barrenness, and then thirteen years of strife between Sarai and Hagar, Abraham exclaimed, "Oh that Ishmael might live before You!" (verse 18). Abraham loved Ishmael and wanted him to be blessed.

But God said, "No, but your wife Sarah will bear you a son, and you shall name him Isaac; and I will establish My covenant with him as an everlasting covenant for his descendants after him."

verse 19

134

Then God promised to bless Ishmael "and make him fruit-ful and multiply him exceedingly" (verse 20). Look closely at what God said next: "He shall father twelve princes, and I will make him into a great nation" (verse 20). Just like Abraham's grandson Jacob (later renamed Israel), Ishmael would be the father of twelve tribes.

Although God said He was making His covenant with Isaac, He gave a prophetic pronouncement about Ishmael that we cannot avoid. If we are to pray properly for Israel, we must have the wider picture and pray for *all* the descendants of Abraham.

Let's dig a little deeper into Ishmael's role as the firstborn son of Abraham, before Isaac came on the scene.

God's Promise for Ishmael

I want to ask you a question: Have you ever given birth to an "Ishmael" in your life? Have you ever experienced the mercy of God while knowing that this was not God's *first* choice? Before we start tossing stones at Sarai, Abram, Hagar and the rest of the company, let's remember that God "causes all things to work together for good to those who love God" (Romans 8:28).

Ishmael may have been the second person (after his father) to receive God's covenant of circumcision. Abraham was a Moabite-Hebrew. The term *Jew* or *Jewish* did not exist yet; and Isaac had not yet even been born. Abraham was circumcised on the day of God's command, at 99 years old (see Genesis 17:26), and "his son Ishmael was thirteen years old when he was circumcised in the flesh of his foreskin" (verse 25).

Circumcision is not a big deal to the Western world. It is simply a medical health procedure performed on newborn baby boys. But the Bible looks at circumcision as an external sign of a covenant being kept between God and His people. The apostle Paul in his letter to the Galatians (and also to the Romans) speaks extensively about the spiritual symbolism contained in this physical act that God commanded Abraham to perform.

I opened this chapter with the story of Hagar and Ishmael being sent away by Abraham. Abraham had made a great feast on the day Isaac was weaned. But Sarah saw Ishmael mocking Isaac and did not like it. She said to Abraham, "Drive out this slave woman and her son, for the son of this slave woman shall not be an heir with my son Isaac" (Genesis 21:10). There was a reason she responded as she did. As we have noted, the combination of one man, two women and two sons is not a recipe for harmony.

But Abraham was greatly unsettled because he cared for Ishmael, a son born of his own flesh. So God exhorted Abraham,

> "Do not be distressed because of the boy and your slave woman; whatever Sarah tells you, listen to her, for through Isaac your descendants shall be named. And of the son of the slave woman I will make a nation also, because he is your descendant."
>
> verses 12–13

Wow! What a demonstration of God's faithfulness to Abraham, even though Ishmael was a byproduct of the flesh trying to work out God's promises. Because Ishmael was Abraham's descendant, God promised to bless him.

Torn yet comforted by these words, Abraham gave Hagar bread and water and sent her away with the boy. Into the wilderness they went.

As Hagar sat a distance away from her son, who was thirsty and crying, the angel of the Lord appeared to Hagar a second time. In their first encounter, while she was a pregnant runaway, the angel had declared to her, "I will greatly multiply your descendants so that they will be too many to count" (Genesis 16:10). Now the angel of the Lord affirmed her son again: "I will make a great nation of him" (Genesis 21:18). God miraculously provided water for Hagar and Ishmael, and they survived. In fact, Genesis 21:20 says, "God was with the boy, and he grew."

What did that say? "God was with the boy"! This was another demonstration of God's divine mercy, blessing the mess that Abraham and Sarah had created.

Hagar was an Egyptian (see Genesis 16:1), so the fruit that came first from Abraham was half Egyptian and half Moabite-Hebrew. Hagar took a wife for Ishmael from the land of Egypt. From Ishmael came twelve princes, twelve tribes, a great nation. The Bible says so three times. The great nation that descended from Ishmael? The Arab people.

All Nations Will Be Blessed

Let's jump back for a moment to Abram's first encounter with the Lord (which we looked at in chapter 4), just after his father, Terah, died. The Lord made it clear from the start that *all* who would come from Abraham would be blessed:

> The LORD said to Abram, "Go from your country, and from your relatives and from your father's house, to the land which I will show you; and I will make you into a great nation, and I will bless you, and make your name great; and you shall be a

blessing; and I will bless those who bless you, and the one who curses you I will curse. And in you all the families of the earth will be blessed."

Genesis 12:1–3

Let me repeat that: Through Abram "*all* the families of the earth will be blessed." All! This includes the descendants of Ishmael—the Arab people. God is aware of who "all" includes.

Now let's skip ahead 24 years to Abram's commissioning. We looked at this passage earlier, but I want to highlight God's promise to establish His covenant with all Abram's descendants, not just one particular generational line. God promised the following to Abraham, whose name means "father of a multitude":

"I will establish My covenant between Me and you and your descendants after you throughout their generations as an everlasting covenant, to be God to you and to your descendants after you."

Genesis 17:7

Descendants and Seed

The apostle Paul emphasized that God "made from one man every nation of mankind to live on all the face of the earth, having determined their appointed times and the boundaries of their habitation, that they would seek God. . . (Acts 17:26–27).

And Jesus said that "God so loved"—who? Just those who love Him? Just Israel? Just believers in Jesus Christ? No, "God so loved the world" (John 3:16). Jesus came to make a way to the Father for all nations, and a way for all the peoples of the earth to be blessed through the covenant God made with Abraham.

138

I appeal to you, then, as an Israel intercessor for decades, to other Israel intercessors: Do not call the Arabs our enemy. Do not treat the Arabs as if they were our enemy, because God promised to establish His covenant with *all* Abram's descendants, including the descendants of Ishmael; and because Paul makes it clear in his letter to the Ephesians that we do not wrestle against people:

> Our struggle is not against flesh and blood, but against the rulers, against the powers, against the world forces of this darkness, against the spiritual forces of wickedness in the heavenly places.
>
> Ephesians 6:12

These forces do operate through people. But we do not wrestle against people. We wrestle against the powers of darkness.

So let me say it a bit more boldly: *The Palestinians are not our enemy.* We must constantly keep a proper biblical perspective or we will get into a wrong kind of romanticism concerning Israel. Israel is the apple of God's eye, but that does not make Ishmael the enemy. You do not have to hate the Arabs to love Israel. You can and should love both peoples.

A dear American friend, Rick Ridings, and his wife, Patti, are prophetic, intercessory-missionary emissaries who, after years of service in Belgium, now live with their family in Jerusalem. Rick says: "If you love the Jews with a soulish love, you will hate the Arabs. If you love the Arabs with a soulish love, you will hate the Jews. But if you love either people, Jews or Arabs, with God's heart, then you will authentically love the others."

With whom did God make a covenant? "The promises were spoken to Abraham and to his seed" (Galatians 3:16)—*seed,* singular, referring to Jesus, the Messiah, as the one seed. Paul went on to say, "If you belong to Christ, then you are Abraham's descendants, heirs according to promise" (Galatians 3:29). So God confirmed His covenant with both the *seed* of Abraham (singular) and the *descendants* of Abraham (plural).

When we are speaking about this enduring covenant, then, there is a distinction between the singular word *seed* and the plural word *descendants*. This seed comes for us through a covenant line of faith, not soul and flesh. The original commission given to Abraham is, in a sense, the same commission later given to the Church: "Go, therefore, and make disciples of all the nations" (Matthew 28:19). These are the same nations that God promised would be blessed through Abraham's seed.

One blessing does not nullify the other. Both the spiritual descendants of Abraham and the physical descendants of Abraham are valid recipients of God's grace. We are not in competition.

Ishmael's Prophetic Destiny

Now we are going to meet two of Abraham's grandchildren. This becomes important if we are going to pray for the descendants of Abraham. Genesis 25 contains "the records of the generations of Ishmael, Abraham's son" (verse 12). God's word to Abraham about twelve princes coming from Ishmael (verse 16) came to pass. The next few verses give us the names of the twelve sons of Ishmael. We will look at only the first two: Nebaioth, the firstborn, and Kedar.

For future reference, note where Ishmael's descendants settled: "They settled from Havilah to Shur which is east of Egypt going toward Assyria" (verse 18). Remember Assyria.

Now let's jump forward to Isaiah 60:7:

"All the flocks of Kedar will be gathered to you, the rams of Nebaioth will serve you; they will go up on My altar with acceptance, and I will glorify My glorious house."

"All the flocks of Kedar will be gathered to you." Where did we hear about Kedar? Who is Kedar? The second son of Ishmael. "The rams of Nebaioth will serve you." Where did Nebaioth come from? He was the firstborn son of Ishmael.

We see here that the descendants of Ishmael—the Arab people—are going to be acceptable before God. They are going to end up glorifying God, and there will be an altar of worship that will come out of Ishmael's seed. Amazing!

This could really mess up some of our narrow thinking, though. Let me simply state: There is a whole lot of prophecy yet to be fulfilled on planet earth. God has an enormous heart, and He has plans for all peoples. Isaiah 60:1–3 states:

"Arise, shine; for your light has come, and the glory of the LORD has risen upon you. For behold, darkness will cover the earth and deep darkness the peoples; but the LORD will rise upon you and His glory will appear upon you. Nations will come to your light, and kings to the brightness of your rising."

Doesn't this sound similar to the words God spoke to Abraham in Genesis 12 and 17?

Praying the Scriptures

Now that our understanding has been expanded, let's consider the relevant Scripture and focused prayers that follow.

[God] made from one man every nation of mankind to live on all the face of the earth, having determined their appointed times and the boundaries of their habitation, that they would seek God, if perhaps they might feel around for Him and find Him, though He is not far from each one of us.

Acts 17:26–27

Father God, You fashioned Ishmael in Hagar's womb and You determined his appointed times and where he would live. You are not far from Ishmael's descendants. Your Word says that You are near to all who call upon You. I ask that the Arab people would seek You, call out to You and find You to be their very present hope in trouble. Deliver them from evil and direct them into paths of righteousness for Your name's sake. Amen.

The Lord is not slow about His promise, as some count slowness, but is patient toward you, not willing for any to perish, but for all to come to repentance.

2 Peter 3:9

Heavenly Father, thank You that You will fulfill every promise that You gave Abraham. Thank You also for Your patience with us. Help us to think correctly concerning the Arab people. Forgive us for judging the descendants of Ishmael instead of interceding on their behalf. You do not wish for them to perish but for all of them to come to repentance. I ask that godly sorrow and Your kindness would draw the Arab people to repentance and faith in the one true God, Yeshua. Send a mighty outpouring of Your Spirit among the descendants of Ishmael, for Jesus Christ's sake. Amen.

"I will make you into a great nation, and I will bless you, and make your name great; and you shall be a blessing; and I will bless those who bless you, and the one who curses you I will curse. And in you all the families of the earth will be blessed."

Genesis 12:2–3

"All the flocks of Kedar will be gathered to you, the rams of Nebaioth will serve you; they will go up on My altar with acceptance, and I will glorify My glorious house."

Isaiah 60:7

Father God, You have made Abraham a great nation. His descendants are indeed uncountable. You said that You would bless those who bless them and curse those who curse them. Forgive us for cursing the descendants of Your son Ishmael. I ask that You bless the Arab people. Make them a blessing to the nations of the earth. Gather them to Yourself and use them to bless Israel. I ask that they would minister to Israel instead of trying to destroy her. May they glorify Your house and be acceptable in Your sight for the sake of Your Son, Yeshua. Amen.

Piercing the Veil

We will not, therefore, write off the whole Islamic issue as a lost cause. I declare that the Islamic veil shall be pierced! A great harvest is at hand. Friend and author Sandra Teplinsky emphasizes this point in her balanced and insightful book *Why Care about Israel?*:

> From God's perspective, it is harvest time for Arab Muslim souls, though a stiff price will likely be paid for it. Amid the world's war on terror, expect to see masses of converted Arabs and prepare to undergird them sacrificially. Remember that for the patriarch's sake they, too, are uniquely loved.[1]

You have probably experienced your own family friction along the way. If not, you have not lived long enough. Families fight. But someday God will have His full way with His family, and these cousins will learn to love each other and love the same God—and His name is not Allah. I believe that love between Arab and Jewish cousins will bloom.

Over the years the Lord has spoken to me about piercing the veil of Islam through the power of the Gospel of the Kingdom, and calling forth the fulfillment of God's great promise. There will be "a great multitude . . . from every nation, tribe, people and language" (Revelation 7:9 NIV) around God's throne. Let's reach into the heart of God for the prophetic destiny of the tribe of the twelve princes of Ishmael, and speak life rather than death.

I have had repeated prophetic declarations and visions in which I have seen a national-level move of God in Egypt. I have prophesied it numerous times over the past twenty years and am beginning to see the fruit of Holy Spirit power at work—gifts of healings and workings of miracles and the like. It is happening.

As a phenomenal example, in 2019 Egypt built the largest church in the Middle East, which some have called a game changer in the region. The building was a gift to the Church from Egyptian president Abdel Fattah el-Sisi, who commissioned the cathedral in 2017 as part of a new capital being built outside Cairo. The new church, he said, should be considered "a message of peace and love to the world." Bestselling American-Israeli author Joel Rosenberg said at the dedication:

> "I think what we have seen here is historic. I really think it's a game changer that a Sunni Arab Muslim President of the world's largest Arab country has built a church, the largest in the Middle East and given it as a gift to the Christians of Egypt. We've never seen anything like it in history. And I think President Sisi is sending a message not just to his own people but to all Muslims that Muslims and Christians can live together in coexistence. That's an extraordinary development."[2]

God remembers sacrifice. Egypt was used to save baby Jesus from being killed. God remembers every sacrifice—yours as well as that of nations.

Another repeated vision I have seen: Entire mosques will have a visitation of the Holy Spirit, resulting in minarets—those tall, slender towers from whose balconies a muezzin calls Muslims to prayer—being transformed into authentic 24/7/365 houses of worship with prayer to the one true God, Yeshua Jesus. I have seen it over and over and over.

When ministering in Sarajevo, the capital of Bosnia and Herzegovina (which was still Yugoslavia at the time), I was in my third-floor hotel room looking out the window, praying. Just across the way, from a minaret, an imam appeared and began chanting. As I prayed and he chanted, we were eyeball to eyeball, and the Lord spoke to me right then: *There will be whole mosques.* I pray that my eyes will not close until I have seen the fulfillment of this prophetic word.

The Bible says that now we see in part and we know in part (see 1 Corinthians 13:12). But there will come a time when we see Him clearly and will experience the Holy Spirit in full splendor. He will enter the land where Daniel was held captive, and this people will at last kneel in prayer and pray for the purposes of God for Jerusalem and the Jewish people.

Where was this place? Babylon. Where is it today? Iran. That is where Daniel prayed his prayers that filled bowls in heaven. Sometimes in the very location where we pray our prayers, the bowls tip over and blessings pour down on that very place.

Listen to the poignant words of a Jewish scholar of scholars and a believer in the land of Israel today, Avner Boskey of Final Frontier Ministries:

> The [Bible's] prophetic word has shaped much of the destiny of the greater Arab nation and its relationship with the world. Fierce independence, a wild and untamable soul, and arrogant animosity can characterize Arab dealings (at their worst) with the world. But the Arab world at its best manifests freedom of abandoned worship, generosity, graciousness and sacrificial zeal. When Messiah Jesus is allowed to transform their hearts, the descendants of Ishmael will find God bringing sweet out of the bitter, and they will discover the beauty of their Abrahamic connection in a totally new way. Peace and cooperation will supplant wildness and strife, and love between Arab and Jewish cousins will bloom again.[3]

Now take a quick breath before we turn our attention to the descendants of Abraham who came through his wife Sarah.

◇ A Personal Prayer ◇

Father God, You have not abandoned Ishmael's descendants. Help me to think correctly concerning the Arab people. Forgive me for judging the descendants of Ishmael instead of interceding on their behalf. You do not wish for them to perish, but for all to come to repentance. I ask that Your kindness will draw the Arab people to repentance and faith in the one true God, Yeshua. Send a mighty outpouring of Your Spirit among the descendants of Ishmael, for Jesus Christ's sake. Amen and amen.

8

The Descendants of Sarah

This is what the LORD Almighty says: "In those days ten people from all languages and nations will take firm hold of one Jew by the hem of his robe and say, 'Let us go with you, because we have heard that God is with you.'"

Zechariah 8:23 NIV

Thirteen years after the birth of Ishmael, God appeared to 99-year-old Abram and said, "I am God Almighty" (Genesis 17:1). This is the first time in Scripture that God reveals Himself, in Hebrew, as El Shaddai—literally, "God almighty" or "all-sufficient One." The Hebrew word *shad* is always translated as "breast." In the same way that a mother provides all that is needed for her newborn's nourishment, God was about to reveal to Abram that He is all-powerful and able to satisfy with "blessings of the breast and womb" (Genesis 49:25).

This is also the way God chose to reveal Himself to Isaac, Jacob, Joseph, Moses and many others. It is the way we must see God if we are to intercede on behalf of the descendants of Sarah.

Laughter Is Born

Sharing Sarah's story is a challenge because most believers know it and may even want to skip over it. But it is delightful, and we cannot let familiarity become a barrier to intimacy. Will you allow her very familiar story to sink down inside of you? The chapters before and after this one may seem newer and more interesting, but Sarah's descendants are the foundation of our faith. I feel the necessity, therefore, to share it—like skimming a stone across the pond while pausing to create a ripple effect of revelation that will settle into and permeate your heart.

So let's look again at what God initially promised to the father of faith, Abraham:

> "I will establish My covenant between Me and you and your descendants after you throughout their generations for an everlasting covenant, to be God to you and to your descendants after you."
>
> Genesis 17:7

Then God had a surprise for Abraham:

> "As for your wife Sarai, you shall not call her by the name Sarai, but Sarah shall be her name. I will bless her, and indeed I will give you a son by her. Then I will bless her, and she shall be a mother of nations; kings of peoples will come from her." Then Abraham fell on his face and laughed, and said in his heart,

"Will a child be born to a man a hundred years old? And will Sarah, who is ninety years old, give birth to a child?"

verses 15–17

God reassured Abraham that it was not Ishmael, the son of Hagar, who would fulfill this promise of a child from his own body:

"No, but your wife Sarah will bear you a son, and you shall name him Isaac; and I will establish My covenant with him as an everlasting covenant for his descendants after him."

verse 19

The Lord visited Abraham again shortly after this exchange. As Abraham sat at the tent door in the heat of the day, three men appeared. He greeted them and asked them to stay and rest and eat. After receiving the food Abraham prepared, the Lord said to him, "I will certainly return to you at this time next year; and behold, your wife Sarah will have a son" (Genesis 18:10).

Sarah was listening nearby at the tent door, and the Bible records that she laughed to herself:

"After I have become old, am I to have pleasure, my lord [Abraham] being old also?" But the LORD said to Abraham, "Why did Sarah laugh? . . . Is anything too difficult for the LORD? At the appointed time I will return to you, at this time next year, and Sarah will have a son." Sarah denied it, however, saying, "I did not laugh"; for she was afraid. And He said, "No, but you did laugh."

verses 12–15

Although Abraham and Sarah were advanced in age, God had decided that they were not too old to receive a very special gift. And Sarah conceived and gave birth to a son.

> Abraham named his son who was born to him, the son whom Sarah bore to him, Isaac. Then Abraham circumcised his son Isaac when he was eight days old, as God had commanded him. Now Abraham was a hundred years old when his son Isaac was born to him. Sarah said, "God has made laughter for me; everyone who hears will laugh with me." And she said, "Who would have said to Abraham that Sarah would nurse children? Yet I have given birth to a son in his old age."
>
> Genesis 21:3–7

It seems as though the Lord derived great enjoyment from this whole affair! Abraham laughed and Sarah laughed, but I guess you could say that God had the last laugh, because Isaac's name means "he laughs." Isn't that great?

What a joyful moment for Sarah and Abraham! This was not another fleshly attempt, motivated out of frustration, to bring to pass the promised child of faith, but God's own fulfillment.

This story may be familiar, but I say to you that God is a God of miracles. I actually declare that almost every day over my life: "Miracles are mine. Miracles are coming to me. And miracles are flowing through me."

If you are barren and married, I speak faith into you right now in the name of Jesus. I speak even as the Lord said to Sarah, "A year from now, I will come back and you will have a child." I say to those who are desperate, "Dream big. Risk again. I dare you to dream."

I speak this word out of my own inheritance. I mentioned earlier that Michal Ann and I were not able to have children; it was documented as medically impossible. But God! If you are barren in the area of dreams and the purposes of God, I say, "But God! This time next year, you will give birth to a dream, in Jesus' name."

The number eight in Scripture—as when Abraham circumcised Isaac at eight days old, as God had commanded him—signifies a time of new beginning. This new beginning was conceived when Abram had faith for the impossible (having descendants as numerous as the stars), and it was birthed as laughter when the promise was revealed.

In the same way we, too, must have faith for what we see as impossible for the nation of Israel, fully confident that our joy will be made full when the impossible comes to pass. I have undaunted faith when it comes to the promises of God concerning the descendants of Sarah. Will you join me?

Sarah's Descendants

Isaac was the only child Abraham and Sarah had through their union. He in turn married the beautiful maiden Rebekah:

> Isaac brought her into his mother Sarah's tent, and he took Rebekah, and she became his wife, and he loved her; so Isaac was comforted after his mother's death.
>
> Genesis 24:67

Time passed and "Isaac prayed to the LORD on behalf of his wife, because she was unable to have children; and the LORD answered him, and his wife Rebekah conceived" (Genesis 25:21).

Rebekah gave birth to struggling twin boys named Esau and Jacob. When they grew up, Jacob, the younger twin, with the help of his mother, deceived his father, Isaac, and stole the blessing of the firstborn son from Esau. Jacob, whose name means "heel-grabber" or "supplanter," fled with Isaac's blessing, which could not be revoked (see Genesis 25:22–34).

Jacob met and became dazzled by Rachel, arranged to marry her and, in turn, was deceived by Laban, her father. It is forever true that what we sow we also reap. Instead of Rachel, Jacob was given Leah, the older and weak-eyed daughter, as a surprise in his tent on his wedding night. But seven days later Jacob got his wish, receiving Rachel as his second and much-sought-after bride, although he had to work another seven years for her (see Genesis 29:1–30).

Leah had no problem bearing sons for Jacob, which caused jealousy and desperation to arise in Rachel. "When Rachel saw that she had not borne Jacob any children, she became jealous of her sister; and she said to Jacob, 'Give me children, or else I am going to die'" (Genesis 30:1). The competition was now on, not only with her sister, Leah, but also with Leah's servant, Zilpah, and her own servant, Bilhah.

Many trials, errors and woes beset Rachel, until finally

> God remembered Rachel, and God listened to her and opened her womb. So she conceived and gave birth to a son, and said, "God has taken away my disgrace." And she named him Joseph, saying, "May the LORD give me another son."
>
> verses 22–24

As the saga unfolded, Jacob, now the father of eleven sons, had a heavenly encounter and wrestled with the angel of the

Lord throughout the night. Jacob prevailed in this wrestling match, received a blessing and had his name changed from *Jacob*, "the deceiver," to *Israel*. Sandra Teplinsky writes in *Why Care about Israel?*:

> The identity *Israel* is given initially to Abraham's grandson Jacob. In his unredeemed nature, Jacob does not always behave honorably, scheming and deceiving his older brother Esau out of his birthright. When Esau seeks revenge, Jacob flees for his life. Frankly, the young man strikes us as an unlikely candidate for *Yahweh's* everlasting favor.[1]

Yes, Jacob wrestled with the Lord until daybreak, pinning Him down to win the divine wrestling match. But who really won? I am persuaded that the Lord let Jacob *think* he won, just as He does with you and me. But perhaps the Lord, in His marvelous and mysterious ways, was the One who really won that arduous, all-night contest. After all, afterward God renamed Jacob *Israel*, and he walked with a limp from that day forward.

Sandra Teplinsky shines light on the origin of the name *Israel*, which means:

> "To strive, persist or exert oneself." Second, *Yisrael* stands for "prince with God," from a play on the Hebrew words *sar* meaning "prince" and *El*. Combining both meanings, we could say that *Yisrael* is a prince who has striven with God and men, and overcome (see Genesis 32:28).[2]

Israel, like Ishmael, the son of Hagar, became the father of twelve sons. Prophetic interpretation tells us that twelve is the number of governmental authority. Jesus, for example, chose twelve disciples. Israel brought forth twelve full tribes, and these became the descendants of Abraham and Sarah who inherited the covenant promises of God.

One of the twelve sons of Jacob was Judah, meaning "thanks" or "praise." The Messiah Himself is known as "the Lion of the tribe of Judah" (Revelation 5:5 KJV). It is from the name Judah—"praise"—that the term *Jew* is derived.

The Jewish People

Not long ago on a Sunday evening, the Lord told me, "You're really good at the macro vision; you're very good at casting My great big vision. But I need people to also see My micro vision. The macro, big vision will not occur unless people allow Me to touch them with a micro vision—a specifically designed vision for individuals to grasp for themselves."

So as we journey through the descendants of Sarah, please know that I am asking the Holy Spirit to touch you with His micro vision. And as you lay hold of God and God lays hold of you, there will be a conception in you of something you may think is impossible—something that will take the Lord God almighty to fulfill. Always remember, with God all things are possible.

I remember hearing international Bible teacher Derek Prince reason through a minefield of questions surrounding subjects like "Who is Israel?" and the role of the Church and Israel in the last days. This beloved pioneer related some of his own pilgrimage in his book *Promised Land*:

There was, I discovered, a distinction to be made between the words *Israel* and *Israelite*, and the words *Jew* and *Jewish*. Linguistically, *Jew* is derived from *Judah*, the name of one of the twelve tribes of Israel. From the time of the Babylonian captivity, however, all the Israelites who returned to the land of Israel were called Jews, irrespective of their tribal background. This usage is carried over into the New Testament. Paul, for example, was from the tribe of Benjamin; yet he called himself a Jew (see Acts 21:39).

In contemporary usage, these four words are not fully interchangeable. *Israel* and *Israelite* focus primarily on national origin and background. *Jew* and *Jewish* focus more on religion, culture and later history. Since the birth of the state of Israel in 1948, the word *Israeli* has been added, referring to any citizen of the state, whether of Jewish, Arab or Druse descent.

One unique feature of the history of Israel, as recorded in the Bible, is that part of it was written after the events, as normal history is, while the remainder was written in advance of the events, as prophecy. Taken together, the historical and prophetic portions of the Bible constitute a complete history of the people of Israel.[3]

Keepers of the Covenant

God's covenant with Israel is one of the oldest legal contracts in history. He made the covenant with Abraham and then renewed it with Isaac. The generational blessing proceeded on to Jacob, whose name was changed to Israel. As Jacob's life was transformed, he passed the torch to his clan of twelve, who inherited the promise. The "Jews" as a unique people of faith came into existence then, and the covenant plan of God was secured. More than three thousand years after it was enacted with Abraham, this covenant contract is still in force today.

The specifics of this contract are laid out in Scripture for all to read. Unlike human contracts, which have time limitations, God's covenant promises are tied to His nature of faithfulness, mercy and love. His plans are eternal—without end—as God's covenant with Abraham was unconditional.

It is, therefore, ultimately God who will keep His Word and see that it comes to pass. I agree with Jeremiah: "Great is Your faithfulness" (Lamentations 3:23). God will keep His covenant promises simply because He said He would, and you can take God at His Word. The descendants of Sarah are the keepers of the covenant purposes and plans of God.

The Land of the Heart

I have probably already rattled your cage in one way or another. While I am at it, then, I guess I might as well go for the jugular and ask you this question: Which is more important in the heart of God: the land of Israel or the people of Israel?

To some people, due to a wrong emphasis or flat-out mis-conception, the answer seems to be "the land." But if that is your answer, you have failed the test. Although there is a land covenant with the descendants of Sarah, which is extremely important in the ways and purposes of the Holy Spirit, it is forever settled in God's heart that the "land of the heart" takes priority.

How, then, should intercessors for Israel pray into the quag-mire that is the Middle East? Asher Intrater, a Messianic scholar and rabbi who lives in Israel (whom I mentioned in chapter 6), is a voice crying in the wilderness:

> All of the land in Israel belongs, by divine covenant, to the Jewish people. Claims of the Islamic world of ownership of the land of Israel are a direct rebellion and challenge to the Word of God.

158

I agree with the most radical proponents of total land possession for Israel. However, land possession is not the *only* issue
involved. When you stress one issue to the lack of others, you
can make a mistake, even when what you are saying is right.
There are other issues in Israel, such as the moral collapse in
schools . . . unemployment, violence, mental and emotional
traumas and on and on. Caring for these issues must also be
on the agenda.

Most of all, there is the issue of evangelism. Praying for
the land without praying for Israel's salvation accentuates only
one aspect of God's purposes for Israel. When evangelism is
avoided, then other issues get a bigger share of the emphasis
than what is due.[4]

Joseph Rabinowitz, the prominent Jewish leader we talked
about in chapter 1 who became absorbed with the Lord Jesus
Christ and with Israel, "the land of the heart," was a forerunner statesman like Jeremiah of old, who cried out that our
hearts of stone would be changed into hearts of flesh. In our
day, thousands of the Jewish descendants of Abraham, Isaac
and Israel have placed their faith in Yeshua Jesus. A worldwide
Messianic movement of Hebrew-Christian congregations has
sprung forth as the eyes of Jewish people have been opened to
behold their glorious Messiah.[5]

May many sons and daughters of Sarah arise and take their
rightful place in leading the processional of praise before the
majesty of the one true God.

So which *is* more important in the heart of God: the land
of Israel or the people of Israel? Both—but God's priority is
always the heart first. People who place external things first
often end up with a "religious" spirit. But when our priority is

people, God can use us to bring in a harvest for His Kingdom. No matter if someone is Arab or Jewish, living in a city or a slum, educated or not, God loves to take a soul for salvation. God loves all people. If all we do is fellowship with people who are like us, we will end up reproducing people of weak faith, because it takes an international family of affection—a cross-pollination of one another—to create God's Kingdom.

When people ask me the greatest thing God has done in recent history prophetically, I still take them back to the fulfillment of biblical prophecy when God's dispersed people will be regathered to their land and God will open their eyes—and they will behold Jesus as their Messiah.

Which brings us right back to the biblical prophecy that God will open the eyes of His Jewish people to behold their Messiah. According to an article in *Christianity Today* in April 2015,

> An estimated 10,000 to 15,000 Ukrainian Jews worship Jesus as Messiah. This makes Ukraine, a nation of 45 million, the region's fulcrum of the Messianic Jewish movement. (By comparison, Ukraine has about 1.7 million evangelical Christians and more than 23 million Orthodox Christians, who constitute about half the country's population.)
>
> Now, as Jews emigrate en masse from Ukraine, its Messianic believers are planting churches around the world.[6]

Praying the Scriptures

Once again, let's practice a prayer session together to intercede for both the nation of Israel and for the Jewish people yet scattered worldwide. I am excited! Are you ready to make a Kingdom impact?

The LORD took note of Sarah as He had said, and the LORD did for Sarah as He had promised. So Sarah conceived and bore a son to Abraham in his old age, at the appointed time of which God had spoken to him. Abraham named his son who was born to him, the son whom Sarah bore to him, Isaac.

Genesis 21:1–3

The redeemed of the LORD will return and come to Zion with joyful shouting, and everlasting joy will be on their heads. They will obtain gladness and joy, and sorrow and sighing will flee away.

Isaiah 35:10

"Listen to Me, house of Jacob, and all the remnant of the house of Israel, you who have been carried by Me from birth and have been carried from the womb; even to your old age I will be the same, and even to your graying years I will carry you! I have done it, and I will bear you; and I will carry you and I will save you."

Isaiah 46:3–4

Gracious Father, take note of Your people, Israel, and do for them as You have promised. Against all odds, may Israel give birth at the appointed time to laughter and joy. Thank You that the redeemed of the Lord will return with joyful shouting to Israel, and that they will have everlasting joy and gladness. You are El Shaddai, the all-sufficient One, who provides completely and satisfies His children. Continue to carry Your people. Bear them up and deliver them for their Messiah's sake, until He returns for His own. Amen.

I do not want you, brothers and sisters, to be uninformed of this
mystery—so that you will not be wise in your own estimation—
that a partial hardening has happened to Israel until the fullness
of the Gentiles has come in; and so all Israel will be saved; just
as it is written: "The Deliverer will come from Zion, He will
remove ungodliness from Jacob." "This is My covenant with
them, when I take away their sins."

Romans 11:25–27

Father God, I ask that we would not be wise in our own
eyes, but that we would understand the mystery of Israel. Thank You for extending Your mercy and grace to
the Gentiles by allowing them [me] to be grafted into
the richness of Your tree of life. Cause the Church to
fulfill her commission to preach the Gospel to the whole
world, so that the full number of Gentiles will come into
the Kingdom and that salvation will come to all Israel.
I ask that You come and deliver the Jews, Your natural
branches, and remove all ungodliness from Israel. Take
away their sins and restore them to Yourself, for Your
great name's sake. Amen.

You remember that Abraham laughed at the prospect of
having a child with Sarah at the age of one hundred. Can you
imagine his surprise and delight when, at an even older age,
he fathered six additional sons through Keturah, his wife after
Sarah's death?

Let's look at the descendants of Keturah as we conclude this
section on praying for the descendants of Abraham.

◇ **A Personal Prayer** ◇

Father God, let Your glory rise upon Israel so that she shines brilliantly with Your presence. In the midst of much darkness in the Middle East and across the earth, I ask, according to Isaiah 60:1–3, that You arise upon Your people. Let Your glory appear upon Israel, and may the God of Israel be exalted. Reveal Your salvation like a burning torch to Your Jewish people worldwide. Pour out Your Spirit of revelation, and grant favor to the completed Jews among the Messianic movement and use them mightily among their people and beyond. I call forth a wind, a fresh move of the Holy Spirit, that will impact all the descendants of Abraham, for Your Kingdom's sake. Amen and amen.

9

The Descendants of Keturah

On that day Israel will be the third party to Egypt and Assyria, a blessing in the midst of the earth, whom the LORD of armies has blessed, saying, "Blessed is Egypt My people, and Assyria the work of My hands, and Israel My inheritance."

Isaiah 19:24–25

I want to speak honestly and transparently as I begin this chapter. I have been reading the Bible for years, and have 45 years of ministry under my belt, yet never in my life have I heard a teaching on Keturah, Abraham's wife, let alone on the prophetic destiny of their children.

While praying over this manuscript for almost a decade, the Holy Spirit kept divinely interrupting my path. Delay after delay occurred, and I often wondered what this "opposition" was all about. But as each delay transpired, God gave me additional understanding.

I am not presenting myself as someone who knows it all; like you, I am a work in progress. With this perspective in mind, let's do some more pioneering by peering into the lives of *all* the descendants of Abraham. The mystery of delay has turned into divine destiny.[1]

Satisfied with Life

Abraham's wife Sarah lived almost forty years after the birth of Isaac. Genesis 23:1–2 says:

> Sarah lived 127 years; these were the years of the life of Sarah. Sarah died in Kiriath-arba (that is, Hebron) in the land of Canaan; and Abraham came in to mourn for Sarah and to weep for her.

Abraham loved Sarah dearly and must have experienced much grief and pain when she died. After her death, and after finding an excellent wife for his son Isaac, Abraham took another wife, whose name was Keturah. Genesis 25:2–4 says that Keturah

> bore to him Zimran, Jokshan, Medan, Midian, Ishbak, and Shuah. Jokshan fathered Sheba and Dedan. And the sons of Dedan were Asshurim, Letushim, and Leummim. The sons of Midian were Ephah, Epher, Hanoch, Abida, and Eldaah. All these were the sons of Keturah.

Keturah bore more children by Abraham than did Sarah and Hagar combined. I think that is interesting.

Before Abraham died, he gave gifts to the sons of Keturah "and sent them away from his son Isaac eastward, to the land

166

of the east" (Genesis 25:6). One of the sons of Keturah was Midian, the father of the Midianites. Some of the descendants of Keturah went to what was called Persia. Others were apparently scattered into Assyria.

Genesis 25:7–8 records:

> These are all the years of Abraham's life that he lived, 175 years. Abraham breathed his last and died at a good old age, an old man and satisfied with life.

What a way to leave this earth—as "an old man and satisfied with life," and with a lineage left behind! I get that because, as I have said, Michal Ann and I could not have children—yet at the time of this writing, I am anticipating the arrival of my eleventh grandchild. And my four married adult kids are probably not finished enlarging the family. I can relate to Abraham.

One Christmas some of the clan were with me. As I was watching the grandchildren—whom my wife never saw before she passed—the Holy Spirit spoke to me: *One miracle. The DNA of every miracle has the capacity to reproduce that miracle. The DNA of one miracle has the capacity to reproduce that miracle.* That fascinated me, as I realized that none of our grandchildren would be alive had we not experienced that first miracle.

Abraham's sons Isaac and Ishmael came together to bury their father in a cave (see Genesis 25:9). What a powerful statement! They came together—they united—to remember their father and put him to rest. I wonder if that could be a picture of things to come. Could it be that our Father will yet do such a work among the descendants of Abraham that they will come together in common purpose at some point and time in history?

Praising the Lord

Isaiah prophesied about the descendants of Keturah, saying to Israel: "A multitude of camels will cover you, the young camels of Midian and Ephah" (Isaiah 60:6). Remember that Midian was a son of Keturah, and Ephah was her grandson.

Isaiah continued in the same verse, mentioning yet another grandson of Keturah: "All those from Sheba will come; they will bring gold and frankincense, and proclaim good news of the praises of the Lord."

Where else have you heard of gold and frankincense together? They were two of the three gifts that the wise men brought to Jesus after His birth (see Matthew 2:11). I cannot confirm that the wise men were descendants of Keturah, but they did come from the east, where the descendants of Keturah had settled, and they certainly fit the description of Isaiah's prophecy.

Whether this prophecy was fulfilled literally at the birth of the Messiah, or whether it is a prophecy for the future yet to come, at least we can agree that there is prophetic destiny on the children of Keturah. These people will rise up as people of wealth and will end up worshiping the one true God. They will bring forth praise to the Lord!

Now let's go to the amazing prophecy of Isaiah, which has not yet been fulfilled. In this passage you will see the descendants of Hagar, Sarah and Keturah come together. As you read, keep in mind that Hagar was an Egyptian and that she found a wife for Ishmael, her half-Hebrew and half-Egyptian son, from Egypt. Remember, too, that the descendants of Keturah settled in Assyria and beyond.

On that day there will be an altar to the Lord in the midst of the land of Egypt, and a memorial stone to the Lord beside its border. And it will become a sign and a witness to the LORD of armies in the land of Egypt; for they will cry out to the LORD because of oppressors, and He will send them a Savior and a Champion, and He will save them. . . .

On that day there will be a road from Egypt to Assyria, and the Assyrians will come into Egypt and the Egyptians into Assyria; and the Egyptians will worship with the Assyrians. On that day Israel will be the third party to Egypt and Assyria, a blessing in the midst of the earth, whom the LORD of armies has blessed, saying, "Blessed is Egypt My people, and Assyria the work of My hands, and Israel My inheritance."

Isaiah 19:19–20, 23–25

God is eventually going to humble Egypt, and Egypt is going to lift a cry for help. The Arabs will cry out due to the severity of their oppressors, and the Lord will manifest Himself as their Savior and Champion. After much pressure, and the probability of all-out war in the Middle East, God will make Himself known to the Arab peoples and they will turn to Him.

Isaiah described the length to which they will go: "They will even worship with sacrifice and offering, and will make a vow to the LORD and perform it" (verse 21). This means not only that they will have a God encounter, but that they will become true disciples and walk in obedience.

Notice that this move of God will also impact Assyria: Turkey, Iraq, Iran and other Middle Eastern territories. Keturah's children were scattered throughout the vast lands of Assyria. They still have an identity today, but it is obscured because, as we saw earlier, Abraham sent them eastward into Transjordan and beyond.

Imagine—the very area of Asia Minor, where the early Church of Jesus Christ once flourished, will rise again out of the ashes into genuine, vibrant worship. Lands that appear to be held captive to the devil through Islam will be delivered and cleansed of their impurity. After thousands of years of broken promises, hatred and enmity between Arabs and Jews, this will be a glorious day in history—a day when the curse is reversed and the blessing of the Lord emerges. What a day that will be!

The Middle East is indeed a complex knot, but the Holy Spirit loves brooding over a mess of darkness, and is expert at this task. Remember the first mention of the Holy Spirit—that He "was hovering" over the face of the deep (Genesis 1:2). God loves bringing order out of chaos. The Holy Spirit is a pro at creating change and making all things new.

The Scripture quotation at the beginning of this chapter is so powerful that I want you to read it again: "Blessed is Egypt My people, and Assyria the work of My hands, and Israel My inheritance" (Isaiah 19:25). There will be, according to Isaiah, a highway from Egypt to Assyria, and people will go freely back and forth, probably right through the middle of Israel, worshiping God together. Blessed are the descendants of Hagar, God's people! Blessed are the descendants of Keturah, the work of God's hands! Blessed are the descendants of Sarah, God's inheritance! I can only imagine.

God is the supreme multitasker. He can accomplish more than one thing at a time. Biblical prophecy indicates that alongside God's gathering of the outcasts of Israel to their homeland, He is setting the stage to do a great work among all the descendants of Abraham. Surprise us all, O Lord. Let it be so!

A Prophetic Blessing

We see, then, that God has declared a prophetic blessing over all the peoples of the Middle East, because all have come from Abraham's seed.

The devil has arisen, however, to thwart God's blessing. A holy war—an unholy war, rather—has raged for thousands of years. The conflict continues to intensify, and a massive, satanic battle is coming. But I am here to declare that the Lord is going to pierce the veil of Islam. A move of God will come from out of Persia (Iran), Iraq, Syria, Lebanon, Egypt and, of course, Israel.

Times of Darkness

Now, just to set the record straight: From the angle that I presently read the Scriptures, I see a lot of intense bickering and warfare yet to occur before the fullness of Isaiah 19 comes to pass. I am not an ostrich with my head buried in the sand. Isaiah 60:1–3 lays out a scriptural principle that says a time of great darkness will precede the unveiling of a great light. Gentiles will come to the brightness of its shining, and even kings will bow to the brilliance of this great light. But first comes "gross darkness" (verse 2 KJV).

Psalm 83 describes vividly a troubling alignment set against a wearied Jewish state:

> They make shrewd plans against Your people, and conspire together against Your treasured ones. They have said, "Come, and let's wipe them out as a nation, so that the name of Israel will no longer be remembered." For they have conspired together with one mind; they make a covenant against You: the tents of Edom and the Ishmaelites, Moab and the Hagrites; Gebal,

Ammon, and Amalek, Philistia with the inhabitants of Tyre; Assyria also has joined them; they have become a help to the children of Lot. . . . Fill their faces with dishonor, so that they will seek Your name, LORD. May they be ashamed and dismayed forever, and may they be humiliated and perish, so that they will know that You alone, whose name is the LORD, are the Most High over all the earth.

verses 3–8, 16–18

Many Bible teachers agree that this text has not yet been fulfilled. This particular group has not yet been brought into an alignment with this degree of hatred. The passage does not say "the peoples of the land of the north," nor does it say "Germany." In fact, even Egypt seems to be missing from this list. Who and what is this alliance that conspires together? Let's turn to the pen of Sandra Teplinsky for more details:

Verses 5–8 tell how every nation in the neighborhood (except Egypt) unites against Israel: Edom and the Ishmaelites (southern Jordan and Saudi Arabia); Moab (central Jordan) and the Hagrites (Syria and Arabia); Gebal (southern Jordan); Ammon (central Jordan) and Amalek (Sinai Desert); Philistia (Gaza Strip area); Tyre (southern Lebanon) and Assyria (Syria/Iraq). Verse 4 sounds their bellicose battle cry: "Come . . . let us destroy them as a nation, that the name of Israel be remembered no more."[2]

In some ways this is nothing new. As I laid out earlier, the enemy has, from Israel's rebirth, been standing close by with a knife to cut her throat.

How did God's prophetic psalmist respond to this threat? How should we respond when we see these things taking place?

The psalmist calls for God to make His great name and His name alone known worldwide:

> May they be ashamed and dismayed forever, and may they be humiliated and perish, so that they will know that You alone, whose name is the LORD, are the Most High over all the earth.
>
> Psalms 83:17–18

God's goal in times of testing is to glorify Himself. He will ultimately use the Arab/Palestinian–Israeli conflict to do it. He wants all peoples to know that He alone is the Most High.

What if the eyes of the entire world were looking on at the moment of Israel's apparent imminent destruction—the moment when God brings humiliation to the enemies of Israel for the purpose of releasing His grace upon them?

Times of Great Light

Darkness comes first, and then the light shines (see John 1:5). There has never been a real contest between light and darkness. When you enter a house, you simply flip the switch and, if it is wired properly, the darkness is driven away by the light. Darkness is a temporary state. I am here not to declare the revival of evil; there are plenty of top-selling authors to do that. I am here to broaden our horizons and help us peer into the redemptive purposes of God, even in the midst of the most stressful, difficult times of the ages. Light will overpower darkness—eventually, somehow!

The Scriptures I have shared regarding God's promises to the descendants of Abraham are for this purpose: to bring light and hope to the dark situation in the Middle East. But even if all we had was Joel's prophecy, we would still be assured that, before this world comes to an end, God says, "I will pour out My Spirit on all mankind" (Joel 2:28).

Praying the Scriptures

Time for more Scripture-based prayers.

> On that day there will be a road from Egypt to Assyria, and the Assyrians will come into Egypt and the Egyptians into Assyria; and the Egyptians will worship with the Assyrians. On that day Israel will be the third party to Egypt and Assyria, a blessing in the midst of the earth, whom the LORD of armies has blessed, saying, "Blessed is Egypt My people, and Assyria the work of My hands, and Israel My inheritance."
>
> Isaiah 19:23–25

Heavenly Father, thank You for the many promises You have given me, and that You will fulfill each one. Thank You that You will also fulfill every promise You made to Abraham and his descendants. Hasten the day when all the descendants of Abraham through Hagar, Sarah and Keturah will worship You together in one accord. I agree with Your Word that says the descendants of Keturah are the work of Your hands and will be a blessing in the earth. I ask specifically that You would bless the descendants of Keturah and lead them to Yourself. Reveal to them that Yeshua is their Messiah. I ask that Jesus would receive the reward of His sufferings through these descendants of Abraham, for the glory of Your holy and righteous name. Amen.

A multitude of camels will cover you, the young camels of Midian and Ephah; all those from Sheba will come; they will bring gold and frankincense, and proclaim good news of the praises of the LORD.

Isaiah 60:6

Father God, I ask that the "young camels" and all the descendants of Keturah would come to You and turn favorably toward Israel. Bless them. Multiply them. Prosper them. I ask that You inspire them to use their wealth to bless Israel and the Kingdom of God. I ask that they would be known in the Middle East and in the earth as bearers of the good news of praises to the Lord. Establish them as worshipers of the God of their father, Abraham, for Your great name's sake. Amen.

Seeing the crowds, [Jesus] felt compassion for them, because they were distressed and downcast, like sheep without a shepherd. Then He said to His disciples, "The harvest is plentiful, but the workers are few. Therefore, plead with the Lord of the harvest to send out workers into His harvest."

Matthew 9:36–38

Father God, Your compassion burned in the heart of Your Son, Jesus. Turn the distress of Abraham's descendants into gladness and blessing. I ask that their souls not be downcast, but that they would put their hope in the God of their father, Abraham. Transform their misguided ways and lead them in Your paths of righteousness. Cause them to hunger and thirst after righteousness. Send out workers into this harvest field to bring Your living waters to a dry and weary land. I ask that Your workers would reap a bountiful harvest for Your Kingdom's sake. Amen.

"I am the good shepherd, and I know My own, and My own know Me, just as the Father knows Me and I know the Father; and I lay down My life for the sheep. And I have other sheep that are not of this fold; I must bring them also, and they will listen to My voice; and they will become one flock, with one shepherd."

John 10:14–16

Jesus, Yeshua, Messiah, You are the Good Shepherd and You know all Your sheep. You have laid Your life down for all the descendants of Abraham through Hagar, Sarah and Keturah. Bring the descendants of Hagar and Keturah into Your fold. Quicken their ears to hear Your voice. I ask that they join with the descendants of Israel so that all Abraham's descendants will become one flock with You as their great Shepherd. You are a mighty God, and You will bring Your Word to pass for Your name's sake. Amen.

The Promised Son

All three national families of Abraham have, by and large, failed to recognize the true Messiah, who is Yeshua, our Lord Jesus Christ. The Jews are still looking for their Messiah to appear, while the others do not even realize they need one. Although most accept Jesus as a prophet (and Muhammad as the final

prophet of God), they do not believe that a Messiah is necessary. Still the prophetic Scriptures predict that these descendants
of Abraham will, at a critical point in time, accept the true
Messiah.

I love the language of Isaiah 19:20: "He will send them a
Savior and a Champion." A Champion shall indeed come. The
Messenger of the New Covenant will be sent to turn away ungodliness from Jacob. Yeshua, Jesus, the true Messiah, said it
succinctly: "I have other sheep that are not of this fold; I must
bring them also, and they will listen to My voice; and they will
become one flock, with one shepherd" (John 10:16). A great
spiritual revival is on God's agenda, and it will encompass all
the descendants of Abraham throughout the Middle East, from
the Nile River to the Euphrates.

As providence would have it, I was recently helping lead an
all-night Worship Watch in my hometown. Our last session,
from 3:30 to 5:00 A.M., was an Israel Prayer Watch. I began to
explain to the group how I had struggled in the composition of
the book you are now reading. I described how, in the process of
writing, I had become the student, having my heart expanded
to pray for all the descendants of the Middle East.

When I finished, two beautiful, anointed young women proceeded to the platform. One was a believing Messianic Jew. The
other was from Iran and had escaped through Iraq to make
pilgrimage into the United States. She was Persian with Jewish
blood but also a believer in Jesus. Here we had the descendants
of Sarah and Keturah right before our eyes.

Many of us were weeping over them in gratitude and intercession when another dark-complexioned believer in the Messiah joined the other two on the platform. The third young
woman was from northern Africa. All three embraced. Now

we had a complete picture before our eyes: three women united in weeping intercession that God's purposes in the Middle East would come to pass.

Yes, God has some surprises in store for all of us. May the descendants of Hagar, Sarah and Keturah all find the one true God and embrace one another, for Jesus' sake.

Here is my closing prayer for all the descendants of Abraham:

Father, I thank You right now. Though I do not fully comprehend how Your Word will unfold, You have a plan in Your heart that is enormous. So I cry out for the descendants of Ishmael, that the blinders would fall off their eyes for the sake of Yeshua's holy name.

You say that one day kings will come to the brightness of Your shining. I pray that the descendants of Keturah, who were sent eastward, will return bringing gold and frankincense to worship the one true God and give Him praise and glory. I thank You that, whether that prophecy has been fulfilled or not, it shall be. Thank You! I call forth Keturah's prophetic destiny to come into being.

And I pray for the descendants of Sarah as well. I pray that the blinders would come off the Jewish people's eyes. The book of Romans says that Israel will be saved when the times of the Gentiles are fulfilled.

I bless the descendants of Keturah and Hagar, who are Gentiles, and ask that the fullness of these Gentiles will come and that they in turn will help release the blinders from the Jewish people's eyes. Amen and amen!

Now on to our appointment in Jerusalem—a city of destiny!

Prophetic Gaze into
the Future

10

Jerusalem: A City of Destiny

"I have chosen Jerusalem so that My name might be there, and
I have chosen David to be over My people Israel."

2 Chronicles 6:6

Maps in ancient times displayed Jerusalem as the center of the
earth. She is mentioned 881 times in the Scriptures, and is the
only city in the entire Bible that we are commanded to pray for
by name. Psalm 122:6–9 declares,

> Pray for the peace of Jerusalem: "May they prosper who love
> you. May peace be within your walls, and prosperity within
> your palaces." For the sake of my brothers and my friends, I
> will now say, "May peace be within you." For the sake of the
> house of the LORD our God, I will seek your good.

While God has given each of us the priestly privilege of
interceding for our respective cities and nations, no city but

Jerusalem is mentioned as one that every God-fearing believer must pray for. Jerusalem is a city where East meets West—a city of great contrasts, great conflicts and a great destiny. She is considered holy by Christians, Jews and Muslims alike. She is indeed unique, both in the world and in the heart of God.

According to the Jerusalem Institute for Policy Research, "Of Jerusalem's 901,300 residents, 60.5% are Jewish, 36.5% are Muslim, 1.8% are Christian and 1.2% specify no religion at all."[1] Jerusalem is approximately 49 square miles, twice the size of Tel Aviv. She is the largest city in Israel, in both area and population. The number of residents migrating out declined from 18,000 a year from 2012–2016 to 17,100 a year in 2017; and that number continues to drop. "Aliyah also impacts on the city's migration, with 2,951 new olim [immigrants on aliyah to Israel] arriving in 2017, 800 of them from the US." Jerusalem is much more observant religiously than the rest of the country. And Jewish women in Jerusalem have more children than their Arab neighbors—4.3 children in 2017 contrasted with 3.3 in the Arab sector.[2]

In my travels around the world, I have found Jerusalem to be a city like no other. She gets under your skin. She slips into your heart. When Michal Ann and I led a prayer tour of Israel with Avner Boskey of Final Frontier Ministries, we listened to the marvelous music of modern-day psalmist Marty Goetz while traveling on our bus. While the setting sun cast golden highlights on the white stones of the city of Jerusalem, we sang the words and wept together. From Isaiah 62:1: "For Zion's sake I will not keep silent, and for Jerusalem's sake I will not keep quiet." How our hearts burned with God's desires for His beloved city!

Jerusalem is indeed a city where the past, the present and the future meet. The psalmist described her this way:

How can we sing the L<small>ORD</small>'s song in a foreign land? If I forget you, Jerusalem, may my right hand forget its skill. May my tongue cling to the roof of my mouth if I do not remember you, if I do not exalt Jerusalem above my chief joy.

Psalm 137:4–6

Do you also carry Jerusalem in your heart?

"Next Year in Jerusalem!"

For centuries the Jewish people wandered, exiled from their homeland and from their beloved Jerusalem, the city of David and the city of God. Rejected by nation after nation, the Jewish people were forced to become pilgrims, without a place to rest their heads. Statistics about the city of Jerusalem are worthy of notice, as are the numbers about Israel.

According to the country's Central Bureau of Statistics, there were just over nine million people as of 2019. Almost seven million of them are Jews of different backgrounds, and almost two million of them are Arabs of different religions. Israel's population is growing at two percent a year. Her Jewish population includes Sephardic Jews, Ashkenazi Jews, Mizrahi Jews, Karaite Jews, Bene Israel, Cochin Jews and Beta Israel, among other groups; and they represent a wide range of Jewish cultural traditions and observance.[3]

Most of the Arabs in Israel are bilingual; their second language is modern Hebrew. Most are Sunni Muslims; some are Arab Christians; others belong to various denominations. Other ethnic groups in Israel include Druze, who were originally Muslims and who speak Arabic; Arameans, Arabic-speaking Christians who may be the descendants of the biblical Aram;

Maronites, who are Arabic-speaking Christians; and Samaritans, who claim to be descendants of the tribes of Manasseh and Ephraim and the ancient Samaritans.[4]

Why am I citing all these facts? To remind us to look at what our Lord has done. If you listen closely enough, you can still hear the weeping of Israel's children down through the centuries, as they dreamed of returning to the Promised Land. A river of tears flows through the pages of time as God's people prayed for deliverance, have been regathering and continue to cry out at the end of every traditional Seder meal: "Next year in Jerusalem!"

Persecution

The First Crusade, launched by the Roman Catholic Church in 1096 to recover the Holy Land from Islam, captured Jerusalem in the summer of 1099. The Crusaders spent their first week in the holy city slaughtering Jews and Muslims alike.

Ownership of this Middle Eastern city has been contested more than any other city in the world. She is sacred, as I said, to Judaism, Christianity and Islam alike. Yet still the cry arises: "Next year in Jerusalem!"

Jews in Muslim countries have been hanged in the public squares. Jews were marked for destruction in the gas chambers in Treblinka and in the ovens of Auschwitz. Still a desperate cry rang out from the heart of a wandering people. From the frozen tundra of Siberia to the hot sands of the Ethiopian desert, they cried out, "Next year in Jerusalem!"

History Speaks

History speaks and we must listen to her wisdom. But often, to our chagrin, history speaks with a deafening silence. It can be argued that the United States has been Israel's greatest ally in recent history. But other pages of American history are not as glorious. Franklin D. Roosevelt was, according to Michael D. Evans in *The American Prophecies*,

> the last American president that could have taken action that might have prevented the Holocaust, yet even into the middle of the war, when more than three million had already been executed, he was still eerily silent on the matter. It appears that the man considered America's greatest Democratic president was also part of our darkest hour as a nation in relating to the children of Isaac.[5]

In that bleak hour, America and the nations of the world closed their ears to the piercing cries of the Jewish people.

The philosophy of Breckenridge Long, a diplomat appointed by Roosevelt to determine who would and would not receive entry permits from Nazi Germany into the United States, was simple and troubling: "Keep them all out; they are all trouble-makers."[6] When once questioned about what should happen to the Jews trying to escape Hitler, Long replied by using his hands as an imaginary machine gun to mow them all down.[7]

I remember visiting the Dachau concentration camp with Michal Ann back in the 1970s. My father's family is primarily of German descent, as I have said, and I was stunned by the lingering evidence of what my people had done. How could such atrocities occur in modern civilization? It was as though I could still hear the cries of the Jewish people echoing in those vacant barracks. Even so, the defiant cry still rang out from inside the Nazi death camps: "Next year in Jerusalem!"

It seems to have been U.S. foreign policy after 1948 not to recognize any part of Jerusalem as "Israel" unless the entire

Arab world did so first. This included the section of west Jerusalem that had been part of Israel since 1948. In that year the
late George C. Marshall, a secretary of state under President
Harry S. Truman, strongly opposed the recognition of the new
Jewish state. In fact,

> General Marshall was so disgusted with Truman's move that
> he stated in an ultra-secret memorandum that if Truman pro-
> ceeded on Israel's recognition, he was going to vote against his
> boss in the next election. Nonetheless, Truman stood his ground
> and signed the note of recognition.[8]

In two detailed memoranda to Truman in March 1948, special presidential counsel Clark Clifford

> emphatically favored both the partition of Palestine and the lift-
> ing of an arms embargo imposed on Jewish forces in Palestine.
> Clifford found himself in direct opposition to the staunchly
> held views of the State Department, particularly . . . Secretary
> of State Marshall.[9]

President Truman did go on to recognize Israel in 1948, as we
have noted. But for years the U.S. and the U.N. have continued to
decry Israel's human rights failures and retaliation for terrorist
attacks against her citizens, with no mention of the continual
attacks against her own innocent civilians.

Change of Course

Jerusalem is Israel's capital and has been for three thousand
years, since the days of King David. But Jerusalem has also
been at the center of the Israeli–Palestinian conflict for decades.

The 104th Congress of the United States of America passed the Jerusalem Embassy Act of 1995 officially recognizing Jerusalem as the capital of Israel and allocating $25 million to move the U.S. embassy from Tel Aviv to Jerusalem. The move was not made, however, for fear of undermining delicate Middle East talks. The real reason was plain and simple: Arab countries did not want to recognize Jerusalem as Israel's capital, and the U.S. bowed to their pressure.

Then, on December 6, 2017, President Donald J. Trump announced that the U.S. was recognizing Jerusalem as the capital of Israel and ordered plans to move the embassy from Tel Aviv to Jerusalem. The day after the U.S. announcement, fourteen out of fifteen members of the U.N. Security Council voted to condemn the decision.

Still, on May 14, 2018, the United States embassy officially reopened in Jerusalem. Here are some of the remarks made at the opening ceremony by the U.S. ambassador to Israel, David Friedman:

> On this exact day 70 years ago, at almost this exact time, David Ben Gurion declared Israel's independence. Just 11 minutes later, President Harry Truman caused the United States to be the first nation to recognize the reborn State of Israel. He later regretted that he waited so long.
>
> 70 years since that memorable event, almost to the minute, the United States finally takes the next step: a step awaited, voted upon, litigated, and prayed for for all these years. Today, we open the United States embassy in Jerusalem, Israel.
>
> Today, we keep our promise to the American people, and we extend to Israel the same right that we extend to every other nation, the right to designate its capital city. A capital city, I

should add, which houses all three seats of government, with a 3,000 year old history dating back to the time when King David made Jerusalem the capital of ancient Israel.[10]

Since that historic embassy move in May 2018, and at the time of this writing, a few other countries have followed suit and moved their embassies to Israel's capital city.

Jerusalem: Her Many Names

The meaning of a name given to a person, family, city or nation often reveals a portion of its prophetic destiny. As we peek through the veil, we see glimpses into divine purpose when we correctly interpret and gain understanding of names.

Cities and regions often live to have more than one name, particularly if they come under the rule of different regimes and cultures. Consider the beautiful city of Saint Petersburg, Russia. This northern port city takes its obvious influence from Church history. But when Communism ruled, it was given a new name—first Petrograd, then Leningrad—representing a contrasting spirit of atheism. Times change, leaders rise and fall, and the names of places often change with each season, leaving behind a special part of history or piece of destiny yet to be fulfilled.

So it is with Jerusalem.

The inspired authors of Scripture have given this unique city many names over the centuries. Let's consider some of her names as recorded throughout biblical history and look at her prophetic destiny.[11]

- City of David (2 Samuel 6:10; 1 Kings 11:27; 2 Chronicles 8:11)

- City of God (Psalm 46:4; Psalm 87:3)
- City of Judah (2 Chronicles 25:28)
- City of joy (Jeremiah 49:25)
- City of peace (Hebrews 7:2)
- City of praise (Jeremiah 49:25)
- City of righteousness (Isaiah 1:26)
- City of the great King (Psalm 48:2; Matthew 5:35)
- City of the Lord (Isaiah 60:14)
- City of truth (Zechariah 8:3)
- Faithful city (Isaiah 1:26)
- Gate of God's people (Obadiah 1:13; Micah 1:9)
- Green olive tree (Jeremiah 11:16)
- Holy city (Nehemiah 11:1, 18; Isaiah 48:2; 52:1; Matthew 4:5; 27:53; Revelation 11:2)
- God's holy mountain (Isaiah 11:9; 56:7; 57:13; 65:25; 66:20; Ezekiel 20:40; Daniel 9:16, 20; Joel 2:1; 3:17; Zephaniah 3:11; Zechariah 8:3)
- Throne of the Lord (Jeremiah 3:17)
- Zion (1 Kings 8:1; Isaiah 60:14; Zechariah 9:13)

Wow! Jerusalem is called everything from "the city of God" to "the holy city." It looks as if there must still be a lot of His Story (history) yet to come to pass in the destiny of Jerusalem.

For a great description of this unique city, let's read a little of what the Psalms have to tell us:

Beautiful in elevation, the joy of the whole earth, is Mount Zion in the far north, the city of the great King. . . . Walk around Zion and encircle her; count her towers; consider her ramparts; go through her palaces, so that you may tell of her to the next generation.

Psalm 48:2, 12–13

Surely Your servants take pleasure in her stones, and feel pity for her dust.

Psalm 102:14

Jerusalem, that has been built as a city that is firmly joined together. . . .

Psalm 122:3

As the mountains surround Jerusalem, so the LORD surrounds His people from this time and forever.

Psalm 125:2

Yes, it is true: Jerusalem is a dusty city surrounded by worn mountains. She is a congested, compacted city full of large and small stones. These stones have been used to build architectural wonders, and they have been hurled as tools of destruction. But there is none like her.

Songs are written about you, Jerusalem. Writers love your winding streets and the diverse personalities of your people. Prophets declare your future. Intercessors weep, as Jesus did, that you would yet come under the wings of your Messiah.

Jerusalem is a place of destiny. God has already set countless divine appointments within this city, the heart of Israel. It was King David's capital. It was home to Levites and priests, and the place where Israel's holy feasts were observed. It was the site of King Solomon's Temple, and where the Holy Spirit was first poured out—the place God's people have always loved. Jerusalem is a place like no other, a city where future appointments on God's calendar are yet to be fulfilled.[12]

A Heavy Stone

Jerusalem is a prophetic city of great contrasts. The prophet Zechariah warned:

> "Behold, I am going to make Jerusalem a cup that causes staggering to all the peoples around; and when the siege is against Jerusalem, it will also be against Judah. It will come about on that day that I will make Jerusalem a heavy stone for all the peoples; all who lift it will injure themselves severely. And all the nations of the earth will be gathered against it."
>
> Zechariah 12:2–3

Nations and entire empires have risen and fallen depending on how they have treated this unusual city and her inhabitants. Their treatment releases either a blessing or a curse; we must choose between the two. Ultimately a day will come, the great and terrible day of the Lord, when all nations of the earth will be caught in a divine vortex as they gather against Jerusalem.

My prayer and expectant hope is that a body of believers will arise to be Israel's best friend in that hour. The shout "Israel, you are not alone!" will be heard from interceding friends whose hearts have been broken with the things that break God's heart. Though Jerusalem is "a heavy stone" to lift, God gives grace to carry the burden. He must; it is His Kingdom way.

As for me and my house, I see no other choice than to care for Jerusalem and the destiny of her inhabitants. I want more than anything to be close to the heart of God. I choose with honor, therefore, to pick up this stone and carry it with the love of Christ. We will look at Zechariah's prophecy in more detail in the next chapter.

Let's consider the Hebrew word for peace—*shalom*. This word has a deeper meaning than the mere absence of conflict or war. A cease-fire is never peace, not even if it becomes permanent. And a cold war was never God's idea.[13] This form of peace is a purely human contrivance for keeping warring parties separated so they do not get the opportunity to destroy one another. Such "peace" is unknown to God.

Shalom has, in the Hebrew, several different facets of meaning, but all have the same intent. Shalom can mean "to be completed" in regard to God's purposes and plans. It can also mean "to be restored," meaning to enter into the fullness of one's calling. When we "pray for the peace of Jerusalem" (Psalm 122:6), we are actually asking the Lord to bring Jerusalem into her divine destiny and to restore her into the fullness of His calling.[14]

Hardly anyone in his or her right mind could ever think that peace will be achieved in the Middle East without a season of conflict, suffering and even war. If a sane person does believe that, he or she is simply not a student of either God's Word or history. The current international peace process has few of God's interests in mind. There will never be true, lasting peace without the Prince of Peace being in the middle of the process.

Shalom can also mean "healing," because the Hebrew words for "restore" and "heal" come from the same root. In the meaning of "healing," we see something interesting about the ongoing peace process.[15] Listen to God's view on the matter: "They have healed the brokenness of the daughter of My people superficially, saying, 'Peace, peace,' but there is no peace" (Jeremiah 8:11).

So what are we to do? There is no such thing as true and lasting peace without a relationship with God. Peace is not just a feeling, not just a condition. True peace is a Person—the Son of God, the Messiah, the King of the Jews. There is no peace for any person, family, neighborhood, city or nation without the Prince of Peace. So when I pray for the peace of Jerusalem, I am ultimately praying that the blinders will fall off the eyes of all unbelievers and that they will behold and embrace the beautiful Messiah Jesus.

He has made peace for us "through the blood of His cross" (Colossians 1:20). You cannot bypass the cross of Yeshua on the path to peace. Yes, let's do all we can to bring an end to conflict, war and terror. Let's sit at the negotiation tables and work for reconciliation. But to pray for the shalom of Jerusalem is to pray that the Jewish people will be reconciled to the God of Israel.

The same is true for all the descendants of Abraham—Arab, Jew and all Gentile peoples alike. The shalom of Jerusalem means that it will be completed in God's purposes and reach its divine destiny in the Messiah. That, and that alone, is true shalom.

Servant leaders are working together from Egypt, Germany, Canada, Brazil, the United States and beyond who are bringing together worldwide interactions of online worship and prayer, holding up all Abraham's descendants to be reconciled to the one true God, and ultimately to one another. Now it is time to get ready and fire our bullets of Scripture-based prayer in defense of Jerusalem, her unique destiny and her role in the earth.

Praying the Scriptures

"Now My eyes will be open and My ears attentive to the prayer offered in this place. For now I have chosen and consecrated this house so that My name may be there forever, and My eyes and My heart will be there always."

2 Chronicles 7:15–16

Father, in the Messiah's great name, we ask that You lean Your ear once again toward Jerusalem, the city You have chosen. Be attentive to the prayers uttered by Your chosen people. Lean Your ear and hear the centuries of cries at the Wailing Wall. You say that Your eyes and Your heart will always be there. Look now and hear the groans of Your covenant people. Answer quickly in Your great mercy, and may Your name be established there forever. O Lord, act for Your holy name's sake. Amen.

Gathering them together, He commanded them not to leave Jerusalem, but to wait for what the Father had promised, "Which," He said, "you heard of from Me."

Acts 1:4

Father God, send an unprecedented outpouring of Your glorious presence upon the city of Jerusalem once again, as You did two thousand years ago. Send a new Pentecost on the believers in the land. Send the promise of the Father on the inhabitants of Jerusalem. Let the fire of Your Spirit fall. Let the wind blow the sound of it forth to gather a crowd. Send forth the promise of the Father on the city of Jerusalem, for Your holy name's sake. Amen.

194

A Special Day Each Year

I doubt there has ever been a more crucial time for believers to gather in prayer for Jerusalem. The battle for Israel and Jerusalem is, ultimately, the battle for Judeo-Christian presence in the world and the future of Western civilization as we know it. American Christians have too often been vague and unempowered in their connection with this world-shaping problem. But the understanding that we must become informed intercessors and empower those in our circle of influence to lift our voices to the Lord is growing in the evangelical Christian community.

An International Day of Prayer for the Peace of Jerusalem (IDPPJ) has, therefore, been declared for the first Sunday of every October—a date near Yom Kippur. This is a call for the global Church to set aside one day each year to fulfill the biblical mandate of Psalm 122:6 and other Scriptures to pray for the peace of Jerusalem and for all her inhabitants. The resolution calling for this prayer observance has been signed by hundreds of Christian leaders of influence from around the world, representing tens of millions of believers.

The IDPPJ is endorsed by a broad coalition of Christian leadership from many nations and church backgrounds. Each of these leaders has joined in signing the call to prayer, calling the Church around the world to pray for the peace of all the inhabitants of Jerusalem. The initiative is co-chaired by Robert Stearns, founder and executive director of Eagles' Wings, and Jack Hayford, founding pastor of The Church On The Way and chancellor of The King's University.

My wife and I were among the many initial endorsers of this strategic prayer initiative. Churches, ministries and individual believers around the globe are encouraged to participate and can learn more from the Day to Pray website: www.daytopray .com. The following is the adopted Resolution to Pray agreed upon by the IDPPJ:

> *RESOLUTION for a CALL to PRAYER*
>
> UNDERSTANDING—that we are children of Abraham by faith, the "wild olive branch" grafted in to the root of God's covenant, and
>
> RECOGNIZING—that God has kept His word to Abraham and his descendants and settled them in their homeland again, according to the word of the prophets, and
>
> RECOGNIZING—that we have a biblical mandate according to Psalm 122, and many other Scriptures, to seek the good and prosperity of Jerusalem, until the Lord makes her a praise in all the earth, and
>
> AFFIRMING—that God's love and intended blessing is for all nations and peoples, and that we have goodwill and love for all mankind, including all inhabitants of the Holy Land, and desire the peace of this entire region;
>
> WE, the undersigned, call upon all men and women of prayer to yearly set aside the First Sunday in October, near the season of Yom Kippur, as the DAY OF PRAYER FOR THE PEACE OF JERUSALEM.[16]

Join me and the growing prayer army across the world in this crucial hour of history, and pray for the peace of Jerusalem, the city of destiny.

◇ **A Personal Prayer** ◇

Father God, let Your glory rise upon Israel so that she shines brightly with Your presence, for Your Kingdom's sake. Father God, send Your shalom to Jerusalem. Let Your Kingdom come. Let the Prince of Peace, the Messiah Himself, be revealed, and let His will be done. May the blinders come off the eyes of both Jew and Gentile alike. Prosper those who love You. Bring Your shalom within the walls of Jerusalem. Prosper the spiritual leadership of Israel and the leaders of all nations. Impart Your heart to all those in governmental authority. Release Your peace and the revelation that the ultimate Source of eternal peace and salvation is the Messiah, Yeshua. Establish Jerusalem as a praise in the earth, for Your glory's sake. Amen.

11

God's Road Map

The LORD said to Abram, after Lot had separated from him,
"Now raise your eyes and look from the place where you are,
northward and southward, and eastward and westward; for all
the land which you see I will give to you and to your descendants forever."

Genesis 13:14–15

I need to ask you a question: Has God rejected Israel?

That may seem like an odd question to ask someone who has
read so far in a book like this. But Paul did not assume that *his*
audience knew the correct answer, since he asked his readers,
"God has not rejected His people, has He?" (Romans 11:1).
So I want to follow Paul's example, for at least two reasons:
first, Satan has attempted to deceive the Church about Israel's

destiny; and second, we cannot afford to be mistaken when it comes to the apple of God's eye.

Has God rejected Israel? Paul answered his own question: "Far from it! . . . God has not rejected His people whom He foreknew" (Romans 11:1–2). We all would say we agree with Paul, because reading the rest of Romans makes the question a no-brainer. A good look at the present circumstances in the Middle East, however, along with the secular opinion of our day, and even the views of many in the Church, might lead us to conclude that God has rejected Israel after all.

Could anyone disagree with the apostle Paul? Well, the prophet Elijah might, in his time, have disagreed. Paul reminded his readers that Elijah pleaded with God *against* Israel, saying, "Lord, they have killed Your prophets, they have torn down Your altars, and I alone am left, and they are seeking my life" (Romans 11:3). But God corrected Elijah: "I have kept for Myself seven thousand men who have not bowed the knee to Baal" (verse 4).

Paul's point was this: Although Elijah felt alone, he was not alone. Although Israel's condition had deteriorated and her religious practices were abominable, God had saved for Himself a remnant who still walked in His ways. God wanted Elijah to know this truth, and He wanted the readers of Paul's letter, which includes you and me, to know this truth as well.

Israel's circumstances today may not appear much better than they did in the time of Elijah. But the God of Israel is not sitting in heaven wringing His hands, in a deep sweat from the stress and worry of Middle East conflict. He is not searching for a politician to bring peace. He has a road map for Israel's future, and that ultimate future is bright and glorious.

Speaking through the prophet Isaiah, God said, "As the heavens are higher than the earth, so are My ways higher than your ways and My thoughts than your thoughts" (Isaiah 55:9). The Word of God will accomplish all that God desires and will succeed completely in every way He intends. He is the Deliverer and the Prince of Peace.

God in heaven is looking for people on earth who will come into agreement with Him about His plan for Israel's future. Are you one of them?

The prophet Isaiah asked, "Can a land be born in one day? Can a nation be given birth all at once?" (Isaiah 66:8). The answer is a resounding *yes!*

Throughout this book, we have noted that the State of Israel came into being against all odds in the most miraculous way. The descendants of Israel have undergone a journey that can hardly be described. They started as a family of seventy who traveled to Egypt to escape famine. Four hundred years later they left Egypt as a people group of well over a million, feared and respected by nations all around. By the year 1020 BC, under King Saul and by divine right of conquest, Israel was a recognized nation. Two generations later, she was one of the richest nations on the Asian continent.

Israel is the only people group or nation that, after thousands of years of exile, has been brought back together according to the Word of God. The Lord declared through the prophet Amos: "I will plant Israel in their own land, *never* again to be uprooted from the land I have given them" (Amos 9:15 NIV, emphasis added).

This miracle is happening in our lifetime. And you do not have to be a Hebrew scholar to know that *never* means *never*. Israel is never, ever to be plucked up from her land again.

Four Cities[1]

In the Six-Day War of 1967, Israel took ownership of all Jerusalem, including the Old City, for the first time since AD 70. But for some years now, enemies of God's purposes have been attempting to force deals in which they get back land in exchange for false peace. Lies and deceptions are commonplace, with political correctness valued instead of the fear of God.

Four important and historic sites are being bartered over as though they were poker chips on a table: "I'll give you this if you will do that." These four cities are the birthplaces of covenants God made with Israel. God says that these covenant promises are "forever" (Genesis 13:15). But many demonic and secular forces are converging in an attempt to usurp and overtake these historic sites in the heartland of Israel. Muslims, other Gentile nations and some Jews are demanding that these four places be given away to make "peace" by replacing them with an Islamic Palestinian state.

Islamic terrorists are among those who willfully defy God's covenants with the aim of driving the Jewish people out of their Promised Land. That is what Islamic terrorism in the Middle East is all about: uprooting and destroying God's covenant people. Their aim is none other than to push the Jews out, inch by inch.

But I want to tell you, you cannot bargain with God's Word. In the middle of all this chaos, God's heart is to see Arabs and Jews reconciled through the Messiah and worshiping Him together as a blessing in the midst of the earth (see Isaiah 19:23–25). The following history demonstrates the biblical foundations of these four sites and the case that the West Bank heartland belongs to Israel.

202

Shechem

When Abram left his roots in present-day Iraq, he built his first altar of worship in Shechem, where the Lord God appeared to him and said, "To your offspring I will give this land" (Genesis 12:7 NIV). Jacob later returned to the city of Shechem and bought the land for one hundred pieces of silver (see Genesis 33:18–19). Hundreds of years later, Joseph's bones were brought up from Egypt and buried in Shechem (see Joshua 24:32). These Scriptures show that the Jewish people have historic ownership of the area of Shechem.

Bethel

When visiting Israel, I realized why Yasser Arafat, a leading Palestinian political leader from 1969 to 2004, did not want to leave the city of Ramallah. Ramallah, which means "God's height" or "the high place of Allah," is only a few miles from the city of Bethel. And Bethel is the place where Israel was "conceived" (see Genesis 28:12–19) and born (see Genesis 35).

After God promised Abram in Shechem, "To your offspring I will give this land" (Genesis 12:7 NIV), Abram "built an altar to the LORD" in nearby Bethel (verse 8).

Many years later the Lord appeared to Abraham's grandson Jacob in this same location in a dream, with angels ascending and descending a ladder from heaven, as he rested at the end of a day's journey.

> Then Jacob awoke from his sleep and said, "The LORD is certainly in this place, and I did not know it!" And he was afraid and said, "How awesome is this place! This is none other than the house of God, and this is the gate of heaven!" So Jacob got up early in the morning, and took the stone that he had placed

as a support for his head, and set it up as a memorial stone, and poured oil on its top. Then he named that place Bethel.

Genesis 28:16–19

Years later God declared to Jacob, "Arise, go up to Bethel and live there, and make an altar there to God, who appeared to you when you fled from your brother Esau" (Genesis 35:1). So Jacob moved his entire household to Bethel, where God reaffirmed His covenant with Jacob and changed his name to Israel.

Then God went up from him at the place where He had spoken with him. So Jacob set up a memorial stone in the place where He had spoken with him, a memorial of stone, and he poured out a drink offering on it; he also poured oil on it. And Jacob named the place where God had spoken with him, Bethel.

Genesis 35:13–15

So Bethel is the place where Israel was conceived and born in the person of Jacob, whose name was changed to Israel. I realized, visiting that ancient and blessed site—"the house of God" and "the gate of heaven" (Genesis 28:17)—what the enemies of Israel are trying to accomplish. They want to destroy Israel's foundations and knock down the pillars at her very heart, the places where God made covenant with His people.

Hebron

The third historic site being bartered over is Hebron, where Abram built an altar after he and his nephew Lot parted ways. Both Lot and Abram had many flocks, herds and tents. The land was unable to sustain them both in the same area, so they

204

agreed to separate. After Lot separated from Abram, choosing the valley of Jordan (before the Lord destroyed Sodom and Gomorrah), the Lord encouraged Abram:

> "Now raise your eyes and look from the place where you are, northward and southward, and eastward and westward; for all the land which you see I will give to you and to your descendants forever. I will make your descendants as plentiful as the dust of the earth, so that if anyone can count the dust of the earth, then your descendants could also be counted. Arise, walk about in the land through its length and width; for I will give it to you." Then Abram moved his tent and came and lived by the oaks of Mamre, which are in Hebron; and there he built an altar to the LORD.
>
> Genesis 13:14–18

Abraham later bought land in Hebron, the Machpelah cave, for four hundred shekels of silver (see Genesis 23:16). This cave was used as a burial site for Sarah, then for Abraham himself and their descendants.

Joshua gave Hebron to Caleb as his inheritance in the Promised Land "because he followed the LORD God of Israel fully" (Joshua 14:14).

David ruled in Hebron for seven years. He later ruled in Jerusalem for 33 years, preparing the way for the Messiah to reign on his throne as King of Jerusalem.

Jerusalem

The fourth Israelite city under contention is Jerusalem, the site of the establishment of God's ultimate covenant—the crucifixion of Jesus Christ at Golgotha. In the days of Abraham, this place was known as Moriah.

God told Abraham to "take now your son, your only son, whom you love, Isaac, and go to the land of Moriah, and offer him there as a burnt offering" (Genesis 22:2). This first sacrifice, the father of faith yielding up his son of promise, foreshadowed the second offering, our heavenly Father sacrificing His only Son on the same mountain. It was on Mount Moriah that the Messiah, sent by Jehovah-Jireh—"The Lord Will Provide"— shed His blood on the cross and opened a new and everlasting covenant for the house of Israel (see Jeremiah 31:31).

Not only did the Messiah die and rise from the dead in Je- rusalem, but He is coming back soon to take up His throne in Jerusalem and to reign as the covenant King of this city forever. Isaiah prophesied:

> Of the greatness of his government and peace there will be no end. He will reign on David's throne and over his kingdom, establishing and upholding it with justice and righteousness from that time on and forever.
>
> Isaiah 9:7 NIV

This is why this city is so significant: Jerusalem belongs to the Messiah, King of the Jews. Jerusalem is His city, to which He shall return and from which He shall reign.

Jerusalem has been restored politically to her rightful owner- ship but is still hotly contested. A demonic scheme is at work, not just to get some Palestinian land back (as news reports would convince you to believe), but to take over the whole nation of Israel. Remember Psalm 83, which we looked at in chapter 9: "They make shrewd plans against Your people" (verse 3). Under certain plans, Shechem, Bethel and Hebron would all be taken out of Jewish possession and turned over to another stewardship.

If this happens, it will not last. There is a reason it will never last, and it is not because God loves the Jews more than He loves Arabs, Hispanics, Africans or Asians. It is because God is faithful to the promises He made to Abraham, Isaac and Jacob. He will demonstrate to the entire world that He is a faithful God and that the Bible, His Word, is true.

Countdown to Zechariah 12

In January 2004 the Lord woke me up in the middle of the night and said, *Watchman, tell Me, what do you see?* I looked up and, in a visionary experience, saw a clock that was not there in the natural, hanging on the bedroom wall. The time on the clock read 11:53 P.M., and above the 12 were the letters *Zech.*

The Holy Spirit said, *Watchman, tell Me, what do you hear?*

Suddenly the external, audible voice of the Lord came: *It is the countdown to Zechariah 12.*

I rested in the presence of God for a while and did not move until His manifest presence withdrew. Then I turned on the light and read Zechariah 12. It is an amazing chapter about a city named Jerusalem. Let's read a portion of it together:

"Behold, I am going to make Jerusalem a cup that causes staggering to all the peoples around; and when the siege is against Jerusalem, it will also be against Judah. It will come about on that day that I will make Jerusalem a heavy stone for all the peoples; all who lift it will injure themselves severely. And all the nations of the earth will be gathered against it. . . .

"On that day the LORD will protect the inhabitants of Jerusalem, and the one who is feeble among them on that day will be like David, and the house of David will be like God, like the angel of the LORD before them. And on that day I will seek to destroy all the nations that come against Jerusalem."

Zechariah 12:2–3, 8–9

The countdown to Zechariah 12 is on. I am not saying this will happen in the next seven minutes, seven years or seventy years. What I do know is that God's prophetic clock is moving toward the *kairos* moment when God's plan for Jerusalem will be consummated. This is the final countdown.

It is easy to identify with the first few verses in this chapter as we hear about the nations coming against Jerusalem. But God has a road map, and it points toward Zechariah 12:10:

> "I will pour out on the house of David and on the inhabitants of Jerusalem the Spirit of grace and of pleading, so that they will look at Me whom they pierced; and they will mourn for Him, like one mourning for an only son, and they will weep bitterly over Him like the bitter weeping over a firstborn."

Let's arise and pray for this, Israel's destiny.

Life from the Dead

Since that revelatory encounter, I have pondered the time shown on the clock: 11:53 P.M. Perhaps it is something like this: Romans 11 will be fulfilled through Isaiah 53. Romans 11—"All Israel will be saved" (verse 26)—will be fulfilled by a revelation of the Messiah in Isaiah 53.

Romans 11:12 says that the Jews' rejection of their Messiah has brought salvation to the Gentiles: "If their wrongdoing proves to be riches for the world, and their failure, riches for the Gentiles, how much more will their fulfillment be!" Verse 15 goes on to say, "If their rejection proves to be the reconciliation of the world, what will their acceptance be but life from the dead?"

What do you think "life from the dead" looks like? The prophet Zechariah gives us a glimpse:

> The LORD, my God, will come, and all the holy ones with Him!
> . . . And on that day living waters will flow out of Jerusalem. . .
> And the LORD will be King over all the earth; on that day the
> LORD will be the only one, and His name the only one. . . .
> People will live in [Jerusalem], and there will no longer be a
> curse, for Jerusalem will live in security.
>
> Zechariah 14:5, 8–9 and 11

The Father will reward His Son, the Messiah, for His sufferings. The salvation of Israel is a key component of that reward, and the Father will not do without it. If we are to align ourselves with the God of Israel, we must align ourselves with His covenants and prophetic promises concerning the salvation of the Jews and the restoration of Jerusalem.

It is not difficult to find political analysts, historians, reporters and even theologians ready to explain their theories and share commentary on Israel's current state of affairs. But despite the abundance of opinions and strong feelings, the future of Israel still remains a mystery to most of the world. Paul, the apostle and bondslave of the Lord Jesus Christ, did not want believers to be "uninformed of this mystery" or to "be wise in [their] own estimation" concerning Israel (Romans 11:25).

Despite what it may look like, Israel has not fallen so far from God that she can never return. In fact, her falling away was ordained by God as a measure of grace to us, the Gentiles. Paul said it this way:

> He redeemed us in order that the blessing given to Abraham might come to the Gentiles through Christ Jesus, so that by faith we might receive the promise of the Spirit.
>
> Galatians 3:14 NIV

The Fullness of the Gentiles

The Gentiles are being embraced by the Jewish Messiah in part "to make [the Jews] jealous" (Romans 11:11). Gentiles are not "natural branches" on God's family tree, but rather cuttings from "a wild olive tree" who must recognize that they have been grafted in. God's plan is once again to graft the "natural branches . . . into their own olive tree" (verse 24), with the result that "all Israel will be saved" (verse 26).

Verse 25 says that "a partial hardening has happened to Israel until—" Until when? Maybe you have read this verse many times. Have you realized that the word *until* is the key word in this passage? "A partial hardening has happened to Israel until—" That means there is a point in time when the hardening will be removed. That time is when "the fullness of the Gentiles has come in" (verse 25).

What does the fullness of the Gentiles look like? Perhaps it harkens back to the day Jerusalem was released from Gentile control in 1967 and restored to Israeli rule. Knowing the God we serve, however, this prophecy probably does not refer only to land but to hearts as well.

What Gentile people group would, in the minds of most people, be the most unlikely to come to faith in the Jewish Messiah? Would it not be the Muslims? What if the Holy Spirit

210

moved powerfully on a remnant of the Islamic people and they turned from their false god to serve the Jewish Messiah? What if a movement of God fell on them with the signs and wonders of an apostolic dimension, and they were grafted in as wild olive shoots to the Master's tree? Talk about provoking the Jewish heart to jealousy!

All I know is that God has a road map, and His will shall be done.

Praying the Scriptures

Seek the LORD while He may be found; call upon Him while He is near. Let the wicked abandon his way, and the unrighteous person his thoughts; and let him return to the LORD, and He will have compassion on him, and to our God, for He will abundantly pardon. "For My thoughts are not your thoughts, nor are your ways My ways," declares the LORD. "For as the heavens are higher than the earth, so are My ways higher than your ways and My thoughts than your thoughts."

Isaiah 55:6–9

Lord, Your ways are higher than our ways. Your thoughts are higher than our thoughts. Let us know Your ways and think Your thoughts concerning Israel. Open the eyes of the hearts of Your people so they see You as the One they have been waiting for. I ask that Israel would seek You with all their hearts. I thank You for Your promise that You will be found by those who seek You. I ask that Israel's encounter with her Messiah will cause the wicked to forsake their way and the unrighteous all their evil thoughts. I call out to Israel, "Come and return to the

Lord. He will have compassion on you and pardon your sins." Thank You, Lord, for Your mercy and kindness and Your willingness to abundantly pardon those who turn to You. In the name of the Lord Jesus. Amen.

"I will restore the fortunes of My people Israel, and they will rebuild the desolated cities and live in them; they will also plant vineyards and drink their wine, and make gardens and eat their fruit. I will also plant them on their land, and they will not be uprooted again from their land which I have given them," says the LORD your God.

Amos 9:14–15

Father, restore the wealth of Your people, Israel. I agree with You that she will rebuild ruined cities and live in them, plant vineyards, make gardens and eat their fruit. Bring Israel's time of barrenness to an end and let her bear fruit for Your Kingdom. Thank You that Israel is being replanted in her land. I call forth righteous leaders who will recognize Israel, reach out to her in relationship and stand with her. Thank You for Your Word that promises that the people of Israel will never again be uprooted from their land. Stir the people of Israel to possess their full inheritance—the land promised to their forefathers. With thanksgiving and praise, through Your Son, the Messiah. Amen.

"On that day the LORD will protect the inhabitants of Jerusalem, and the one who is feeble among them on that day will be like David, and the house of David will be like God, like the angel of the LORD before them. And on that day I will seek to destroy all the nations that come against Jerusalem. And I will pour out on the house of David and on the inhabitants of Jerusalem the Spirit of grace and of pleading, so that they will look at Me whom they pierced; and they will mourn for Him, like one mourning for an only son, and they will weep bitterly over Him like the bitter weeping over a firstborn."

Zechariah 12:8–10

Lord God, I thank You that a day is coming when You will defend the inhabitants of Your city, Jerusalem. Hasten that day, Lord. Stretch out Your mighty hand and strengthen the weak. Pour out on the house of David and all the inhabitants of Jerusalem Your Spirit of grace and supplication. Open their eyes to see the One our sin has pierced. Prick their hearts. I ask that godly sorrow would draw them to repentance and faith in Your holy Son, their elder brother, Yeshua. Amen.

God's Plan Includes You

The story of Israel is all about a God who keeps His promises. From this point of restoration—after a nation was born in one day, never to be plucked up again—God's road map calls for a body of believers to carry His heart, watchmen who see from His perspective and hear Him when He speaks.

The road map leads to Romans 11 and goes through Isaiah 53. It is the salvation of all Israel through the revelation of her suffering Servant. When Israel is grafted back in, it will be nothing less than life from the dead. When we labor for Israel, we are laboring for the greatest worldwide outpouring of the Holy Spirit that there has ever been.

Our God is the holy Lord of heaven, and His Word never fails. He is the Judge of all, living and dead, and has the final word on your life and on the Middle East. And He is looking for a people who will come into agreement with Him.

Will we allow those four sites of covenant foundation—Shechem, Bethel, Hebron and Jerusalem, pillars of the house of Israel—to be toppled by Islam, or will we take a stand and agree with the covenant God of Israel, even, if necessary, against all odds? We are children of Abraham by faith. We have been bought with the price of Yeshua's covenant blood. We belong to the high and Holy One who inhabits eternity and who is the King of Jerusalem. Will you take a stand? God is looking for allies. Will you be one? Are you willing to give your life, like Esther and Mordecai, as a sacrifice for God's purposes?

◇ A Personal Prayer ◇

God has a plan for every person, family, city and nation. Indeed, the Lord of Hosts has a glorious future for Israel and all the nations of the Middle East.

Believe it? Then join me and countless thousands of others to pray these promises into being. Join me now in this personal prayer of dedication:

Father God, it was for such a time as this that I have
come into Your Kingdom. If I die, I die, for my life is but
a gift from You and is not my own. Place Your mighty
hand on me to be a Mordecai who helps the Esthers be
a forerunner voice crying in the wilderness. Let a people

214

arise who will cry out for the destiny of Israel and intercede effectively for Your purposes in the Middle East. As for me and my house, I want to be possessed by You for Your purposes. Come, Lord Jesus, and do this for Your name's sake, that You may receive the reward for Your suffering on behalf of Jews and Gentiles alike. I dedicate myself to Your grace and for Your purposes. I declare that Your Word, God, is the final road map for Israel and the entire Middle East.

Thank You for Your mercy and Your lovingkindness and Your willingness to pardon those who turn to You, in the name of the Lord Most High, the host of the armies, almighty God. For the glory of Jesus' sake. Amen and amen.

12

The Great Hope

Looking for the blessed hope and the appearing of the glory of
our great God and Savior, Christ Jesus.

Titus 2:13

It has been an honor to journey with you as together we discover
treasures in the Word of God, treasures in the heart of God, and
treasures deposited within the people of God. I am grateful.
This is the closing chapter on an amazing subject.

I do not believe that you, the reader, have just stumbled onto
the subject of this book, the mystery of Israel and the Middle
East. God has planted a seed in your heart and mind to explore
this topic.

There are some who are religious and even spiritual, who
love history or are perplexed over how Israel fits into today's
complex discussion of the Middle East, yet who do not really
know Jesus. If that is you, I pray that the blinders come off
your eyes and heart and that the Holy Spirit does what He
does best—makes Jesus wholly real to you. In fact, I pray that

our heavenly Father opens the eyes and hearts of all of us to the majesty of His plan—which includes you, me and all the descendants of Abraham—to touch lives, inspire us and change us for the times in which we live. Amen.

I love the theme verse for this important and timely focus:

Looking for the blessed hope and the appearing of the glory of our great God and Savior, Christ Jesus.

Titus 2:13

I encourage you to "pray-read" this verse again and again throughout your daily routine: "I am looking for the blessed hope and the appearing of the glory of our great God and Savior, Christ Jesus."

What is the great hope? The coming of the Messiah.

I have prayed a lot into the teachings I have shared in this book. I have written other books on this subject and have been involved in this vital discussion for quite a few years. But this book presents a different posture. It is the culmination of the ages—a look into finality, a place of grandeur, the mystery that is revealed when the Spirit and the Bride say, "Come."

The Spirit and the bride say, "Come." And let the one who hears say, "Come." And let the one who is thirsty come; let the one who desires, take the water of life without cost.

Revelation 22:17

Is that you? Are you thirsty? We are each offered the water of life without cost because Jesus has already paid the price—through grace, faith and His sacrifice. The sin of all history past, all history present and all history future was laid upon Him.

218

The Spirit and the Bride say, "Come." I am persuaded that there will literally be a time—maybe not just a day, but a season, a period of time—when this occurs, when the awakened Church, who is the Bride, and the Holy Spirit cry out together.

We are like a bride who has been separated from her husband, perhaps for many years, and yearns to have him back home and close in her arms. You see, Jesus Himself likewise has a burning desire to come to us, His Bride, the awakened Bride, the Church comprising all His children. And that awakened Bride cries out, "Come, come!" The Holy Spirit and the Bride come into unison and lift a cry, "Come!"—for revival and divine connection and the Second Coming of Jesus. Global revival in the last days will set the stage and ultimately usher in the Messiah's return.

Divine Relationship

There is a divine relationship between the mighty outpouring of the Holy Spirit and the Second Coming of the Messiah through faith and prayer, evangelism, acts of compassion and moving in the power of the Spirit. We each have a part to play that only we can play.

Revival begins in the heart of one man and one woman of God, and it becomes a fire that spreads. Luke 12:39–40 says,

> "Be sure of this, that if the head of the house had known at what hour the thief was coming, he would not have allowed his house to be broken into. You too, be ready; because the Son of Man is coming at an hour that you do not think He will."

When Jesus said, "If the head of the house had known at what hour . . ."—it doesn't say "what second" or "what minute." So we, too, must be ready at an hour we do not expect. As believers we are called to know the "times and the seasons" (1 Thessalonians 5:1 KJV), which includes discerning the purposes of God and our appropriate actions and responses needed during that period of time.

Let's add another consideration—the pattern. Believers have not talked much about the Second Coming of the Messiah, but we should. When we believe in the literal Second Coming of the Lord Jesus Christ, it does something inside us; it makes us want to be ready at any hour to welcome Him. Whether in our generation or the next or the next, the revelation of His coming helps make us ready and expectant. It creates a hunger in us to want to tell others about the Messiah, which causes revival to break out, which will ultimately usher in the Second Coming of the Messiah.

The pattern is actually pretty simple:

- Awakening
- Revelation of the Second Coming
- Readiness
- Receiving His presence
- Revival
- Second Coming of the Messiah

The depth of your hunger is the length of your reach to God. It is true. The pattern is simple, but remember, it includes a shaking to be awakened.

Back in chapter 3 we looked at the gentle awakening, followed by the rude awakening, that will work together for good unto the Great Awakening. When the Spirit says, "Come," it includes shaking to be awakened:

> This expression, "Yet once more," denotes the removing of those things which can be *shaken*, as of created things, so that those things which cannot be shaken may remain."
>
> Hebrews 12:27, emphasis added

Everything that can be shaken will be shaken, so that what "cannot be shaken may remain." Has your life ever been shaken? Shaking comes into every life. And God can use it redemptively for His purposes to reveal the foundation of that life. The foundation of a person's life determines his or her endurance. How long will the foundation stand when shaken under work pressure, relationship storms and inevitable personal troubles?

Our awareness of God's presence, His jealousy toward us, His passionate pursuit of us—all of these and more wake us out of our slumber and complacency and instill in us a sense of divine urgency.

A friend of mine recently completed 170 days in a row of prophetic street evangelism. One by one he prayed for people, telling them about the good news of the Messiah. I am not saying that is your calling, but I am saying that each of us has a part to play. Don't we? Our part is to wake up out of the slumber that the greater Church has fallen into.

How does it happen? One member at a time. One member awakens another out of slumber and complacency. One member at a time instills in another member the divine urgency to be ready to receive the outpouring of the Holy Spirit. One member at a time shares His desire for us—and His longing to return empowers us to be spiritually vigilant, spiritually alert and even passionate and full of zeal.

Parallel Restoration

The Spirit and the Bride say, "Come!" How will all this happen? Through a fresh Pentecost—the baptism with the Spirit and fire falling afresh on believers, both individuals and the Church as a whole, the Bride. John the Baptist promised that Jesus "will baptize you with the Holy Spirit and fire" (Matthew 3:11). We need a fresh baptism of His burning fire in our lives, which collectively will change everything on a personal, regional, national and global level.

I pause right here, right now, to say to you:

> Receive a fresh falling of the fire of God, like the fire of Acts 2, on your life. I speak forth that the Spirit and the Bride say, "Come," because we are both filled with the fire of God. I speak forth a returning, a restoring, a completion of the baptism of the Spirit and fire. I bless you, that you will enter into an immersion of the Holy Spirit that causes empowering, filling and sanctification, because fire cleanses. I speak that for you in Jesus' name. The Spirit and the Bride say, "Come."

We saw in chapter 3 that parallelism between the natural and the spiritual realms occurs during awakening. One mirrors the other. One reflects the other. The natural and spiritual realms trigger one another; they are a divine response and reaction.

It is marvelous to recognize the parallel restoration of the nation of Israel and spiritual awakening in the Body of Christ.

222

There have been three different parallel movements of the Holy Spirit. (I mentioned these briefly in chapter 3.) The restoration of the nation of Israel parallels various restoration movements in the Church today. So when God is moving on natural Israel, there is a great parallel restoration in the Church, the Body of Messiah. And a parallel awakening will occur in the Church when Israel takes her proper place and role in God's destiny.

A study on the seven feasts of Israel would be marvelous, but here I just highlight the great parallel restoration and the three great feasts: Passover, Pentecost and the Feast of Tabernacles.

Passover

Passover is mentioned in both Old and New Testaments: The Passover lamb of the Old Testament is fulfilled in the sacrifice of the Lamb of God, Jesus the Messiah, who was slain on our behalf. In the Old Testament, all of Egypt was under a plague, and the Israelites, in quarantine, brushed the blood of a lamb on their doorposts so the death angel would pass over and not kill their firstborn, as happened to every Egyptian. In the New Testament, Passover was fulfilled through the Lamb of God, Jesus, who shed His blood on behalf of all of us. This restoration has been fulfilled.

Pentecost

Pentecost is also mentioned in both Old and New Testaments. In the Temple period, Pentecost was an agricultural festival, the Festival of Weeks or Shavuot, marking the beginning of the wheat harvest. The original Pentecost was the giving of the law to Moses on Mount Sinai, filled with the glory and awe and wonder of God. Then Moses came down the mountain with the Law and was radiant, glowing. There were signs and wonders all around the first Pentecost.

The giving of the Holy Spirit to believers in Acts 2 is the New Testament fulfillment: "When the day of Pentecost had come, they were all together in one place" (verse 1). The writer describes "a violent rushing wind" and "tongues that looked like fire" (verses 2–3) and the Holy Spirit resting on each one who had gathered. "And they were all filled with the Holy Spirit" (verse 4).

Pentecost, Old Testament and New. We see Moses receiving the commandments in the Old, considered to be a shadow; and the fulfillment in the New, when believers received the Holy Spirit, with signs and wonders.

The Feast of Tabernacles

The Feast of Tabernacles, or Sukkot, the Feast of Ingathering, is the feast that the Jewish people celebrate every year in the fall, marking the end of the harvest and representing a shadow of something yet to come. What could it be? This feast has yet to find its greater fulfillment under or in the New Covenant, but it is coming; it is greatly coming. It is the final harvest of souls, the great ingathering.

We are right at the door, at the beginning of the greatest global harvest the world has ever seen.

Reconciliation and Healing

What is required for this global harvest? The following is from two of my friends, Asher Intrater and Dan Juster, Messianic Jewish scholars living in Israel:

Covenant relationships and integrity are demonstrated by the fact that the first-century believers were in one place (unity), and in one accord (love), and that they were praying (holiness) under the direction of the apostles (congregational authority). [1]

In other words, if we cannot act in unity, love, purity and under authority, we will not ultimately experience the glory of God. They go on:

The relationship between our unity and the glory of God has been pointed out by many in reference to John 17:22, where Yeshua prays that we might receive the same glory God gave to Him and that we would all be one.[2]

This is what Jesus said in John 17:22:

"The glory which You have given Me I also have given to them, so that they may be one, just as We are one."

I suggest you go back and read Intrater's and Juster's quote again. As God gave glory to Jesus, Jesus gave His glory to His disciples—and this will make us one.

Before we look at an unusual prophecy about reconciliation and healing, let's review the more familiar dry bones passage for the original historical context:

The hand of the LORD was on me, and he brought me out by the Spirit of the LORD and set me in the middle of a valley; it was full of bones. He led me back and forth among them, and I saw a great many bones on the floor of the valley, bones that were very dry. He asked me, "Son of man, can these bones live?"

I said, "Sovereign LORD, you alone know."

Then he said to me, "Prophesy to these bones and say to them, 'Dry bones, hear the word of the LORD! This is what the Sovereign LORD says to these bones: I will make breath enter you, and you will come to life. I will attach tendons to you and make flesh come upon you and cover you with skin; I will put breath in you, and you will come to life. Then you will know that I am the LORD.'"

So I prophesied as I was commanded. And as I was prophesying, there was a noise, a rattling sound, and the bones came together, bone to bone. I looked, and tendons and flesh appeared on them and skin covered them, but there was no breath in them.

Then he said to me, "Prophesy to the breath; prophesy, son of man, and say to it, 'This is what the Sovereign LORD says: Come, breath, from the four winds and breathe into these slain, that they may live.'" So I prophesied as he commanded me, and breath entered them; they came to life and stood up on their feet—a vast army.

Ezekiel 37:1–10 NIV

This "dry bones" prophecy provides the context for the unusual prophecy in the same chapter of Ezekiel:

"Now you, son of man, take for yourself one stick and write on it, 'For Judah and for the sons of Israel, his companions'; then take another stick and write on it, 'For Joseph, the stick of Ephraim and all the house of Israel, his companions.'"

verse 16

This portion of Scripture has been twisted and mishandled, but let's not let fear of misuse cause us to go to no use. The symbolic word and act of Israel and Judah being joined can be interpreted and applied in many different manners, but each suggests the ingredients of a great outpouring of the Holy Spirit in the end times.

Historical Perspective

First, the two sticks coming together represent the healing of the division between the Northern Kingdom, Israel, and the Southern Kingdom, Judah. The prophets foretold that they would come back united, the Jewish nation as one whole. That is the historic perspective.

Parallel Restoration

Second, let's look at the parallel restoration, the healing of the Body of Christ. The two sticks of Ezekiel 37:16 may be interpreted as reconciliation and healing—a true unity movement within the body of believers globally.

This is a supernatural work, not a manmade ecumenical movement that boils differences down to a very low common denominator. No, this is not a lowering of any standard. It is humans coming into agreement with God's values and God's Word. In that way, the level of healing in the body of believers is not just manmade but supernatural.

Healing of Division

Third, the two sticks of Ezekiel 37:16 can be seen as the healing of the historic division between the Church and the Jewish people, as the reconciliation between Gentile believers and Messianic believers. You may ask, "But aren't we all believers in Yeshua?" Yes, but there is still a lot of pain and prejudice. This reconciliation will be a miracle because the Church has persecuted the brothers of Jesus.

The level of forgiveness and reconciliation needed is part of the mystery and the destiny of the Bride of Christ becoming healed and whole, with two opposing parties coming to peace through the blood of the cross. As the reconciliation between Gentile believers and Messianic believers occurs, the result is wider unity outside church walls.

And hold on for a moment. As goes the Church, so goes the world. We live in a time of incredible polarity. We need healing—of races, of ethnic groups, of cities and nations. Do you think it matters how much division and schism there is in the Body of Christ? Do you think that a healing reconciliation movement, with our bond as Jesus and the Word of God, would affect what the world looks and acts like? I believe the Bible indicates so:

> He Himself is our peace, who made both groups into one and broke down the barrier of the dividing wall, by abolishing in His flesh the hostility, which is the Law composed of commandments expressed in ordinances, so that in Himself He might make the two one new person, in this way establishing peace.
>
> Ephesians 2:14–15

This great work of parallel restoration in the natural and spiritual realms results in the generation of "greater works" (see John 14:12) arising. The fulfillment of the Feast of Tabernacles, the great harvest, and then the ultimate ushering in of the Second Coming of the Messiah—all are related.

Considering the timing of this glorious event brings us back to the question we asked in chapter 4: Can we hasten (or accelerate) the day of His appearing?

The Day of His Appearing

Some would say we absolutely cannot hasten the return of the Lord, because in their theological take on the providence of God, everything is preordained.

I believe very much in the sovereignty of God. I also believe that He gave us free will, and that He invites us into the mystery and destiny of being a co-laborer with Christ.

As we consider whether we can hasten His appearing, let's ask another question: Is it possible that we can cause it to be delayed? It is an interesting concept, is it not?

The Bible seems to suggest that we *can* either hasten or delay the coming of the Lord:

> What sort of people ought you to be in holy conduct and godliness, looking for and *hastening the coming of the day of God*, because of which the heavens will be destroyed by burning, and the elements will melt with intense heat!
>
> 2 Peter 3:11–12, emphasis added

Without majoring on the dimensions of calamity in this passage, let's look at our part in the coming of the day of God. Peter suggests that "holy conduct and godliness" will hasten "the coming of the day of God." Your life and your lifestyle can be part of hastening the coming of Messiah, when the Spirit and the Bride say, "Come!"

I also firmly believe that prayer can change the course of events. One of our models is Daniel in captivity in Babylon. He read the prophetic promise of an earlier generation—but he did more than just read it. He sought God earnestly that the promise would be fulfilled:

I, Daniel, understood from the Scriptures, according to the word of the LORD given to Jeremiah the prophet, that the desolation of Jerusalem would last seventy years. So I turned to the Lord God and pleaded with him in prayer and petition, in fasting, and in sackcloth and ashes.

Daniel 9:2–3 NIV

What was the promise? That at the end of seventy years of captivity in Babylon, Judah would be released and return to her homeland. Daniel read the prophecy of Jeremiah from an earlier generation, then sought God to remove the hindrances that stood in the way, so the promise could be fulfilled. He did not assume that the timeline would automatically take place. He took on himself the mandate to remind God of His Word and see God's Word come to pass.

That is the dynamic of intercession—how we can hasten a promise to come to fruition.

"In Like Manner"

Now to another question: How will Jesus appear? The angels told the disciples, "This same Jesus, who was taken up from you into heaven, will so come *in like manner* as you saw Him go into heaven" (Acts 1:11 NKJV, emphasis added). This absolutely amazes me.

Since I like to ponder phrases, let's consider the phrase *in like manner*. What could that mean? Surely Jesus will come back down out of heaven, but to where? The Mount of Olives on the outskirts of Jerusalem.

But there is more to it than that.

What are some possible "in like manner" scenarios? I believe there are at least four:

1. He will return in similar historic circumstances to the demographic and political situation in Israel and the entire Middle East at the time He left.

2. He will return in like manner to the Jewish people living in the Promised Land as when He was taken up, as today many Jews live in the land and more continue to return from the nations of the earth.

3. He will return in similar spiritual circumstances to when He lived in the land, when there were scribes and Pharisees as well as ordinary Jews who were believers in Yeshua. Today there are Orthodox Jews and Messianic believers in the land.

4. He will return in like manner as when He was taken up, since the world powers of Greece, Magog, Babylon and Persia are realigning themselves.

Restoration

Before the return of the Lord Jesus Christ, there must be a restoration of all things. Let's listen to Peter on the Day of Pentecost:

> "Therefore repent and return, so that your sins may be wiped away, in order that times of refreshing may come from the presence of the Lord; and that He may send Jesus, the Christ appointed for you, whom heaven must receive until the period of restoration of all things, about which God spoke by the mouths of His holy prophets from ancient times."
>
> Acts 3:19–21

Restoration happens in reverse order. Let me explain that with a simple analogy.

I mentioned that my earthly father was a carpenter. He made furniture and was very involved with antiques. So I grew up around shellac, which was applied to wood furniture as a stain and sealer. Some old pieces of furniture have layers of shellac as well as layers of paint, as the owners over the years have added their preferences to the pieces. Well-made furniture passed down through generations of a family can have a dozen layers of finish. To restore the piece to its original beauty, each layer starting from the top needs to be removed.

In the same way, God is restoring His creation, from where we are (at the "top") to return to the original (at the very base). Think of it, in a sense, as the book of Acts reversed.

Consider that God's restoration involves five stages, starting with stage 5 and moving back to stage 1:

Stage 5: Worldwide evangelism, along with the realignment of the political systems of the nations. That is the end of the book of Acts.

Stage 4: The regathering of the Jews, the restoration of Israel and the restoration of unity in the Body of Christ.

Stage 3: Intercession, persecution, tribulation, and signs and wonders with a revival focus, including a back-to-Jerusalem movement.

Stage 2: The fire of the Holy Spirit falling, accompanied by a glory realm of God and the nations entering the valley of decision.

Stage 1: Jesus will return in like manner to the way He departed. The return, the great hope, the Second Coming, the return of Messiah Jesus!

Back to the Beginning

When Peter preached on the Day of Pentecost, he quoted the book of Joel. In my summation of this book, I am going to do likewise—take us to the place of the beginning, which is also the place of the ending: the book of Joel.

Peter saw on the Day of Pentecost what Joel had declared prophetically: "This is what has been spoken through the prophet Joel" (Acts 2:16). Hundreds of years earlier, Joel had prophesied, "I will pour out My Spirit on all mankind" (Joel 2:28). So if *this* was *that*, then let's go to the model of Joel and see what else he might have to tell us regarding the great hope—the Second Coming of Jesus.

The book of Joel evokes a chain reaction that is significant as it relates to Acts 2—the empowering of the early Church by the Holy Spirit and its relation to the Second Coming of our Lord Jesus Christ. Joel ties together three elements to create a chain reaction, an acceleration, the consummation of the ages:

1. Intensive intercession, the global prayer movement today.
2. The fire of revival in the midst of shaking world events.
3. The return of Jesus Christ as the conquering King.

1. Intensive Intercession

There is intensive intercession and prayer taking place today. Two separate but purpose-united gatherings took place on the National Mall in Washington, D.C., on September 26, 2020. Tens of thousands attended the Washington Prayer March 2020 led by evangelist Franklin Graham; the same number watched via the internet.[3] A separate gathering on the same day in the same city was "The Return—National and Global Day of

Prayer and Repentance," led by Jonathan Cahn, a Messianic rabbi. It was attended by tens of thousands, with reports of twelve million worldwide watching online.[4] Speakers at these two events included believers in the White House, both houses of Congress, churches, synagogues, missionaries and people from all walks of life, all crying out to God for the globe to open hearts, minds and spirits to the Lord Jesus, Yeshua Messiah.

The world is reaching out to God in prayer like no other time in history. When searching for "global prayer" online, I found 35 million results, including books, websites, events, YouTube videos, Facebook pages, networks, 24/7 call-in for prayer sites—and the list goes on and on.

Just one example of 24/7 prayer is found in the prayer room of the International House of Prayer in Kansas City, Missouri, founded by Mike Bickle. On September 19, 1999, Mike and dedicated intercessors started "a movement of unceasing worship with prayer . . . which, in the grace of God, shall continue till Jesus returns."[5] The prayer room continues to keep prayer and worship going 24/7 and is open to the public.

As another example, The Voice of the Martyrs website chose November 1, 2020, as the International Day of Prayer for Persecuted Christians.

2. The Fire of Revival

When internationally known evangelist Billy Graham died on February 21, 2018, at the age of 99, he had preached the Gospel of Jesus Christ to some 215 million people in more than 400 crusades, simulcasts and evangelistic rallies in more than 185 countries and territories.[6]

In 1967 German evangelist Reinhard Bonnke started evangelizing in Africa. As a result of Bonnke's ministry, more than 79 million people gave their lives to Jesus Christ. (He died in 2019.) Bonnke's largest in-person event drew 1.6 million in Lagos, Nigeria, on a single night.[7]

Daniel Kolenda, Bonnke's successor at the ministry he founded, Christ for all Nations, has continued the massive open-air evangelistic campaigns in remote regions, leading more than 22 million people to Christ.[8]

Another Jesus people movement in 2020 started bringing thousands to Christ in the midst of a global pandemic and chaos on the streets of major U.S. cities. Worship leader Sean Feucht began holding worship gatherings across the nation aimed at engaging millennials. Prompted by the restrictions placed on churches and worship meetings by state governments, Feucht felt called to stand up to the restrictions, believing that the nation is "on the cusp of a revival that will sweep America!"[9] He and his worship team have seen thousands of people saved, healed and baptized.

His "Burn 24-7" outreach is a global worship and prayer movement spanning six continents and 250 cities.[10] Its mission is "to plant a sustainable furnace of 24-7-365 worship, prayer and supernatural explosive outreach . . . in every community, people group, city and nation in the world."[11]

The fire of revival is indeed burning in the midst of soul-shaking world events.

3. The Return of Jesus

I said earlier that, to restore a piece of furniture, each layer of paint or shellac needs to be removed, starting from the top, to recover the original beauty. In the same way, as God restores His creation, God is "reversing" the book of Acts, to return to the original.

What was the original? We heard Peter say on the Day of Pentecost, "This is what has been spoken through the prophet Joel" (Acts 2:16). So for our beginning, we go back to the book of Joel. He conveyed warnings, much like the book of Revelation, concerning Jesus' return:

> "Woe for the day! For the day of the LORD is near, and it will come as destruction from the Almighty."
>
> Joel 1:15

> Blow a trumpet in Zion, and sound an alarm on My holy mountain! Let all the inhabitants of the land tremble, for the day of the LORD is coming; indeed, it is near.
>
> Joel 2:1

> The LORD utters His voice before His army; His camp is indeed very great, for mighty is one who carries out His word. The day of the LORD is indeed great and very awesome, and who can endure it?
>
> verse 11

Guess what? Modern-day people did not make up the word *awesome*. The New American Standard Bible uses that very word in this translation—in fact, "very awesome." Other translators use the word *terrible*.

And finally:

> The sun will be turned into darkness, and the moon into blood, before the great and awesome day of the LORD comes.
>
> verse 31

This is the passage Peter quoted (see Acts 2:20) on Pentecost, the coming of the Holy Spirit and the birthday of the Church. And this is the consummation of the battle between good and evil on the earth, which brings us to John's revelation on the Isle of Patmos and the book of Revelation—so we end where we started: "The Spirit and the Bride say, 'Come.'"

The purposes of God include the mighty, glorious outpouring of the Holy Spirit while the nations rage and the devil and his demonic hordes are attempting to take one last stand to conquer the earth. The dual conflict of the fire of judgment and the glory of God is God's plan. God the Father desires this to take place. But eventually He says, "Enough." God wants the battle between humankind and the devil to end. That is the great and terrible day of the Lord. This mystery—which is the mystery of Israel and the Middle East and praying for the peace of Jerusalem—is ultimately fulfilled in the Prince of Peace Himself.

We have done a quick romp, a restoration in reverse of the book of Acts. We have looked at some ways that the Lord Jesus can return "in like manner." We have seen parallels between the book of Acts and the book of Joel and the book of Revelation. That starts with fire and ends with "And the Spirit and the Bride say, 'Come.'"

More prayer and fasting are happening right now in this generation than in all of history—and they have not even reached their zenith. There are global moments of praying, dreaming and envisioning by the Spirit of God.[12]

As we come to the end of this book, I pray that you have been renewed in the washing of the water of the Word, and are prepared to receive the fire of Pentecost, the birthmark of the Church. I believe you can receive right now, right where you are, because His plan is personal and includes you.

Behold, He is coming with the clouds, and every eye will see
Him, even those who pierced Him; and all the tribes of the earth
will mourn over Him. So it is to be. Amen.

Revelation 1:7

Here is the resolution of the conflict of the ages—when the
Son of Man, the Son of God, splits the skies and comes with
His saints and angels, and every eye will behold Him. The
mystery has now been revealed: that Christ Jesus is the Messiah
of Jew and Gentile alike. He is the answer to every person's
questions. He is the risen Savior and Lord, and we will behold
Him, the Lamb of God.

Will you come into agreement with God's heart for His great
plan for Israel, the Middle East and all the nations of the earth?

◇ A Personal Prayer ◇

Father, we declare that it is a great honor and privilege to
live in these days that are like none other, yet were spoken
of by the holy prophets of old. So pour out Your Spirit
on all people. Release dreams and visions and revelations.
Join the generations for such a time as this. Pierce the
Islamic veil. Convict us of our idols. Cleanse our house.
Restore Your house with fire and power and character and
integrity. We declare that the mystery and the destiny of
Israel ultimately is about the great hope, the Second Coming of the Messiah.

We do come into agreement with Your great plan for
Israel, the Middle East and all the nations of the earth.

We lift our hearts to You, our Lord and our King, and we cry out together. The Spirit and the Bride say, "Come." Even so, Prince of Peace, come quickly. Lord Jesus, come for Your honor and for Your glory and for the great global end-time harvest, when You, Jesus, will receive the reward of Your sufferings. Amen and amen.

Appendix A

Overview of Israel's History

November 29, 1947. The United Nations (U.N.) partitions Palestine into two independent states—one Jewish and the other Arab. Arab nations renounce the Jewish state and vow to seize all of Palestine by force.

May 14, 1948. The British Mandate for Palestine expires. The Israeli Declaration of Independence is signed, proclaiming the State of Israel. The Israel Defense Force is formed.

May 15, 1948. Arab nations surrounding Israel suddenly attack the world's newest nation. (This Pan-Arab force includes armed forces from Egypt, Transjordan [present-day Jordan], Syria, Lebanon and Iraq.)

January 7, 1949. A cease-fire agreement ends Israel's War of Independence. (In an armistice agreement, however, signed July

1949, the Arab League closes its frontiers to Israel and declares itself "in a permanent state of war" with Israel.)

February 1949. The first Knesset (Israeli Parliament) meets in Jerusalem and elects Chaim Weizmann (the Jewish chemist who helped Great Britain prior to the Balfour Declaration) as its first president.

May 11, 1949. Israel is admitted to the U.N.

1948–51. The Knesset enacts the Law of Return, which states, "Every Jew has the right to come to this country as an immigrant." Israel's population more than doubles with 684,000 new arrivals from North Africa and the Middle East and the airlift of entire Jewish communities from Yemen (43,000) and Iraq (113,000).

1951. World Zionist Congress meets for the first time in Jerusalem.

1952–56. West Germany signs a reparations agreement to pay the State of Israel $719 million for material losses to Jews under Nazism and $100 million to individuals. Arabs continue to be actively hostile, with three thousand clashes between armed Arab forces and Israeli soldiers.

Egypt, Syria and Jordan sign a military pact to defend one another in the event of war (with Israel).

October 1956. Egypt nationalizes the Suez Canal and cuts off international shipping through it. Faced with Arab threats of war, Israel launches a preemptive attack called the Sinai Campaign, with support from Britain and France (who fear their shipping will be endangered).

March 1957. Israel withdraws from Sinai. U.N. peacekeeping troops are sent to ensure the Suez Canal remains open to most international—but not yet Israeli—shipping.

1958–59. End of first decade as a new state: Jewish population reaches 1.8 million, raises the standard of living and achieves agricultural self-sufficiency. Arab and Druse communities share in progress, participate in free elections and have their own representation in the Knesset.

Israel provides technical and scientific assistance to emerging nations in Africa and Latin America; many of them establish embassies in Jerusalem and support Israel in the U.N.

1964. Pope Paul VI becomes the first pope to visit Israel, though Israel's statehood is not recognized by the Vatican. The Palestinian Liberation Organization (PLO) is founded in Egypt with the express goal of destroying Israel through armed struggle. Yasser Arafat soon becomes head of this terrorist organization.

1967. Prelude to the Six-Day War. Al Fatah, a Palestinian terrorist organization, sends trained terrorists into Israel for sabotage. Kibbutz settlements in Galilee are bombed by Syrians.

May 14, 1967. Egyptian leader Gamal Abdel Nasser moves large numbers of troops into Sinai.

May 16–June 4, 1967. Nasser expels U.N. peacekeeping forces from Sinai, blocking shipping lanes in the Gulf of Aqaba, and announces that Egypt is "prepared to wage war on Israel." Jordan and Iraq place their military forces under Nasser's command.

June 4, 1967. The Six-Day War starts. Israel mobilizes for defense, leaving older men, women and children to keep necessary, basic services going, bring in agricultural harvests and pack export orders.

June 5, 1967. Israel bombs airfields of Egypt, Syria, Jordan and Iraq, destroying 452 planes in three hours. Israeli ground forces move against Egyptian forces in the Sinai at four points. Israel notifies King Hussein of Jordan that she will not attack Jordan if his troops will keep the peace. In response, Jordanian troops open fire on Israel along the entire armistice line and occupy U.N. headquarters in Jerusalem.

June 6–7, 1967. Israel counterattacks and takes all of Jerusalem, including the Old City, for the first time since AD 70.

June 9, 1967. Israel drives Syrians from the heavily fortified Golan Heights, penetrates the Sinai to the Suez Canal and takes Gaza Strip. Israeli naval forces capture Sharm El Sheikh on the Red Sea.

June 10, 1967. Cease-fire called after Israel's miraculous victory against overwhelming odds. Israel establishes free access to Jewish, Christian and Muslim holy sites and removes barriers between East and West Jerusalem. The result is an unprecedented awakening of Jews abroad to Israel's importance for world Jewry.

1967–73. The war of attrition brings on continual harassment by Egypt on Sinai borders and increasing Soviet involvement in Egypt, including Soviet planes, anti-aircraft missile bases and troops. Prelude to Yom Kippur War: Egyptian and Syrian troops gather on cease-fire lines. Israel begins mobilization of reserve forces on eve of Yom Kippur (Day of Atonement).

September 5–6, 1972. The Munich Massacre occurs, in which Palestinian terrorists break into the Munich (Germany) Olympic Village, kidnapping and killing eleven members of the Israeli Olympic team.

October 6, 1973. Yom Kippur War: Israeli Cabinet meets on the holy day itself, confirms Prime Minister Golda Meir's decision not to make a preemptive air strike, despite "unmistakable signs of imminent attack." The purpose is to make the responsibility for aggression unmistakably clear. As the Israeli Cabinet is meeting on Yom Kippur, Arabs attack on two fronts at 2 P.M.

October 7–25, 1973. Israel stops advance on both fronts within two days, but at a heavy cost and high casualties.

October–November 1973. The "Oil War" begins after the cease-fire; Arab nations dramatically reduce oil supplies to the West.

January 18, 1974. Egypt and Israel sign a disengagement agreement. U.S. officials (evidently unaware of biblical prophecy and the spiritual history of the region) claim it is the first step toward permanent peace in the Middle East.

May 1974. Syria and Israel sign a disengagement agreement, and Israeli forces withdraw slightly west of the cease-fire lines on the Golan Heights.

September 1975. Israel withdraws from portions of the Sinai, and Egypt reopens the Suez Canal to Israeli shipping for the first time since 1951.

January 1976. Syria takes advantage of civil war in Lebanon to move troops into Lebanon and join forces with the PLO. With much of southern Lebanon under her control, she bombards northern Israel with Soviet Katyusha rockets.

July 1976. Israeli forces stage a daring rescue operation and free more than one hundred hostages from Arab terrorists in a hijacked plane in Entebbe Airport in Uganda.

July 1977. Israeli Prime Minister Menachem Begin presents a plan for Middle East peace to U.S. President Jimmy Carter in Washington, D.C.

November 1977. Egyptian President Anwar Sadat visits Jerusalem at the invitation of Prime Minister Begin to initiate direct peace talks.

September 1978. Prime Minister Begin, President Sadat and President Carter meet at Camp David, Maryland, to formulate peace accords.

1979. In response to increasing Israeli civilian casualties, Israel begins preemptive strikes against terrorist bases in southern Lebanon.

March 26, 1979. Israel and Egypt sign a treaty in which Israel agrees to relinquish the Sinai Peninsula to Egypt in exchange for peace. They agree to recognize and respect each other's right to live in peace within secure and recognized borders and to establish regular diplomatic relations.

1981. PLO and Syrian forces bombard northern Israel daily, forcing residents, including children, to spend weeks in bomb shelters. Israel responds by bombing the PLO headquarters in Beirut.

June 7, 1981. Israel destroys Iraq's Osirak nuclear reactor and neutralizes Iraqi nuclear weapons capacity through Operation Opera.

January 7, 1982. Foreign Minister Yitzhak Shamir meets with Pope John Paul II.

April 25, 1982. Prime Minister Begin returns to the Sinai Peninsula to meet with President Hosni Mubarak of Egypt.

June 4, 1982. The attempted assassination of Shlomo Argov, Israel's ambassador to the U.K., triggers Operation Peace for Galilee, an Israeli invasion of southern Lebanon to remove PLO Katyusha rockets and dismantle their Soviet-armed terrorist camps.

September 16, 1982. Lebanese Maronite–Christian soldiers enter Palestinian refugee camps in West Beirut and slaughter hundreds. One week later, 400,000 Israelis (ten percent of the entire population) gather in Tel Aviv to demonstrate their horror and demand a commission of inquiry.

October 1982. Arafat is exiled from Lebanon to Tunisia, which serves as PLO headquarters until 1993.

November 23, 1983. Israel trades 4,765 terrorists for six Israeli soldiers held prisoner by Arafat's Fatah terror forces.

June 28, 1984. Israel trades 291 Syrian prisoners for eleven Israeli soldiers (five of them deceased).

January 4, 1985. Operation Moses airlifts six thousand Ethiopian followers of Judaism to Israel.

May 20, 1985. Israel trades 1,150 terrorists for three Israeli soldiers held by Ahmed Jibril's PLO-related forces.

October 1, 1985. Israel bombs PLO Headquarters in Tunis, Tunisia, in response to the murder of Israeli yachters in Cyprus.

December 1985. Seventeen El Al airline passengers are murdered and 109 wounded by PLO attacks at airports in Rome and Vienna.

February 1986. Natan Sharansky, a Russian Jewish human rights activist who had been imprisoned for many years in Russia's notorious labor camps, is finally freed by the U.S.S.R. and arrives in Israel.

April 17, 1986. Agents of the Syrian Air Force attempt to smuggle a suitcase bomb onto an El Al London-to-Tel Aviv flight, but security guards discover and successfully dismantle the bomb.

July 22, 1986. Prime Minister Shimon Peres pays a surprise public visit to King Hassan II of Morocco.

October 26, 1986. Mordechai Vanunu, an Israeli peace activist, is kidnapped back to Israel by agents of Israel's legendary Mossad security apparatus, after accepting a bribe to publicize information about Israel's purported nuclear capabilities.

February 15, 1987. Yosef Begun, a so called prisoner of Zion, is freed from Russian imprisonment after being sentenced in 1983 to twelve years in prison/exile for distributing anti-Soviet propaganda. (Begun had applied to leave Russia twelve years earlier, but his application was denied.)

October 15, 1987. Ida Nudel, another prisoner of Zion, arrives in Israel following sixteen years of refused permission to leave Russia.

December 9, 1987. The Intifada, an organized Palestinian revolt against Israeli occupation of the Gaza Strip, begins. By the end of December, 21 Palestinians are dead and 179 wounded; 41 Israeli soldiers and 27 civilians are wounded.

March–April 1988. Abu Jihad, Arafat's military deputy, is killed in his Tunis home by commandos purported to be Israeli elite troops. Abu Jihad had masterminded an attack on a bus full of civilians (mostly mothers) in southern Israel and was guiding the Intifada revolt. Israel has never claimed responsibility.

July 1989. Islamic terrorist forces Jerusalem-bound bus into a gorge, killing 16 and wounding 27.

July 1989. Israeli commandos kidnap Hezbollah leader of south Lebanon, Sheikh Abdel Karim Obeid, as a bargaining chip in negotiating the release of three Israeli soldiers held captive in Lebanon.

1989–94. More than 500,000 Jewish immigrants reach Israel.

February 4, 1990. Nine Israeli tourists are killed and seventeen wounded by Muslim fundamentalists on a tourist bus on the way to Cairo.

May 1, 1990. The Jewish Agency, which oversees Jewish immigration to Israel, reports record numbers of Russian Jews leaving the U.S.S.R. Over the next decade, more than 820,000 Jews emigrate from the former U.S.S.R. to Israel.

August 2, 1990. Iraq invades Kuwait, and Israel distributes gas masks to all citizens in anticipation of a chemical weapons attack by Iraq.

October 8, 1990. Muslim fears that Jews are building a third Temple on the Temple Mount in Jerusalem lead to a riot in which thousands of Arabs attack an Israeli police station. 26 Jews are injured, 140 Arabs are injured and 21 Arabs are killed.

January 1991. Coalition air forces attack Iraq. In response, Iraq fires salvos of ground-to-ground missiles into Israel. Over a period of more than a month, approximately 38 Iraqi versions of Scud missiles fall (33 El Hussein missiles and 5 El Tijara missiles) in nineteen missile attacks. These missiles mainly hit the greater Tel Aviv region and Haifa, although western Samaria and the Dimona area are also hit by missiles. Directly these attacks cause 2 civilian deaths, and indirectly they cause 4 heart attacks, 7 deaths as a result of incorrect use of biological/chemical warfare kits, 208 injuries and 225 cases of unnecessary injection of atropine. Damage to general property consists of 1,302 houses, 6,142 apartments, 23 public buildings, 200 shops and 50 cars. Israel assents to American requests not to respond. On February 28 a cease-fire is declared.

May 1991. Operation Solomon brings more than 14,000 Ethiopian followers of Judaism to Israel, who are resettled in less than two days.

October 1991. The U.S.S.R. and Israel restore diplomatic ties. The Madrid International Middle East Peace Committee meets, discussing "land for peace."

January 1992. Israel establishes full diplomatic relations with China and India.

March 1992. The terrorist group Islamic Jihad bombs the Israeli embassy in Argentina, killing 29 and injuring 242.

June 1992. Yitzhak Rabin is elected for a second time as prime minister of Israel, defeating Yitzhak Shamir.

September 13, 1993. Lacking support by the Israeli public, the U.S.–brokered Oslo Accord (Oslo I) is signed between the PLO and Israel. This accord is understood as promoting land for peace and expressing the PLO's desire to solve disputes in a peaceful manner.

February 1994. Lone activist Baruch Goldstein kills 29 Muslims and wounds a hundred in an attack on a Muslim service in Hebron's Machpelah Cave on Purim, the Feast of Esther. Two of his friends had been murdered on December 6 by terrorists.

June 12, 1994. Rabbi Menachem Mendel Schneerson, head of the Lubavitch Hasidic movement, dies at age 92. Many of his followers believed that he was the messiah and would be resurrected.

July 1994. Arafat arrives from Tunisia (via Egypt) to cheering crowds in Gaza and four days later in Jericho.

July 18, 1994. Terrorists detonate a car bomb, blowing up the Jewish community center in Buenos Aires, Argentina, killing 85 and injuring hundreds.

July 26, 1994. Terrorists detonate a car bomb at the Israeli embassy in London, injuring fourteen and causing widespread damage.

October 19, 1994. A Hamas suicide bomber blows up a Tel Aviv bus, killing 22 and injuring more than 40.

October 26, 1994. Israel and Jordan sign a peace treaty.

December 10, 1994. Yitzhak Rabin, Shimon Peres, and Yasser Arafat are awarded the Nobel Peace Prize "for their efforts to create peace in the Middle East."

January 22, 1995. Two Islamic Jihad suicide bombers blow themselves up at Beit Lid Junction, between Tel Aviv and Haifa, killing 21 and injuring 34.

July 24, 1995. Six Israelis are killed and 32 injured by a suicide bus bomber in Tel Aviv.

August 21, 1995. Five are killed and 107 injured in Jerusalem suicide bus bombing. Both bombs were built by Yahya Ayyash, "the Engineer."

October 26, 1995. Fathi Shaqaqi, one of Islamic Jihad's leaders, is killed by gunmen in Malta.

November 4, 1995. Prime Minister Yitzhak Rabin is assassinated by Yigal Amir, a 26-year-old law student and opponent of the Oslo Accords.

January 5, 1996. Hamas bomb-maker Yahya Ayyash, "the Engineer," is killed by a booby-trapped cellphone in Gaza.

February 25, 1996. Twenty-seven Israelis are killed and 78 injured by two suicide bombs in Jerusalem and Ashkelon.

March 3, 1996. Eighteen Israelis are killed and dozens injured by a suicide bus bomb in Jerusalem.

March 4, 1996. Fourteen Israelis are killed and 157 injured by a suicide bomb at Dizengoff Center, Tel Aviv, on the Feast of Purim.

May 29, 1996. Benjamin Netanyahu becomes prime minister of Israel.

September 1996. An archaeological tunnel along the Western Wall opens in Jerusalem. Rioting by Muslims spreads, with tens of thousands attacking Israeli forces. Fourteen Israeli soldiers and eighty Palestinians are killed.

January 15, 1997. Israel redeploys in Hebron, according to the Oslo Accords.

March 1997. A Jordanian soldier kills seven Israeli eighth-grade schoolgirls on the Island of Peace, between Jordan and Israel on the Jordan River.

July 30, 1997. Fourteen Israelis are killed and 150 injured by Hamas suicide bombers in Jerusalem.

October 23, 1998. Prime Minister Netanyahu and Yasser Arafat sign the Wye River Memorandum, consisting of steps to implement Oslo II (signed September 28, 1995).

May 4, 1999. Deadline set forth in Oslo I passes without establishing the permanent status of a Palestinian entity.

July 1999. Labor Party leader Ehud Barak is elected prime minister of Israel.

September 4, 1999. Sharm El Sheikh Memorandum, signed by Ehud Barak and Yasser Arafat, extends deadline for implementation of Oslo I. It also attempts to restart stalled negotiations and ensure compliance with Oslo I and II and the Wye River Memorandum. Deadline for completion is set for September 13, 2000.

September 5, 1999–May 22, 2000. A flurry of diplomatic activity between the Israelis and Palestinians attempts to push forward the peace process.

March 21, 2000. Pope John Paul II visits Israel. He is credited by Israel with unprecedented and significant improvement in Catholic-Jewish relations.

May 2000. Israel withdraws her peacekeeping forces from the strategic military buffer zone in southern Lebanon, resulting in the proliferation of the terrorist group Hezbollah. Barak cuts off talks with Palestinians due to violence in Arab-occupied Israeli territories.

June 6, 2000. U.S. Secretary of State Madeleine Albright meets separately with Barak and Arafat to push for the resumption of negotiations.

July 11–25, 2000. At Camp David summit meetings initiated by U.S. President Bill Clinton, Barak offers the following: Israeli withdrawal from virtually all the West Bank and all the Gaza Strip to create a Palestinian state; the removal of isolated Jewish settlements and transfer of resulting vacated lands to Palestinian control; the exchange of other Israeli lands for certain West Bank settlements, to remain under Israeli control; and Palestinian control over East Jerusalem, including most of the Old City and the Temple Mount. In summary, Barak's offer concedes to approximately 95 percent of Arafat's demands. Refusing Barak's offer or further negotiation, Arafat walks out of the meetings without making a counteroffer.

September 2000. Palestinian terror attack in Gaza kills an Israeli soldier. With legal permission of Palestinian officials, Ariel Sharon visits the Temple Mount. In protest of his visit, an uprising of terror begins against Israel, known as the Al-Aqsa Intifada.

September 28, 2000–September 2005. Terrorism inside Israel escalates dramatically. The Palestinian Authority communications director states that this uprising was planned weeks earlier, when Barak offered to meet 95 percent but not 100 percent of Arafat's demands at Camp David. The Al-Aqsa Intifada continues "officially" until September 2005. More than one thousand Israelis are killed by terrorism during this period.

2000–2006. First wave of aliyah (Jewish immigration to Israel) from the West occurs. More than eleven thousand Jewish immigrants move to Israel from France, with more than seven thousand from North America and ten thousand from Argentina.

February 2001. Ariel Sharon is elected prime minister of Israel.

April 30, 2001. U.S. Senator George Mitchell releases an analysis of the causes behind the Al-Aqsa Intifada. The Mitchell Report concludes that Sharon's visit to the Temple Mount was not the cause of the intifada. The report is intended as an effort to restart peace negotiations and calls for the Palestinians to stop violence as a precondition to further negotiation.

September 11, 2001. Al Qaeda Islamic extremists, with links to the Palestinian groups Hezbollah and Hamas, destroy the twin towers of the World Trade Center in New York City and damage the Pentagon, killing nearly three thousand in suicide airplane attacks. In Gaza and the West Bank, Palestinians dance in the streets, chanting their support for the leader of Al Qaeda, Osama bin Laden.

October 2, 2001. George W. Bush becomes the first U.S. president to publicly call for establishment of a Palestinian state, stating, "The idea of a Palestinian state has always been part of the vision."

January 3, 2002. Israel intercepts the cargo freighter *Karine A*, carrying fifty tons of weapons shipped from Iran to the Palestinian Authority.

March 27, 2002. Hamas suicide bombing at the Park Hotel in Netanya during a Passover Seder kills 30 Israelis and injures

140. Days later Israel launches Operation Defensive Shield to dismantle terror nests in Jenin (West Bank).

March 29, 2002. Records are discovered implicating Arafat in the continued financing of terrorism, including his order for weapons associated with *Karine A*. As a result, Israel confines him to his headquarters in Ramallah for the remainder of his active life.

June 24, 2002. President Bush declares that there can never be a Palestinian state while Arafat is leader of the Palestinians and that he no longer considers him a partner in the peace process.

January 2003. Prime Minister Sharon wins a landslide reelection on a platform that includes condemnation of the notion of Israeli withdrawal from Gaza.

April 2003. The U.S., in cooperation with Russia, the European Union and the U.N. (known as the Quartet), presents its Roadmap to Peace to Israel and the Palestinian Authority. The plan is a performance-based, goal-driven plan, with clear phases, timelines and benchmarks. It involves reciprocal steps by the two parties in the political, national security, economic and humanitarian spheres. The goal is to create a Palestinian state, based on the premise that this will resolve the Israeli-Palestinian conflict.

November 11, 2004. Yasser Arafat dies in France from an undisclosed illness, and within hours Mahmoud Abbas is chairman of the PLO Executive Committee.

January 9, 2005. Abbas is elected president of the Palestinian National Authority.

August 15, 2005. At Prime Minister Sharon's direction, Israel unilaterally withdraws from Gaza, forcibly evicting Jewish citizens who fail to leave voluntarily. This causes a significant rift in Israeli society. Shortly thereafter, Qassam rockets are launched regularly in terror attacks from Gaza into the western Negev, particularly Sderot, and continue to the date of this writing. (An online clock tracks how long Israel has been rocket-free: https://www.israel21c.org/online-clock-tracks-how-long-israel -has-been-rocket-free/.)

September 2, 2005. The International Atomic Energy Agency announces that Iran has been concealing development of nuclear technology.

December 24, 2005. Ultra-Orthodox Jewish anti-missionaries opposed to the Gospel (who for decades have harassed or persecuted Messianic Jews) physically attack Jewish believers during a congregational Sabbath service in Beersheba.

January 4, 2006. Sharon suffers a severe stroke, ending his political career and leaving him in a coma.

January 25, 2006. The terrorist group Hamas is elected as the majority representative of the Palestinian National Authority.

April 24, 2006. President Mahmoud Ahmadinejad of Iran (from 2005–2013) announces to the world, "Israel cannot logically continue to exist." He regularly and publicly reiterates this statement, including that Israel must be "wiped off the map." He is a staunch Holocaust denier.

April 2006. Ehud Olmert, a protégé of Sharon, is elected prime minister of Israel (2006-2009).

June 25, 2006. Israeli soldier Gilad Shalit is kidnapped in Gaza by Hamas. He will be held captive for more than five years.

June 28–November 26, 2006. Israel Defense Forces intermittently strike Hamas in Gaza as a result of increased Palestinian Qassam rocket fire into western Israel.

July 12–August 14, 2006. Hezbollah attacks northern Israel, killing three Israeli soldiers and kidnapping two others. Israel and Hezbollah fight a war in southern Lebanon and northern Israel. A U.N. ceasefire creates a peacekeeping force in Lebanon to disarm Hezbollah and ensure Israeli withdrawal. Israel withdraws, but Hezbollah is not disarmed.

2006–2007. Israel's economy grows faster than that of any Western nation.

June 7–15, 2007. Hamas wins military and political control over Gaza through a civil war with the Fatah party of President Abbas. As a result, Abbas loses control over Gaza. Sharia (Islamic) law is established in Gaza.

September 6, 2007. Israeli Air Force bombs suspected nuclear reactor development site in Syria.

October 2007. After receiving several Islamic death threats, Rami Ayyad, Arab Christian manager of the only Christian bookstore in Gaza, is found murdered.

November 27, 2007. U.S. President Bush convenes a summit in Annapolis, Maryland, to jumpstart the peace process between Israel and the Palestinian Authority.

2008–2009. The Gaza War. More than two thousand rocket and mortar attacks are launched from Gaza into the Negev. Negotiations between the governments of Israel and the Palestinian Authority continue.

March 6, 2008. A Palestinian from East Jerusalem opens fire on students at Jerusalem's Mercaz HaRav Yeshiva, killing eight and wounding eleven.

March 22, 2008. A terrorist bomb disguised as a Purim holiday gift is delivered to the home of a Messianic Jewish family in Ariel, severely injuring their teenage boy. In the following months, national and international interest in Messianic Jewish faith in Israel significantly increases. The perpetrator, an American-born Israeli religious nationalist, is later sentenced to life imprisonment.

April 2008. Prime Minister Olmert announces his intent to divide Jerusalem and concede governmental control over much of the city either to Palestinians or to an international peace-keeping force.

May 2008. Israel's sixtieth anniversary is honored in an un-precedented manner when vast numbers of Christians come for celebrations and prayer gatherings.

May 14, 2008. After sixty years of statehood, Israel's population stands at approximately 7,282,000. Approximately 5.5 million Israelis are Jewish, representing about 43 percent of the world's total Jewish population. https://www.jewishvirtual library.org/israeli-population-statistics-1960-2008

May 2008. Prime Minister Olmert is implicated in an international finance scandal that threatens to remove him from office.

June 2008. Indirect peace negotiations begin between Israel and Syria in Turkey. Included are discussions of Israeli withdrawal from the Golan Heights.

July 2, 2008. A Palestinian terrorist and resident of East Jerusalem drives a bulldozer into cars, buses and pedestrians in downtown Jerusalem, killing 3 Israelis and wounding 45.

July 30, 2008. Under pressure of criminal investigation, Prime Minister Olmert announces that he will resign his office.

January 2009. The Gaza War ends with a unilateral Israeli cease-fire.

February 2009. Benjamin Netanyahu elected as prime minister of Israel.

March 15, 2011. The Syrian civil war begins. Millions of refugees flee the war to neighboring countries and Europe, and ISIS takes advantage of these conditions in an attempt to establish its caliphate. Fighting continues at this writing.

October 2011. Hamas releases Israeli soldier Gilad Shalit, held for more than five years, in exchange for 1,027 prisoners.

November 2012. Israel launches week-long military campaign against Hamas following months of escalating rocket attacks on Israeli towns in western Negev.

December 2013. Israel, Jordan and Palestinian Authority sign agreement to try to save the Dead Sea from drying up by pumping water from the Red Sea.

July–August 2014. Israel responds to attacks by armed groups in Gaza with a military campaign by air and land to destroy missile-launching sites and attack tunnels.

March 2, 2015. Israeli Prime Minister Netanyahu delivers address to Joint Session of U.S. Congress warning of the impending nuclear deal with Iran.

July 2015. Iran Nuclear Deal is signed by the U.S. and several other world powers. Israeli Prime Minister Benjamin Netanyahu says it will guarantee that Iran becomes a nuclear power.

September 2015. A wave of Palestinian terror begins over issues of the Temple Mount and Eastern Jerusalem. In twenty months 49 people are killed, and 731 people are injured through 177 stabbing attacks, 144 shootings and 58 vehicular ramming attacks.

December 2016. United Nations Security Council resolution 2334 calls East Jerusalem, including the Old City, "occupied" Palestinian territory, and condemns all Israeli settlements.

January 20, 2017. U.S. President Donald Trump's administration sets a different tone toward Israel and signals the end of eight years of cold relations with the Obama administration.

April 2017. Egyptian President el-Sisi and Jordan's King Abdullah II visit the White House, signaling a closer relation to the U.S., a united front against Iran and closer relationships with Israel.

May 9, 2017. Turkish President Erdogan vows to help the Palestinians guard against the "Judaization" of Jerusalem. Jerusalem's mayor Nir Barkat tells Erdogan the connection of the Jewish people goes back more than 3,000 years and says, "Jerusalem is and will remain the eternal, united capital forever."

May 22, 2017. President Donald Trump is the first sitting U.S. president to visit the Old City of Jerusalem. He and his wife, Melania, also visit the Church of the Holy Sepulchre, the traditional site of Jesus' crucifixion, burial and resurrection, and the Western Wall, Judaism's most revered religious site.

December 2017. U.S. President Donald Trump recognizes Jerusalem as the capital of Israel.

January 22, 2018. Mike Pence is the first U.S. vice president to speak in the Knesset, the national legislature of Israel. He promises, "The USA will never compromise on the safety and security of the State of Israel."

March 2018. U.S. President Donald Trump recognizes Israeli sovereignty over the Golan Heights.

October 26, 2018. Prime Minister Benjamin Netanyahu visits Oman, the first prime minister to visit a Gulf state in 22 years.

November 2019. The U.S. considers the Israeli settlements on the West Bank to be legal.

February 6, 2020. Following a Hamas call for a Palestinian uprising against Israelis, twelve Israeli soldiers are injured when a man rams his car into them in Jerusalem. Later that day a terrorist shoots at police officers near the entrance of the Temple Mount. A third attack takes place at a military post in the West Bank.

May 17, 2020. Benjamin Netanyahu is sworn in as prime minister after three deadlocked and divisive elections in fewer than two years. He has served as Israel's prime minister longer than any other leader, including the country's founding father, David Ben-Gurion.

August 13, 2020. The Trump administration is instrumental in brokering the Abraham Accords between the United Arab Emirates and Israel. The UAE becomes the first Gulf state to establish diplomatic relations with Israel. Bahrain and Sudan also normalize relations with Israel in 2020.

August 31, 2020. The first -ever direct El Al flight from Tel Aviv, Israel, to Abu Dhabi, United Arab Emirates, over Saudi Arabian airspace, carrying delegations from Israel and the United States.

October 2020. Israel Defense Forces conduct a historic drill called Lethal Arrow, simulating a war along the northern border, where tensions with enemies, including Hezbollah, are consistently high.

November 8, 2020. A flight carrying Jewish Israelis and Arab Israelis are the first tourists to arrive in Dubai. In a remarkable breakthrough, UAE and Israel have agreed to launch regular commercial flights between their two countries.

June 13, 2021. With 60 votes in favor and 59 opposed (1 abstention), Israel's 120-member Knesset votes in a new eight-party coalition government, naming Naftali Bennett prime minister for the first two years and Yair Lapid for the last two years of the term. Benjamin Netanyahu remains head of the largest party in the Israeli parliament.

Author's Note: This overview of Israeli history was developed from information compiled and provided by Avner Boskey and from information appearing in Derek Prince's book *The Key to the Middle East* (Chosen, 2013), pages 155–185. For further information on Derek Prince Ministries, visit www.derekprince.org. Special appreciation to Kerry and Sandra Teplinsky and to Angela Rickabaugh Shears for their invaluable expertise in revising and adding to this timeline, particularly with more recent history.

Appendix B

Come Humbly to Israel!

Don Finto

As a non-Jewish believer who has come to some understanding of the purposes of God for the nation of Israel and the Jewish people in this end-time generation, let me encourage you to consider several things as you pursue connections with Jewish friends, acquaintances and co-workers and look forward to an upcoming visit to Jerusalem.

Come humbly to Israel; come humbly to Jerusalem. This is the land of your inheritance. Here Jesus was born, lived, taught, ministered, was crucified as a common criminal and buried, rose from the dead and ascended from the Mount of Olives, where He will return as King, Emperor and Supreme Ruler over all nations in a future world empire of peace (see Acts 1:11; Zechariah 14:9).

Israel is the only nation of the world whose land deed was signed by the Almighty Himself. Look at His words to Abraham,

Isaac, Jacob and Joshua in Genesis 15:18–21; 26:3; 35:12 and Joshua 1:4, and His words through the psalmist in Psalm 105:8–11. The land belongs to Abraham's descendants through Isaac and Jacob (Israel) in perpetuity, even though she will not have full possession until she is walking in the commandments of God (see Deuteronomy 28:15ff.).

Jesus predicted that Jerusalem would be destroyed and "taken as prisoners to all the nations" (Luke 21:24 NIV). Ezekiel 37:1–11 described Israel as dry bones that would be resurrected and into which the breath of God would enter. Jeremiah called the return of Israel "out of all the countries where he had banished them" a greater miracle than the Exodus from Egypt (see Jeremiah 23:7–8 NIV).

God sees Jerusalem as "the center of the nations, with countries all around her" (Ezekiel 5:5 NIV). And: "Whoever touches you [Jerusalem] touches the apple of [God's] eye" (Zechariah 2:8 NIV). Even the boundaries of the nations relate somehow to the tribes of Israel (see Deuteronomy 32:8).

Believers in our day are learning to honor the host nations on every continent. Israel is the host nation of all nations. Of no other city does the Lord say, "Give yourselves no rest, and give him no rest till he establishes Jerusalem and makes her the praise of the earth" (Isaiah 62:6–7 NIV). No other city has a divine injunction to be remembered in prayer (see Psalm 122:6).

You, as a believer in Jesus, are grafted into the Jewish olive tree (see Romans 11:17). Grafted in, not replacing. This is our family of faith. Even Jewish people who have not yet come to faith in their Messiah are a part of our yet-to-be-redeemed family.

Enjoy the diversity of Abraham's sons and daughters who have returned from two thousand years of exile from more than a hundred nations and languages. Listen as people speak the language of Moses and the prophets. Enjoy especially the fellowship with your Jewish brothers and sisters whose eyes and hearts have been opened to their own Messiah.

Go to be blessed, but also go to bless others. Walk in the blessing God spoke to Abraham: "I will bless those who bless you, and whoever curses you I will curse; and all peoples on earth will be blessed through you" (Genesis 12:3 NIV). Israel was created as a blessing to all nations, but you have now become part of that heritage, so you are both to receive and to carry the blessing wherever you go.

Those of us who have learned to love Israel and the Jewish people, however, must never forget her blood cousins, the Arab nations, the sons and daughters of Ishmael and other related peoples. Ishmael was not Abraham's son of the covenant and was sent away from his family home at an early age; but Abraham also blessed him and his descendants. The Lord told him, "*As for Ishmael*, I have heard you: *I will surely bless him*" (Genesis 17:20 NIV, emphasis added).

The surrounding Arab nations also have a destiny in God. Egyptians and Assyrians (who would represent today's Iraq, Syria and other nations adjacent to Israel) are also a people of destiny. They, along with Israel, will one day be a blessing to the whole earth (see Isaiah 19:23–25). Be alert to both Jewish and Arab believers who are united and often risking their lives to see that their people learn of their common Redeemer.

Ours is a unique day in history, the day predicted by Jesus, the day for which the prophets and apostles yearned:

1. Israel will be returned from centuries of exile and established as a nation. The return from Egypt was from

269

the south, the return from Babylon was from the east, but this return is from the north (think Russian Jews), south (Ethiopia), east and west (think America and other Western nations) (see Isaiah 43:5–6).

A. Israel entered into exile as two distinct nations: the Northern Kingdom of Israel and the Southern Kingdom of Judah. But the prophets knew they would come back united as one. Jeremiah, Hosea and Ezekiel all foresaw our day when she would return as one people (see Jeremiah 3:18; Ezekiel 37:20–22; Hosea 1:11).

B. Eighty percent of those who have returned from the nations are secular Jews, often with very little faith and little knowledge of their own God. Some may wonder why Israel has come back in our day, since so many of the Jewish people are no longer committed to their God, but Ezekiel made it clear that Israel's return from exile would not be because she had become righteous, but rather "for the sake of my holy name, which you have profaned among the nations where you have gone" (Ezekiel 36:22 NIV).

C. Jeremiah knew Israel's return would not be a time of peace. "Cries of fear are heard—terror, not peace" (Jeremiah 30:5 NIV) was his description. "Why do I see every strong man with his hands on his stomach like a woman in labor, every face turned deathly pale?" (verse 6).

D. This return from the nations is often described in great detail. Jeremiah spoke of "women in labor" (31:8 NIV) who would be among the returnees, a reference applicable to both Ethiopian and Yemenite Jews who gave birth en route. Isaiah foresaw airplanes and ships bringing back "your children from afar" (see Isaiah 60:8–9).

2. "Jerusalem will be trampled on by the Gentiles until . . ." (Luke 21:24 NIV) were Jesus' words that day on the Mount of Olives. In other words, the Gentiles would dominate the city for a season, but the Jews would be back. That coming back happened in the Six-Day War of 1967, when Israel again took sovereign control of the city of Jerusalem.

3. For the first time since the first century, tens of thousands of Jewish eyes are opening to the Gospel of Yeshua/Jesus, just as predicted. God told Isaiah that Israel's eyes would be closed "until the cities lie ruined and without inhabitant, until the houses are left deserted and the fields ruined" (Isaiah 6:11 NIV). Isaiah's "until" is fulfilled in our day; Jewish eyes are opening to their Messiah.

   A. Congregations or synagogues of Jewish believers have sprung up all over the world, with more than a hundred groups inside Israel alone.

   B. Hosea described a time when Israel would be "many days" without a king and without a sacrifice. "Afterward the Israelites will return and seek the LORD" (Hosea 3:4–5 NIV).

   C. Ezekiel foresaw a time when "you, my people, will know that I am the LORD, when I open your graves and bring you up from them" (Ezekiel 37:13 NIV).

D. The apostle Paul spoke of a "hardening in part until . . ." (Romans 11:25 NIV), indicating that at a future time Israel's eyes would open.

E. And Jesus told the Jewish leaders of His day that they would not see Him again until they were ready to receive Him (see Matthew 23:39).

F. The predicted future time is now!

4. The amazing awakening of faith among nations long held in darkness is yet another sign that we are living in prophecy-fulfilling days. Both Paul and Ezekiel connect this international revival of faith to the return of the Jewish people; and Jesus specifically says that every nation (*ethnos*, ethnic group) of the world must hear the Gospel of the Kingdom before the end (see Matthew 24:14; see also Ezekiel 36:23; Romans 11:12).

As we ponder world evangelization, we would do well to remember the words of the first century's most prominent evangelist. "First to the Jew," Paul reminded the Romans (see Romans 1:16). Though Paul was called to the Gentiles, he always went first to the Jewish synagogues to witness to his own people before turning to the Gentiles in that very city (see Acts 13:5, 14; 14:1; 17:2, 10, 17; 18:4; 19:8). I am convinced that all our worldwide evangelism will prosper if we place the Jewish people in the proper priority in our ministry and witness.

5. The Church from the nations has a growing awareness of her relationship to the Jewish people. For centuries

the Church proclaimed loudly that Jewish people must give up their Jewishness to become Christians. Believers in the nations assumed that the Lord had severed His relationship with the nation of Israel. But in recent years the Church has come to see that we are now "fellow citizens with God's people" (Ephesians 2:19 NIV), that we are "heirs together," "members together," "sharers together" with the Jewish people (see Ephesians 3:6 NIV).

As you look forward to your time in Israel, let me encourage you to rethink the way in which you relate to the Jewish people, and offer some suggestions for expressing your faith while walking among them.

First, remember that the Jewish people are the parents of our faith. When Malachi spoke of the hearts of the fathers being turned to the children, and the children to their fathers (see Malachi 4:6), he was referring to family relationships. But there is another sense in which these words refer to us from the nations as we relate to the parents of our faith, the Jewish people.

Jewish people are turning to acknowledge their own Messiah. Perhaps we have become accustomed to thinking of Jewish "converts" to the faith. Though this is true—in the sense that *convert* means "to turn," and that all of us who have come to Jesus have turned from sin—there is another sense in which Jewish people do not "convert" when they come to faith. They are simply returning to the God of their fathers.

Jewish believers prefer to use the words *congregation* or *synagogue* rather than *church*. The whole Christian world speaks freely of "the Church," but the Greek word for *church* (*ekklesia*) can also easily be translated "congregation." To the Jewish ear, the word *church* evokes scenes of the Crusades, when Jewish people were locked in their synagogues and burned to death; pogroms, when Jewish people were required to reside only in certain areas and were subjected to repeated persecution; the Inquisition, when "Christian" rulers of Spain led the charge to confiscate Jewish wealth and drive the Jews from their country; and the Holocaust, spawned and executed in "Christian" Germany, Austria and Poland. Think, therefore, in terms of "congregations" of Jewish believers, even "synagogues," rather than "churches." It is a matter of terminology, but it shows love and respect for our centuries-long persecuted Jewish family.

Christ is the transliteration of the Greek *Christos*, meaning "Anointed One." In speaking of Jesus, Jewish believers prefer to use the Hebrew equivalent, *Messiah*. Even the name *Christ* brings up memories of persecution and horror to the Jewish mind. *Christ-killers* was a derogatory term spoken over countless Jewish people through the centuries. "Die in the name of Christ!" was often scrawled across the death chambers of Europe during the years of the Nazi reign of terror. Jesus made it clear, however, that it was not only the Jewish leaders who would be responsible for His death, but that the Son of Man also would be "handed over to the Gentiles" who would "mock him, insult him and spit on him . . . flog him and kill him" (Luke 18:32–33 NIV).

Messiah is Jewish and scriptural! In deference to the soul of the Jewish nation, which has suffered much at the hands of "Christians," I choose to refer to Jesus as "Messiah," especially when speaking to my Jewish friends.

Most of the Jewish believers I know do not refer to themselves as Christians. The term *Christian* has little meaning in today's world. It may simply imply that one was born into a family that has been nominally Christian for generations. In other words, there are "Christian atheists" or "Christian skeptics" who have no faith at all in God, in His Word or in His Son. In the New Covenant Scripture, the name *Christian* appears only three times, and each time it was a name that others applied to the believers of the day (see Acts 11:26; 26:28; 1 Peter 4:16).

Christian Zionism—the belief that Israel has a right to be in the land of her inheritance—is a growing phenomenon in our day. Believers from the nations are beginning to bless Israel. But even among Christian Zionists, there is great diversity, with sometimes totally unbiblical teaching.

1. Some would have us believe that the Jewish people do not need their own Messiah—that God has a different plan for them. This would be hard for the apostle Paul to accept. He said, "I could wish that I myself were cursed and cut off from Christ for the sake of my people, those of my own race, the people of Israel" (Romans 9:3–4 NIV).

2. Others believe that the Jewish people will come to faith one day, but that this is not their day. No need to tell them about Yeshua, since all Israel will eventually be saved. These people believe that Jesus did not intend to be the Messiah of Israel the first time He came; that event, they believe, awaits future fulfillment. The apostle Peter, however, would have differed. "God has made this Jesus, whom you crucified, both Lord and Messiah," he told the gathered people from the nations on that first Shavuot (Pentecost) after the resurrection (Acts 2:36 NIV).

3. Christian Zionists have wonderfully sown millions of dollars into the land of Israel, bringing in millions of believers from around the world and establishing great storehouses of humanitarian aid. This is right and good. Paul said that since we have received spiritual blessings from the Jewish people, we "owe it to the Jews to share with them [our] material blessings" (see Romans 15:27). But Paul also adds, speaking to the Galatians, that we should always especially remember "those who belong to the family of believers" (Galatians 6:10 NIV). Not only are we related to Israel and the Jewish people; we are doubly connected to those in the family of faith.

As you interact with Jewish brothers and sisters and actually travel the land, listen to the voice of the Holy Spirit. Speak when He calls you to speak, and be silent when He calls you to be silent. Plant seeds of salvation, water the seeds already sown and, yes, be ready to reap the harvest. Remember that it is the work of the Holy Spirit to draw people to Himself. We are simply His instruments to do His bidding in the process.

Come to Israel! Come humbly!

Come under the blessing. Be a blessing (see Genesis 12:1–3).

Obey the biblical injunction regarding prayer for Israel (see Psalm 122:6; Isaiah 62:7).

Pray for the eyes of the Jewish people to be opened to their Messiah (see Isaiah 6:8–13).

Include also the Arab family in your prayers (see Genesis 17:20; Isaiah 19:19–25).

Do not forget the special connection to "those who are of the household of the faith" (Galatians 6:10).

Walk forth in the mystery revealed—Jew and Gentile together in Messiah Yeshua/Jesus (see Ephesians 3:6).

For more information about Don Finto or to order one of his books, *Your People Shall Be My People* or *God's Promise and the Future of Israel,* visit The Caleb Company website: www.caleb.global/.

Appendix C

Praying for Israel and the Middle East

The material in this section is adapted from an appendix in my book *The Prophetic Intercessor* (Chosen, 2007).

Foundational Scriptures about Israel's future: Jeremiah 31:8–10; Hosea 1:10

Scriptures about aliyah, the return to the land: Isaiah 11:11–12; 43:5–6; Jeremiah 16:14–15; 23:7–8; 30:3

Scriptural response to prophetic words about Israel: Isaiah 12:1; 49:13; 51:3; 52:9; 61:2–7; 66:13; Jeremiah 31:10–14; Romans 11:25–27

Biblical Intercessory Prayers for Israel

From the Life of Moses

- Exodus 32:11–13, 31–32 (Moses' cry to the Lord on behalf of the Israelites, based on God's reputation and covenant, as well as for the sake of His glory)

- Deuteronomy 9:18–19, 25–29 (Moses' fasting for forty days, intervening for Israel in a time of great crisis)
- Deuteronomy 30:1–10 (the proclamation of restoration as taught to the descendants of the Israelites in the desert)
- Numbers 14:13–19 (a plea for God to demonstrate His power, followed by an intense cry for pardon according to God's great lovingkindness)

From the Life of Nehemiah

- Nehemiah 1:4–11 (a compassionate plea before God to forgive His people)

From the Life of Solomon

- 1 Kings 8:46–53 (a simple prayer for God to forgive, now and in the future as He has in the past)

From the Lives of Asaph and the Sons of Korah

- Psalm 44 (verse 26: "Rise up, be our help, and redeem us!")
- Psalm 74 (an appeal to God amid the devastation of the land by the enemy)
- Psalm 79 (a lament over the destruction of Jerusalem and a cry for help)
- Psalm 80 (verses 2–3: "Save us! . . . Restore us!")
- Psalm 83 (a prayer for the Lord to confound His enemies)
- Psalm 85 (a prayer for God's mercy on the nation)
- Psalm 123 (verse 3: "Be gracious to us, LORD")

From the Life of Joel

- Joel 1:8, 13–14 (call to a solemn assembly)
- Joel 2:12–17 (an intercessory cry to "spare Your people, LORD," verse 17)

From the Life of Isaiah

- Isaiah 58:1 ("Cry loudly, do not hold back")
- Isaiah 62:1, 6 ("For Zion's sake I will not keep silent, and for Jerusalem's sake I will not keep quiet. . . . All day and all night [God's watchmen] will never keep silent")
- Isaiah 63:15–64:12 (a desperate prayer for mercy and help)

From the Life of Jeremiah

- Jeremiah 9:1 ("I . . . weep day and night")
- Jeremiah 14:7–9, 17–22 (verse 7: "LORD, act for the sake of Your name! Our apostasies have indeed been many, we have sinned against You")
- Jeremiah 15:5 (a plea in the midst of judgment)
- Lamentations 3:40–51 (verses 49–50: "My eyes flow unceasingly, without stopping, until the LORD looks down and sees from heaven")
- Lamentations 5:19–22 (verse 21: "Restore us to You, LORD, so that we may be restored")

From the Life of Daniel

- Daniel 6:10 (praying three times each day)
- Daniel 9:3–19 (verse 19: "Lord, hear! Lord, forgive! Lord, listen and take action! For Your own sake, my

God, do not delay, because Your city and Your people are called by Your name." Daniel's prayer of confession on behalf of his people is our biblical model to follow today.)

Practical Prayer Suggestions

Perform acts of identificational repentance. Cry out to the Lord with brokenness that our Father would forgive us, the Church, for our apathy and fear and for not speaking up and acting with righteousness in past times of history.

Pray for an awakening. Ask the Lord to awaken the global Church of Jesus Christ in this hour to the immediacy and urgency of this message. Intercede that the Lord would raise up modern-day Esthers, Josephs, Daniels and Deborahs "for such a time as this."

Pray for an extension of time. Petition the Lord for an extension of a time of mercy and freedom so that the Jews from Russia and elsewhere may flee to Israel.

Pray for protection. Pray for places of safety and refuge to be raised up in anticipation of times of persecution of the Jewish people. Intercede that the enemy's plans would be thwarted and that God's destiny for the Jewish people would be fulfilled in this generation.

Pray for a movement of signs and wonders. Petition the Lord to release an increase of His presence with a movement of signs and wonders. Pray that the blinders would fall off the eyes of the Jewish people and that they would recognize and receive Jesus Christ as their sovereign Lord.

Pray for Peace

Use God's favor on you to pray for peace: "Glory to God in the highest heaven, and on earth peace to those on whom his favor rests" (Luke 2:14 NIV).

- The world is full of tribulation but in Him nations can experience peace: "I have told you these things, so that in me you may have peace. In this world you will have trouble. But take heart! I have overcome the world" (John 16:33 NIV).
- God is peace: "Gideon built an altar to the LORD there and called it The LORD Is Peace" (Judges 6:24 NIV).
- God can heal every relationship—personal and far away, "'creating praise on their lips. Peace, peace, to those far and near,' says the LORD. 'And I will heal them'" (Isaiah 57:19 NIV).
- Israel is a small country amid known and unknown enemies. "But I will restore you to health and heal your wounds . . . because you are called an outcast, Zion for whom no one cares" (Jeremiah 30:17 NIV).
- If persecution is because of righteousness, God blesses people and places: "Blessed are those who are persecuted because of righteousness, for theirs is the kingdom of heaven" (Matthew 5:10 NIV).
- Peace in hearts and nations must begin with love: "I tell you, love your enemies and pray for those who persecute you" (Matthew 5:44 NIV).

- Blessings and peace are rewards of praying for those who are deceived: "Bless those who persecute you; bless and do not curse" (Romans 12:14 NIV).
- God will judge the nations for their treatment of God's people: "I will gather all nations and bring them down to the Valley of Jehoshaphat. There I will put them on trial for what they did to my inheritance, my people Israel, because they scattered my people among the nations and divided up my land" (Joel 3:2 NIV).

Reasons to Pray for the Middle East[1]

- Daniel prayed for the nations. He understood how prophecy affects politics, and vice versa. He studied Scripture to understand how to pray. He meditated and sought prophetic understanding of how prophecy applied to his generation. He compared the biblical promise and timing with the date and conditions in which he lived (see Daniel 9:1–3).
- Daniel took the Scriptures as a mandate to pray for the prophecies to be fulfilled with the expectation that his prayers were part of causing those prophecies to come to pass. The destiny of all the nations is connected spiritually with the restoration of Israel. An understanding of the prophetic significance of events in the Middle East, therefore, should influence the prayers of the saints wherever they live in the world (see Daniel 9:2–3).
- Daniel prayed with humility and repentance—not primarily about his own sins, but about the sins of his people. He repents on their behalf as he makes

intercession for them (see Isaiah 53) and stands in the gap for them (see Ezekiel 22; Daniel 9:4–6).

- Our prayers can affect the world because God commissions mighty angels to respond to our prayers. The connection between our prayers and the work of angels not only changes history, but gives us prophetic revelation and insight into the plans and purposes of God (see Daniel 9:20–23).

Notes

Chapter 1: The Birth of a Nation

1. Lance Lambert, *The Uniqueness of Israel* (Eastbourne, England: Kingsway, 1991), 55.

2. Ibid.

3. Merrill C. Tenney, *New Testament Survey* (Grand Rapids: Eerdmans, 1961), 45. In addition, Lambert, 160, mentions the emperor Hadrian's attempt to rename Jerusalem and remove every trace of Jewish history from it.

4. James Goll, "Say to the North," *Engage* newsletter, 2002.

5. Kai Kjæ-Hansen, *Joseph Rabinowitz and the Messianic Movement: The Herzl of Jewish Christianity* (Grand Rapids: Eerdmans, 1994; and The Stables, Carberry, Scotland: Handsel Press, 1995), 17–19.

6. Ibid., 19. My narrative of Joseph Rabinowitz's supernatural revelation on the Mount of Olives has been reconstructed from several sources, including transcripts of actual messages and the report of a student attending a meeting in Leipzig, Germany, on February 13, 1887, where Rabinowitz gave his testimony. According to author Kai Kjæ-Hansen, the details contained in this student's report "are probably the closest we can get to a description of Rabinowitz's conversion."

7. Ibid., 22.

8. Ibid., 33.

9. Ibid.

10. Ibid.

11. Lambert, *Uniqueness*, 129–30. Quoting Theodor Herzl, *The Jewish State*, trans. S. D'Avigdor (Leipzig: Verlags-Buchhandlung, 1917), 15.

12. Ibid., 79.

13. Ibid., 130, emphasis mine.

14. Herzl, diary entry for September 3, 1897; quoted in Tom Hess, *Let My People Go! The Struggle of the Jewish People to Return to Israel* (Washington, D.C.: Progressive Vision, 1988), 116.

15. Ramon Bennett, *Saga: Israel and the Demise of Nations* (Jerusalem: Arm of Salvation Press, 1993), 149–50. The specific application of acetone in the manufacture of cordite is briefly described in *Merriam Webster's Dictionary*, 10th Ed., s.v. "cordite."

16. Ibid., 150.

17. Hess, 57.

18. Quoted in Bennett, 150.

19. Ramon Bennett, *When Day and Night Cease* (Jerusalem: Arm of Salvation Press, 1992), 92.

20. Quoted in James W. Goll, *The Prophetic Intercessor: Releasing God's Purposes to Change Lives and Influence Nations* (Grand Rapids: Chosen, 2007), 131.

21. Steve Lightle, *Operation Exodus II* (Tulsa, Okla.: Insight Publishing, 1999), 154; and *Holocaust Encyclopedia*, U.S. Holocaust Memorial Museum, s.v. "Nazi Camps," https://encyclopedia.ushmm.org/content/en/article/nazi-camps.

22. Ibid.

23. Ibid., 158.

24. Ulf Ekman, *The Jews: People of the Future* (Minneapolis: Word of Life Publications, 1993), 70.

25. Gordon Lindsay, *The Miracle of Israel* (Dallas: Christ For The Nations, Inc., 1987), 46.

26. Ibid.

27. Ibid., 47.

28. Ibid., 51.

Chapter 2: When the Walls Came Tumbling Down

1. The Commonwealth of Independent States (CIS) was formed in December 1991, after a tripartite agreement among Russia, Ukraine and Belarus created the nucleus of the new political center of the former U.S.S.R. It marked the end of Mikhail Gorbachev's political career as general secretary of the fallen Communist Party and the temporary rise of Boris Yeltsin.

2. *Microsoft Encarta Online Encyclopedia 2000*, s.v. "Berlin Wall."

3. Lightle, 20–21, 27–29; and Gustav Scheller with Jonathan Miles, *Operation Exodus: Prophecy Being Fulfilled* (Tonbridge, England: Sovereign World, 1998; distributed in U.S. by Renew Books), 29–30.

4. Lightle, 45–47.

5. Ibid.

6. Scheller, 7.

7. Lightle, 55–59.

8. Hess, 34–36.
9. Ibid., 36.
10. Ibid., 36–37.
11. Lightle, 105.
12. Ibid., 106–107.
13. "East German Border Claimed 327 Lives, Says Berlin Study," BBC News, June 8, 2017, https://www.bbc.com/news/world-europe-40200305.
14. "Total Immigration to Israel from the Former Soviet Union," Jewish Virtual Library, https://www.jewishvirtuallibrary.org/total-immigration-to -israel-from-former-soviet-union, accessed March 3, 2021.

Chapter 3: The Winds of Awakening

1. Ed Silvoso, Ekklesia (Minneapolis: Chosen, 2017), 24.
2. Interestingly some have proclaimed a "New Jesus People Movement" in the U.S. as thousands have gathered in numerous cities from the West Coast to the East Coast during the pandemic of 2020 to worship and share the Gospel. See Andrea Morris, "Thousands Rejoice, Worship Together 'to See the Love of God' During West Coast 'Revival in America,'" CBNNews .com, September 6, 2020; https://www1.cbn.com/cbnnews/us/2020/september /thousands-rejoice-worship-together-to-see-the-love-of-god-during-west -coast-revival-in-america.
3. Jewish Voice Ministries International, https://www.jewishvoice.org /learn/messianic-jews.

Chapter 4: Appointed a Watchman

1. Johannes Facius, *Hastening the Coming of the Messiah* (Kent, England: Sovereign World Ltd., 2001), 14.

Chapter 5: Praying for the Fulfillment of Aliyah

1. Dr. Richard F. Gottier, *Aliyah, God's Last Great Act of Redemption* (Kent, England: Sovereign World Ltd., 2002), 10.
2. Malcom Hedding, *Understanding Israel* (Oklahoma City, Okla.: Zion's Gate International, 2002), 145.
3. William W. Orr, quoted in Hedding, 19.
4. James W. Goll, *Kneeling on the Promises* (Minneapolis: Chosen, 1999). The contents of this chapter were shaped by the same truths that I searched out while writing this earlier book.
5. Bennett, *When Day and Night Cease*, 122–23.
6. Derek Prince, *Promised Land, God's Word and the Nation of Israel* (Charlotte, N.C.: Derek Prince Ministries, 2003), 75–76.
7. Please see: https://www.jewishvirtuallibrary.org/russia-virtual-jewish -history-tour.

Chapter 6: The Mordecai Calling

1. Paul Yonggi Cho, *Daniel: Insight on the Life and Dreams of the Prophet from Babylon* (Lake Mary, Fla.: Creation House, 1990), 144. Paul Yonggi Cho later changed his name to David Yonggi Cho.

2. James Strong, *Strong's Exhaustive Concordance of the Bible* (Nashville: Abingdon, 1980), s.v. *pergamum*, 4010, 4444, 4456, 4463.

3. *Encyclopaedia Britannica*, s.v. "Humann, Karl," accessed February 12, 2021, https://www.britannica.com/biography/Karl-Humann.

4. Don Finto, November 27, 2020, personal email. See also Gordon Robertson, "The Seat of Satan: Nazi Germany," *CBN*, 2021, https://www1.cbn.com/700club/seat-satan-nazi-germany and "The Nazis and the Altar of Satan," *CFI-USA*, December 28, 2019, https://cfi-usa.org/pergamon-to-berlin/.

5. Paul Goble, "Russia: Analysis from Washington: Rise of Anti-Semitism in Russia," *Radio Free Europe / Radio Liberty*, July 28, 1999, https://www.rferl.org/a/1091831.html.

6. David Rising, "Survey: About 1 in 4 Europeans Hold Anti-Semitic Beliefs," *AP News*, November 21, 2019, https://apnews.com/article/f18c9fa70b794974b214b6e9f1552cfd.

7. "The State of Antisemitism in America 2020," AJC (Global Jewish Advocacy), October 26, 2020, https://www.ajc.org/AntisemitismReport2020.

8. CNN staff, "Antisemitic incidents in the US reached the highest on record in 2019, ADL says," *CNN.com*, accessed September 8, 2020, https://www.cnn.com/2020/05/12/us/antisemitic-incidents-highest-2019/index.html.

9. Michal Ann Goll recorded the dream in her diary and told me the details.

10. If you are serious about effectual fervent prayer, I encourage you to pick up copies of the following books: Norman Grubb, *Rees Howells: Intercessor* (Fort Washington, Penn.: Christian Literature Crusade, 1952); and Doris M. Ruscoe, *The Intercession of Rees Howells* (Fort Washington, Penn.: Christian Literature Crusade, 1988).

11. Scheller, 150–51.

Chapter 7: The Descendants of Hagar

1. Sandra Teplinsky, *Why Care About Israel?* (Minneapolis: Chosen, 2004), 161.

2. Chris Mitchell, "Egypt's El Sisi Builds Middle East's Largest Church, A 'Game Changer' in the Region," *CBNNews.com*, January 7, 2019; https://www1.cbn.com/cbnnews/israel/2019/january/egypts-el-sisi-builds-middle-easts-largest-church-a-game-changer-in-the-region.

3. Avner Boskey, *A Perspective on Islam* (Nashville: Final Frontier Ministries, 2001), 16.

Chapter 8: The Descendants of Sarah

1. Sandra Teplinsky, 84–85.
2. Ibid., 85.
3. Derek Prince, 17–18.
4. Asher Intrater, quoted in Ari and Shira Sorko-Ram, *Praying for Israel: How?* (Tel Aviv, Israel: Maoz Israel Report, 2004), 2. For more on this article and subject, please see: http://www.revive-israel.org.
5. For more on the subject of the modern-day Messianic movement, I commend to you an outstanding book: Don Finto, *Your People Shall Be My People* (Minneapolis: Chosen, 2016).
6. Lincoln Brunner, "Messianic Judaism Flourishes in Holocaust Towns," *Christianity Today Online,* April 23, 2015, https://www.christianitytoday .com/ct/2015/april/messianic-judaism-flourishes-in-holocaust-towns-ukraine .html; and *Jews for Judaism,* https://jewsforjudaism.org/news/messianic -judaism-flourishes-in-holocaust-towns.

Chapter 9: The Descendants of Keturah

1. Robert Somerville, *The Three Families of Abraham* (Huntsville, Ala.: Awareness Ministry, 2002). Though I have not quoted directly from this book, this short manuscript was placed in my hands at just the right moment and its contents supported the direction of this chapter.
2. Sandra Teplinsky, 237.

Chapter 10: Jerusalem: A City of Destiny

1. Peggy Cidor, "Jerusalem 2019: Facts and figures," *The Jerusalem Post,* June 6, 2019, https://www.jpost.com/Israel-News/Jerusalem-2019-Facts-and -figures-591764.
2. Ibid.
3. Benjamin Elisha Sawe, "What Is the Ethnic Composition of Israel?," *WorldAtlas,* July 17, 2019, https://www.worldatlas.com/articles/what-is-the -ethnic-composition-of-israel.html.
4. Ibid.
5. Michael D. Evans, *The American Prophecies* (New York: Time Warner Books, 2004), 85–86.
6. Ibid., 86.
7. Ibid.
8. Steve Clemons, "Mitt Romney, George Marshall, and Israel-Palestine," *The Atlantic,* October 8, 2012, https://www.theatlantic.com/international /archive/2012/10/mitt-romney-george-marshall-and-israel-palestine/263 365/.
9. "Truman Advisor Clark Clifford Opposes State Department on Partition," *Center for Israel Education,* 2021, https://israeled.org/clark-clifford/.

10. Gary Willig, "US embassy opens in Israel's capital," *Arutz Sheva,* IsraelNationalNews.com, May 14, 2018; https://www.israelnationalnews.com/News/News.aspx/245941.

11. Ruth Ward Heflin, *Jerusalem, Zion, Israel and the Nations* (Hagerstown, Md.: McDougal Publishing, 1999), 4–16. I used her book as a reference for this chapter, although I took no direct quotations.

12. Ibid., 19–30; 47–48; 53–57.

13. Facius, *Hastening the Coming of the Messiah*, 84.

14. Ibid., 85.

15. Robert Stearns, "Prayer for the Peace of Jerusalem," *Kairos Magazine,* 2003, 8–9.

16. Robert Stearns, Jack Hayford and Paul Cedar, "The Day of Prayer for the Peace of Jerusalem," http://www.daytopray.com/Resources/FREE_DPPJ_Equipping_Packet_Download.

Chapter 11: God's Road Map

1. Portions of this section were drawn from the teaching ministry of Tom Hess. See *Appointed a Watchman for Israel*, untitled teaching material by Tom Hess (Jerusalem: Jerusalem House of Prayer for All Nations, 2003), 1–2.

Chapter 12: The Great Hope

1. Keith Intrater and Dan Juster, *Israel, the Church and the Last Days* (Destiny Image, 2005), 117.

2. Ibid.

3. BGEA, "The Faces of Prayer March 2020," https://billygraham.org/gallery/the-faces-of-prayer-march-2020.

4. Myra Kahn Adams, "Messianic Rabbi Shares Reaction to Huge Turnout for 'The Return'"; October 10, 2020; *Townhall.com;* https://townhall.com/columnists/myrakahnadams/2020/10/10/jonathan-cahn-interview-we-are-overwhelmed-by-what-the-lord-did-at-the-return-n2577734; accessed November 10, 2020.

5. Please see: https://www.ihopkc.org/prophetichistory/.

6. Please see: https://memorial.billygraham.org/official-obituary/.

7. Kate Shellnut, "Died: Reinhard Bonnke, Record-Setting Evangelist to Africa," *Christianity Today*, December 7, 2019, https://www.christianitytoday.com/news/2019/december/reinhard-bonnke-died-evangelist-christ-for-all-nations-afri.html.

8. Please see: https://new.cfan.org/daniel-kolenda.

9. Brandon Showalter, "Worship leader: US on 'cusp of revival,' time to change narrative of burning cities with worship," *The Christian Post*, August 2, 2020, https://www.christianpost.com/news/worship-leader-us-on-cusp-of-revival-time-to-change-narrative-of-burning-cities-with-worship.html.

10. https://www.seanfeucht.com/about

11. Please see: https://www.burn24-7.com/about.

12. If you would like to learn more about prayer, I have written a book and a whole course titled *Praying with God's Heart*. The online class is "The Power and the Purpose of Prophetic Intercession"; I developed this one point in another whole series.

Appendix C: Praying for Israel and the Middle East

1. I am grateful to Asher Intrater for his article "Strategic Prayers for the Middle East," *Revive Israel*, August 13, 2020, from which some of these reasons to pray have been adapted. https://tribe.reviveisrael.org/strategic-prayers-for-the-middle-east/.

Glossary

I trust this simple glossary of terms will help clarify the meaning of a few terms I have used throughout this book. This is by no means a thorough and comprehensive professional dictionary. Rather, I have simply defined a few terms in my own words. I hope this will be of help to you, thus making the book a bit more reader- and user-friendly.

Aliyah: The Hebrew word for the return of the Jews to their homeland in Israel. It means literally "going up."

Anti-Semitism: Intense dislike, hostility, hatred or discrimination against Jewish people, religious practices, culture or ethnicity.

Ashkenazi-Ashkenazim: A name that in its more popular use describes those Jewish people originating in northwest Europe, particularly Germany, central Europe, eastern Europe and Russia. It has become a designation of culture and way of life for Jewish people from those areas, as contrasted with the Sephardic culture.

Day of Atonement: The most holy day for the Jews, an annual day of fasting, penitence and sacrifice for sin. Before the destruction of the Temple, the high priest would enter the Holy of Holies on the tenth day of the seventh month of the Hebrew calendar and offer sacrifices for the sanctuary, the priests and the people. This foreshadowed the entrance of Jesus, the great High Priest, who offered Himself as the eternal sacrifice once for all, having purchased for us eternal salvation. This day, also known as Yom Kippur, is observed today with fasting and confession of sins.

Diaspora: A dispersion of the Jews from their homeland, such as the Jewish people being sent into Egypt in the time of Moses.

Eretz Israel: This Hebrew term means "the land of Israel."

Fasting: To abstain from food as a sacrifice to God for spiritual release of power and intervention. Also an act of humbling one's soul before God.

Fishers and Hunters: This phrase, based on Jeremiah 16:16, refers first to "fishermen," benevolent messengers sent to the Jewish people to encourage, woo and entice them to obey God's call to flee danger in foreign lands and return to Israel; and then to "hunters" operating under the influence of the spirit of Haman or some other satanic force, to hunt down and round up every Jewish person they can find with one ultimate goal: absolute annihilation of the Jewish people.

Gemara: A rabbinical commentary on the Mishnah and the second part of the Talmud. *Gemara* means "completion" or "tradition." There are two Gemaras, one compiled in Tiberias in the fourth century and the other compiled in

Babylon around AD 500. The Mishnah with the Tiberias Gemara is popularly called "the Jerusalem Talmud," and the Mishnah with the Babylonian Gemara is called "the Babylonian Talmud."

Gentile: This Hebrew word literally means "a nation," but it is used to describe any person who is neither of Jewish origin nor an adherent of Judaism. (See "Righteous Gentile.")

Harp and Bowl: This is a term taken from Revelation 5 and 8, describing worship and intercession. The harp symbolically represents worship, and the bowl filled with incense is a description of the prayers of believers. Therefore, the phrase *harp and bowl* is often used to describe the combined activities of worship and intercession.

Hasid–Hasidism (also **Chassid–Chassidism**): A popular religious movement within Judaism that began in the latter part of the eighteenth century. At first it was bitterly contested by Orthodox Judaism, but it was finally accepted and recognized. It is characterized by religious ecstasy, mass enthusiasm, a close-knit and cohesive community life and charismatic personalities in leadership.

Holocaust: It is the name given to the most tragic period of the second Jewish exile. Spanning twelve years from 1933–1945, it was the Nazi-inspired "final solution" to the so-called Jewish problem, and it called for the systematic destruction of the Jewish people. It is estimated that at least six million Jews died in this tragic period.

Identificational Repentance: This is a form of intercession in which one confesses the generational sins of the family, ethnic group, city and/or nation of one's background. The intercessor discerns the generational iniquity of his or her family and/or people group and then repents before God for this sin or injustice. For more on this subject, read my book *Intercession: The Power and the Passion to Shape History.*

Intercession: The act of making a request to a superior, or expressing a deep-seated yearning to our one and only superior, God.

Intercessor: One who reminds God of His promises and appointments yet to be fulfilled; who takes up a case of injustice before God on behalf of another; who makes up the "hedge" (that is, builds up the wall in time of battle); and who stands in the gap between God's righteous judgments and the people's need for mercy.

Kairos: A Greek word in the New Testament for the word "time." *Kairos* refers to when time and promise meet, creating a strategic time when God's plans, purposes and destiny unfold in that specific moment. *Chronos* is another Greek word describing the chronology of ordered events.

Land of the North: This Old Testament term is used to describe those regions located geographically directly north of Jerusalem. This term especially is used to describe the region of the former Soviet Union.

Mishnah: The "oral Torah," the collection of oral laws or traditions of the elders (as opposed to the written law of God), chiefly compiled and edited by Rabbi Judah ha-Nasi (AD 230). Its object: to preserve the law of God and apply it to everyday life. In Jewish eyes it has ranked second only to the Hebrew Bible (what Christians call the Old Testament). The word *mishnah* comes from a root meaning "to repeat" and thus "to teach by repetition."

Neo-Nazi: This term describes new Nazis—those today who agree with or follow the programs and principles of Hitler's Nazi party, particularly his extreme anti-Semitism.

Olim: Those "going up" to Israel from other lands.

Pogrom: This Russian word meaning "destroy" or "devastate" describes the organized or officially encouraged slaughter of Jewish people through militia-led riots in Russia, the Ukraine, Poland, Romania and parts of eastern Europe (particularly during the time of the Russian tsars).

Priest: One who pleads the needs of the people before God. In the Old Testament the tribe of Levi was set apart for this purpose. In the New Testament each believer in Christ is a priest unto the Lord.

Prophet/Prophetess: A man or woman who represents the interests of God to the people. Having stood in the council of God, the prophet releases a clarion call to the people of what is in God's heart at the moment. Some refer to this as one of the fivefold ministry gifts listed in Ephesians 4:11.

Prophetic Intercession: The act of waiting before God in order to hear or receive His burden—His word, concern, warning, condition, vision or promise—and responding back to Him and the people with appropriate actions.

Replacement Theology: The theological teaching that God is finished with the Jewish people and that the Church has replaced Israel in the plan and purpose of God. According to this view, God's promised blessings to Israel in the Hebrew Scriptures are now the exclusive property of the Church because God has cursed and rejected Israel. The Church is seen as the new or true Israel because of the role the Jewish people played in rejecting and crucifying

Jesus the Messiah. It is clear, however, that Jew and Gentile worked together to crucify the Savior of the world and that He died to bring forgiveness and new life to both Jew and Gentile through His own death and resurrection.

Righteous Gentile: A term used by the government of Israel to officially honor those non-Jews who risked their lives, freedom, safety, reputation and livelihood to save, protect, shield or assist Jewish people from their pursuers during World War II and at other times.

Sephardic/Sephardim: *Sepharad* means "Spain" in Hebrew. Thus the term refers to the Jewish people of Spanish and/ or Portuguese origin or descent. Many Sephardic Jews live in Central and South America today.

Supplication: To entreat, seek, implore or beseech God in earnest prayer.

Talmud: This Hebrew word means "study" or "learning." It is used most commonly to describe that body of teaching comprising the commentary and discussions of scholars. Composed between AD 200 and AD 400, it consists of the Mishnah and the Gemara. The influence of the Talmud on Jewish life, thought and conduct is inestimable.

Travail: Prayer that brings forth a birthing in the spirit, which creates or enlarges an opening for an increased dimension of the Kingdom of God.

Visitation: A supernatural experience in which a distinct sense of the presence of God is accompanied by fear of the Lord. This may come in the form of an angelic visitation, as in the book of Acts, or by other biblical means.

Watch of the Lord: A gathering in Jesus' name (see Matthew 24; Mark 13; Luke 21) to watch, pray and be vigilant for the life of a church, city or nation. It is also a position on the wall of the Lord to see outside the city, in order to alert the gate-keepers of approaching enemies or envoys from the King; and to see inside the city, in order to recognize and confront disorderly, unlawful activity of the enemy.

Watchmen: Those who serve in the position of watching during a watch of the Lord.

Yeshua: This is the Hebrew name of Jesus Christ the Messiah—the One who saves.

Zion: A term used in the Hebrew Bible for Jerusalem. See, for example, 2 Samuel 5:7.

Zionism: The movement birthed by Theodor Herzl in the late 1800s in Switzerland purporting that the true destiny of the Jewish people could be found only in Zion, their ancient covenant home in Palestine. These "Zionists" or "lovers of Zion" urged the Jewish people, decades before Hitler's storm troopers began to herd millions of European Jews to their destruction, to flee Europe and return to their ancient homeland in the Middle East.

Index

Abbas, 259
Abdullah II, 264
Abraham, 132, 135–38, 142–43,
   150–58, 162, 167, 171, 174–78,
   193, 204–6, 269
Africa, 99, 177, 207, 234
Ahmadinejad, Mahmoud, 259–60
AJC (Global Jewish Advocacy), 114
Al-Aqsa Intifada, 256, 257
Alexander II, 19
aliyah, 15–16, 20, 92, 104–5, 126,
   182, 256, 295
Albright, Madeleine, 255
Allenby, Edmund, 25–26
Amir, Yigal, 253
angels, 50, 57, 58–59, 137, 285
Anna, 83–84
antichrist, 112, 125
Anti-Defamation League, 114
anti-Semitism, 17, 19–20, 27, 52,
   107, 112–14, 119, 120, 295
Arab Christians, 183
Arab-Israeli War (1948), 34

Arabs, 137, 139, 142, 143, 144, 146,
   147, 169, 183, 207
Arafat, Yasser, 203, 243, 248, 252,
   253, 254, 256, 258
Arameans, 183
Argov, Shlomo, 247
Artaxerxes, 107
Aryan supremacy, 27
Asaph, 280
Ashkenazi Jews, 183, 295
Asians, 207
assembly, 61
Assyria, 140, 167, 168–69, 170, 269
atheism, 27, 38, 188
Auschwitz, 31, 184
Austria, 29, 113
authority, 119, 123–25, 127, 225
awakening, 55–70, 220, 282
Ayyad, Rami, 261
Ayyash, Yahya, 253

Babylon, 96–97, 98, 109, 110, 146,
   157, 229–30, 321

303

Baker, Sharon, 122
Baker, Trevor, 122
Balfour, James, 25
Baltimore, 56
Barak, Ehud, 255, 256
Barkat, Nir, 264
Bar Kokhba, 17
barrenness, 132–33, 134, 152–53, 212
Basel, 23–24
Begin, Menachem, 246, 247
Begun, Yosef, 249
Bene Israel, 183
Ben-Gurion, David, 34, 187, 265
Bennett, Ramon, 26, 98–99
Bergen-Belsen, 31
Berlin, 108–12
Berlin Wall, 37–40, 53, 127
Bernis, Jonathan, 101
Beta Israel, 183
Bethel, 203–4, 206, 214
Bible, 80
Bickle, Mike, 234
Bilhal, 154
bin Laden, Osama, 257
birthing, 18, 27, 51, 153
blessing, 68, 171, 191
blitzkrieg, 30
Bonhoeffer, Dietrich, 127
Bonnke, Reinhard, 234–35
Boskey, Avner, 75, 146, 182, 266
Boskey, Rachel, 75
Bosnia and Herzegovina, 145
"Boycott, Divestment and Sanc-
   tions" (BDS), 81
Brazil, 193
Brezhnev Doctrine, 51
"Burn 24-7" outreach, 235
Bush, George W., 257, 258, 261

Cahn, Jonathan, 234
Cain, Paul, 37–38
Caleb, 205
Caleb Global, 111
calling, 86
Camp David, 256
Canada, 193
car bomb, 252
Carter, Jimmy, 246, 247
Cathedral of the Archangel, 46
charismatic renewal, 10
China, 99, 251
Cho, Paul Yonggi, 108, 110
Christ For The Nations, 32
Christianity Today, 160
Christian Zionism, 275–76
church, 61, 79, 162, 272–73
Churchill, Winston, 25
Church On The Way, 195
church restrictions, 235
circumcision, 134, 135–36
clay pots, 74
Clifford, Clark, 186
Clinton, Bill, 256
Cochin Jews, 183
cold war, 192
commissioning, 86, 140
Commonwealth of Independent
   States (CIS), 38, 288
Communism, 27, 38, 45, 46, 47, 48,
   52, 110, 188
compassion, 77–78
complacency, 221
conflict, 112, 192, 238
congregation, 273–74
consummation, 237
covenant, 134–35, 138–39, 140,
   157–58, 162, 196, 202

creation, 232
crisis intercession, 84, 118, 121, 124, 128
Crusades, 184, 274
curse, 191
Czech Republic, 108

Dachau, 31, 185
Daniel, 110–11, 146, 229–30, 281–82, 284
darkness, 171–73
David, 80–81, 84
Day of Atonement, 296
death, spirit of, 45
delay, 166, 229
deliverance, 126
demonic, 120, 127, 206, 237
descendants, 140
destiny, 190–91, 192, 269
Diaspora, 95, 296
divine urgency, 221
division, 228
double portion, 68
dreams, 114–17
Druze, 183
"dry bones" prophecy, 225–26
Dunkirk, 121–22

Eagles' Wings, 195
East Germany, 37, 39, 40, 51
Egypt, 34, 137, 144–45, 168–69, 170, 171, 172, 193, 241, 242, 269
ekklesia, 61, 273–74
Ekman, Ulf, 30
Elijah, 200
El Shaddai, 149, 161
el-Sisi, Abdel Fattah, 145, 264
Ephah, 168, 175

Ephraim, 184
Erdoğan, Recep Tayyip, 264
Eretz Israel, 296
Esau, 154, 155, 204
Esther, 84–87, 107, 117–18, 120, 126, 128, 214
ethnicity, 76
Europe, 104, 113–14
evangelism, 63, 159, 221, 232, 272
Evans, Michael D., 185
Évian, 29–30, 31, 49–50
exile, 17, 201, 268, 270
exodus, 126
Ezekiel, 96, 270, 271, 272

Facius, Johannes, 41, 43, 83
false teachings, 76
familiarity, 150
family friction, 144
fasting, 84–87, 118, 120–21, 237
Fatah, Al, 243
Feast of Tabernacles, 224, 228
Festivals of Jewish Music and Dance, 101
Feucht, Sean, 235
Final Frontier Ministries, 75, 146, 182
"final solution," 30
Finto, Don, 111–12, 277
First Crusade, 184
first regathering, 95–97
First Zionist Congress, 23
fishermen, 20, 23, 24, 27–28, 31, 103, 127, 296
forgiveness, 228
free will, 229
Friedman, David, 187–88
fulfillment, 86, 275

gatekeepers, 119
Gaza, 172, 259, 260
Gemara, 296–97
General Assembly of the United
  Nations, 24
generational sins, 50
genocide, 108
Gentiles, 60, 68–69, 162, 210–11,
  227, 271, 272, 297, 300
gentle awakening, 63–65, 86, 127
Germany, 27–31, 37, 172, 193
Glickstein, Richard, 113
God
  faithfulness of, 69, 87
  glory of, 237
  Israel as pupil of, 75–76, 100, 110
  as multitasker, 170
  nature of, 93
  presence of, 86, 194, 221
  promises of, 158
  sovereignty of, 229
  supernatural intervention of, 35
Goetz, Marty, 182
Golan Heights, 246, 262, 265
Goldstein, Baruch, 252
Goll, James, 9–10, 313–14
Goll, Michal Ann, 10, 50–51, 74,
  114–17, 132, 153, 167, 182, 185
Gorbachev, Mikhail, 38, 41, 43, 44,
  46, 48, 51, 288
Gordon, S. D., 81
Graebes, Fritz, 127
Graham, Billy, 234
Graham, Franklin, 233
Great Awakening, 62, 64, 66–67,
  68, 86, 125, 221
Greece, 231
Greenblatt, Jonathan A., 114

Gromyko, Andrei, 32
Grubb, Norman, 121–22

Hadrian, 17–18
Haganah, 31–32, 33
Hagar, 131–47, 151, 168, 174, 176,
  178
Haider, Jörg, 113
Haman spirit, 107, 117, 119, 125
Hamas, 257, 259, 260, 263
harp and bowl, 297
Hasidism, 297
Haskala Jews, 21
Hassan II, 249
Hayford, Jack, 195
healing, 192, 227–28
heart, 77–78, 159
Hebron, 204–5, 206, 214
Hedding, Malcolm, 94–95
Herzl, Theodore, 22–24, 27
Hess, Tom, 45–47
Hezbollah, 255, 257, 260, 266
Hispanics, 207
history, 184–86, 189
Hitler, Adolf, 27–31, 49, 92, 111–
  12, 113, 121
Holocaust, 18, 30–31, 32, 92, 114,
  115, 185, 260, 274, 297
Holy Spirit
  vs. chaos, 170
  drawing of, 276
  outpouring of, 221
holy war, 171
Hosea, 94–95, 271
Howells, Rees, 121–22, 128
Howells, Samuel, 122–24
Humann, Karl, 110
human rights failures, 186

humility, 284
Hungary, 113

identification, 124–25
identificational repentance, 50–51,
    282, 297–98
immigration, 26, 29, 31, 32, 46, 52,
    81, 299
India, 251
inheritance, 212, 267, 275
Inquisition, 274
Instrater, Asher, 224–25
intercession, 124–25, 128, 230, 232,
    233–34, 298
Intercessors for Denmark, 83
International Atomic Energy
    Agency, 259
International Christian Embassy
    Jerusalem, 40
International Day of Prayer for Per-
    secuted Christians, 234
International Day of Prayer for the
    Peace of Jerusalem (IDPPJ),
    195–96
International House of Prayer, 234
Intifada, 249–50
Intrater, Asher, 111–12, 158
Iran, 146, 169, 171, 177, 259, 263
Iraq, 34, 169, 171, 172, 177, 250,
    251, 269
Irgun, 31–32
Iron Curtain, 40, 43, 51–52, 53
Isaac, 10, 135, 136, 152, 153, 159,
    161, 167, 206
Isaiah, 97–98, 168, 169, 271, 281
Ishmael, 10, 132, 134–37, 140–44,
    147, 151, 155, 167, 269
Ishtar Gate of Babylon, 108, 110

Islam, 143, 158, 170, 184, 202, 214
Israel
    prayer for, 76–84
    priority of, 60–61
    as pupil of God's eye, 75–76, 100
    rejection of, 199
    salvation of, 79–80
    State of, 201, 241–66
Israel Awakening, 57, 58–59, 70
Israeli, 157
Israelites of the New Covenant, 22
Israel Prayer Watch, 80, 132, 177

Jacob, 135, 154, 157, 161, 203, 204
Jeremiah, 93–94, 96, 270, 281
Jericho, 38–39
Jerusalem
    destiny of, 181–97
    establishing of, 78–79, 268
    fulfillment of, 34–35
    peace of, 80–81
    restoration of, 205–7, 214
Jerusalem Embassy Act of 1995, 187
Jerusalem Institute for Policy Re-
    search, 182
Jesus Christ
    crucifixion of, 205–6
    as Lamb of God, 223
    as Messiah, 176–77, 274
    as Prince of Peace, 193
    second coming of, 83–84, 218–22,
        228–32, 235–38
Jesus People Movement, 10, 62, 70,
    91, 235, 289
Jewishness, 157
Jewish people
    persecution of, 19
    restoration of, 15
    returning of, 102

Jewish Voice Ministries International, 62
jihad, 33
Jihad, Abu, 250
Joel, 173–74, 233, 236, 281
John Paul II (Pope), 247, 255
John the Baptist, 222
Jones, Bob, 38
Jordan, 172, 242
Joseph, 203
Joshua, 205
Judah, 227
judgment, 94, 237
Juster, Dan, 224–25

kairos, 208, 298
Karaite Jews, 183
Kedar, 140–41
Kellough, Sue, 122, 123–24
Keturah, 10, 162, 165–78
KGB, 42, 43–44, 46, 48, 52
kindness, 68
King's University, 195
Kishinev, 19, 20
Kjæ-Hansen, Kai, 287n6
Knesset (Israeli Parliament), 242, 243
Kohl, Helmut, 51
Kolenda, Daniel, 235
Kremlin, 46–47
Kristallnacht, 30
Kuwait, 250

Laban, 154
Lambert, Lance, 17
Land of the North, 18, 22, 35, 38, 100–101, 298
land possession, 158–60

Latin America, 104
laughter, 151–52
Law of Return, 242
League of Nations, 29
Leah, 154
Lebanon, 171, 172, 241, 246
Leningrad, 46, 47, 188
Lenin, Vladimir, 27, 38, 42, 45, 47, 48
light, 173
Lightle, Steve, 29, 41, 43–44, 47–48
Lindsay, Gordon, 32–33, 34
Long, Breckenridge, 185
Lot, 204–5
love, 67–68, 146, 225

Maccabees, 85
Madrid International Middle East Peace Committee, 251
Magog, 231
Malachi, 273
Manasseh, 184
Maronites, 184
Marshall, George C., 186
Marx, Karl, 27
Mein Kampf, 27, 30
Meir, Golda, 245
Messiah, 176–77, 274
Messianic Jewish movement, 22, 62, 159, 160, 177, 224–25, 231, 261
Michael, 46
micro vision, 156
Middle East, 104, 158, 163, 169, 170, 171, 192, 217, 284–85
Midian, 167, 168, 175
miracles, 126, 127, 152, 167, 201
Mishnah, 298
Mizrahi Jews, 183

Moldova, 19
Moravians, 122
Mordecai, 40, 84–87, 107–8, 112,
    113, 117–18, 120, 125–26, 128,
    214
Moriah, 205–6
Moscow, 45, 46, 47, 51, 113
Moses, 224, 279–80
mosques, 145–46
Mount of Olives, 21–22, 46, 230,
    271, 287n6
Mubarak, Hosni, 247
Muhammad, 176
Munich Massacre, 245
Muslims, 21, 144, 202, 210–11
mystery, 162, 166, 209, 228, 229, 237

Nasser, Gamal Abdel, 243–44
Nazis, 113, 115–17, 185, 242
Nebaioth, 140–41
Nebuchadnezzar, 96, 108
Nehemiah, 280
Neo-Nazis, 116, 299
Netanyahu, Benjamin, 254, 263, 265
new covenant, 224
New York City, 49
North America, 104
"north country," 18, 22, 35, 38,
    100–101, 298
Nudel, Ida, 249
Nuremburg, 28–30

Obama, Barack, 264
obedience, 16
Obeid, Sheikh Abdel Karim, 250
occult, 127
October Revolution (1917), 47
Odessa, 42–43, 44

olim, 182, 299
olive tree, 210, 211, 268
Olmert, Ehud, 260, 261, 262
Open Heavens Conference, 55
Operation Peace for Galilee, 247–48
Operation Solomon, 251
opposition, 165
Orr, William W., 95
Orthodox Christians, 160
Orthodox Judaism, 231, 259, 297
Oslo Accords, 252, 253, 254–55

Palestine, 20–21, 25, 32, 98, 139,
    173, 186, 202
Palestinian Liberation Organization
    (PLO), 243, 247, 248, 252
pandemic, 81, 235
parallelism, 61–62, 222, 227–28
Partition Plan, 33
Passover, 223
Paul
    as a Jew, 157
    on Gentiles, 210
    on grace, 93
    on Israel, 79–80, 199–200, 209, 272
    on Jerusalem, 81
    on Jewish people, 276
    on the Messiah, 275
Paul VI (Pope), 243
peace, 146, 192–93, 196, 247, 283
Pence, Mike, 265
Pentecost, 194, 222, 223–24, 233,
    237, 275
Pentecostalism, 9
Peres, Shimon, 249, 253
Pergamum, 109–10
persecution, 19, 112, 184–88, 232,
    274

Persia, 167, 171, 231
Petrograd, 188
Pharisees, 231
pleading, 101
plumbline, 64, 65
Pogrom, 299
Potemkin Stairs, 42–43
power, 127
prayer
  authority in, 123–25
  for awakening, 63, 65
  commandos, 41
  of dedication, 214–15
  of Esther, 118
  as global, 237
  for Israel, 120–21, 127, 195, 279–85
prejudice, 76
Priddy, Kingsley, 124–25
priests, 299
Prince, Derek, 91, 95, 99, 104, 156, 266
Promised Land, 53, 103
promises, 158
prophecy, 16, 63, 120, 141, 168, 170, 225–26
prophetic intercession, 97, 171, 299
Purim, 85, 86

Rabinowitz, Joseph, 20–22, 24, 110, 125, 159, 287n6
Rabin, Yitzhak, 252, 253
Rachel, 154
Ramallah, 203, 258
Reagan, Ronald, 46
Rebekah, 153–54
rebellion, 94
reconciliation, 82, 193, 227
refugees, 116

refuseniks, 46, 52
regatherings, 95–99
reparations, 242
repentance, 50–51, 282, 284, 297–98
replacement theology, 60, 76, 299–300
restoration, 15, 62, 97, 213, 222, 231–32
resurrection, 82
revival, 82–83, 94, 219, 233, 234–35, 272
Ridings, Patti, 139
Ridings, Rick, 139
righteous Gentile, 300
Rishon LeZion, 20
Roman Catholic Church, 184
Roosevelt, Franklin D., 29, 185
Rosenberg, Joel, 145
rude awakening, 65–66, 86, 127
Russia, 19, 27, 32, 38, 52, 101, 112–13, 127

Sadat, Anwar, 246, 247
Samaritans, 184
Samuel, 44
Sarah, 132–34, 135, 136, 149–63, 166, 174, 176, 178, 205
Sarajevo, 145
Satan, 27, 109–10
Saudi Arabia, 172
Saul, 44, 201
Scheller, Gustav, 41, 43, 44, 124
schism, 228
Schneerson, Menachem Mendel, 252
scribes, 231
Second Coming, 83–84, 218–22, 228–32, 235–38
Second Great Awakening, 67

second regathering, 97–99
seed, 139–40
Seleucid Dynasty, 85
sensationalism, 76
Sephardic Jews, 104, 183, 300
September 11 terrorist attacks, 257
Shalit, Gilad, 260, 263
shalom, 81, 192–93, 197
Shamir, Yitzhak, 247, 252
Shaqaqi, Fathi, 253
Sharansky, Natan, 249
Sharia (Islamic) law, 260
Sharon, Ariel, 257, 258, 259
Shavuot, 275
Shears, Angela Rickabaugh, 266
Shechem, 203, 206, 214
Simeon, 83–84
sin, 94
sings and wonders, 282
Six-Day War (1967), 10, 34, 61, 202, 243–44, 271
Sjöberg, Kjell, 41
sleeping, 59
slumber, 221
Solomon, 280
Sons of Korah, 280
Sorger, Matt, 55, 59
South America, 99
Soviet Union, 53, 99
Speer, Albert, 111
spiritual warfare, 65
Star of David, 75
Stearns, Robert, 195
Stern Gang, 31–32
Suez Canal, 242–43, 244, 246
suicide bombing, 253, 257
Sunni Muslims, 183
supplication, 300

Swansea Bible College, 121–22, 128
synagogue, 273–74
Syria, 34, 171, 172, 241, 242, 246, 261, 262, 263, 269

Talmud, 300
Taylor, Hudson, 18–19
Tel Aviv, 187, 248
ten Boom, Corrie, 127
Teplinksy, Kerry, 266
Teplinksy, Sandra, 143–44, 155, 172, 266
terrorism, 112, 144, 186, 202, 245, 248, 250, 256, 258
Third Great Awakening, 67
Titus (Roman commander), 17, 98
tourism, 81
training, 86
Transjordan, 26, 34, 169, 241
travail, 300
Treblinka, 31, 184
tribulation, 232, 283
Trotsky, Leon, 27
Truman, Harry S., 34, 186, 187
Trump, Donald J., 187, 264, 265, 266
trumpet call, 100, 101
Trump, Melania, 264
Turkey, 24, 169, 262
twelve, 155–56

Ukraine, 160
United Arb Emirates, 266
United Nations, 24, 29, 32, 241, 242
United States, 113–14, 185–86, 193
unity, 225
U.S.S.R., 33, 34, 41, 249, 251, 288

Vannu, Mordechai, 249
visitation, 300
Voice of the Martyrs, 234

Wagner, C. Peter, 109
Wall Street, 48–49
Wannsee Conference, 30
war, 65
Washington Prayer March (2020), 233
watchmen, 88, 119, 301
watch of the Lord, 300–301
weeping, 101
Weizmann, Chaim, 25
Western civilization, 195
Western Wall, 21, 194, 254
wilderness, 133, 136
winds, 58
World War I, 24–27

World War II, 18, 30–31, 39, 115, 121–22, 126, 128, 300
World Zionist Congress, 242
World Zionist Organization, 23
worship, 170
Wye River Memorandum, 254

Yeltsin, Boris, 38, 288
Yeshua, 301
Yisrael, 155
Yom Kippur, 46, 62, 195, 196
Yom Kippur War, 245
Yugoslavia, 108, 145

Zabotinsky, Jeb, 28
Zechariah, 207–8, 209
Zilpah, 154
Zionism, 9, 19, 275–76, 301

James W. Goll is the founder of God Encounters Ministries. He is an international bestselling author, a certified Life Language Coach, an adviser to leaders and ministries, and a recording artist. He is also the founder of Worship City Alliance and Prayer Storm, and the co-founder of Compassion Acts and Women on the Frontlines. James is a member of the Harvest International Ministries International Apostolic Team and the Apostolic Council of Prophetic Elders. He serves as a core instructor at Wagner University. James is also the founder of GOLL Ideation, where creativity, consulting and leadership training come together.

After pastoring in the Midwestern United States, James was thrust into the role of international equipper and trainer. He has traveled to more than fifty nations, sharing the love of Jesus and imparting the power of intercession, prophetic ministry and life in the Spirit. His desire is to see the Body of Christ become the house of prayer for all nations and to see Jesus Christ receive the reward of His suffering.

James has recorded numerous classes with corresponding curriculum kits, and also offers a yearlong mentoring program available globally at mentoringwithjames.com. He is the author or co-author of more than forty books, many of which are listed at the front of this book.

James was married to Michal Ann for 32 years before her graduation to heaven in the fall of 2008. He has four married children and a growing number of grandchildren. He makes his home in Franklin, Tennessee.

For further information, please contact James at

God Encounters Ministries
P.O. Box 1653
Franklin, TN 37065
(877) 200-1604
info@godencounters.com

Websites:
godencounters.com
mentoringwithjames.com
GOLLIdeation.com

Facebook, Instagram, YouTube, Vimeo, GEM Media, XP Media, Kingdom Flame, *Charisma* blog, iTunes podcasts

More from James W. Goll

The key to effective prayer, says bestselling author James W. Goll, is to align our heart and prayers with God's heart. With wisdom and insight, he walks you through how to simply, humbly hold the needs of people before God, lean into His heart for them, and pray what you see and hear as empowered by the Holy Spirit.

Praying with God's Heart

Bestselling author James Goll takes you on an adventure into the heart of what it means to hear God, and how to do it. On this journey, both beginners and those who have been listening to God for years will explore biblical principles about prayer, starting from square one. Let this be the start of a lifestyle of hearing God in your daily life!

Hearing God's Voice Today

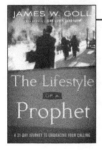

This unique, hands-on 21-day guide will help you develop the intimacy with God essential to hearing His voice clearly. Reflection questions, devotional prayers and practical applications will help you proclaim His words faithfully—and step boldly into your calling.

The Lifestyle of a Prophet

✓Chosen

Stay up to date on your favorite books and authors with our free e-newsletters. Sign up today at chosenbooks.com.

 facebook.com/chosenbooks

 @Chosen_Books

 @chosen_books

CPSIA information can be obtained
at www.ICGtesting.com
Printed in the USA
LVHW080152160921
697935LV00013B/485